The Multivariate Social Scientist

Introductory Statistics
Using Generalized Linear Models

To Andrea and Alexandra
Graeme Hutcheson

Στους π. Θεμιστοκλής και Ελιάνα Χατζηιωάννου
Nick Sofroniou

The Multivariate Social Scientist

Introductory Statistics
Using Generalized Linear Models

Graeme D. Hutcheson and Nick Sofroniou

SAGE Publications

London · Thousand Oaks · New Delhi

First published 1999

SAGE Publications Ltd
6 Bonhill Street
London EC2A 4PU

SAGE Publication Inc
2455 Teller Road
Thousand Oaks, California 91320

SAGE Publications India Pvt Ltd
32, M-Block Market
Greater Kailash - I
New Delhi 110 048

British Library Cataloguing in Publication data

A catalogue record for this book is
available from the British Library

ISBN 0 7619 5200 4
ISBN 0 7619 5201 2 (pbk)

Library of Congress catalog card record available

Typeset by Graeme D. Hutcheson and Nick Sofroniou using LaTeX.
Printed in Great Britain by The Cromwell Press Ltd, Trowbridge, Wiltshire

Contents

Preface

One of the most important contributions to the field of statistics in the latter part of this century has been the introduction of the concept of *generalized linear models* by J. Nelder and R. W. M. Wedderburn in 1972. This framework unifies the modelling techniques for categorical data, such as logistic regression and loglinear models, with the traditional linear regression and ANOVA methods. Within one paradigm we have both an integrated conceptual framework and an emphasis on the explicit analysis of data through a model-building approach allowing the estimation of the size of effects, predictions of the response variable, and the construction of confidence intervals. This move away from the simplistic hypothesis testing framework that has come to characterize much of social science research, with its binary conception of 'scientific truth', can only be for the better — allowing the researcher to focus on the practical importance of a given variable in their particular domain of interest.

It is an unfortunate fact that the widespread assimilation of these methods into the social sciences is long overdue, and this was one of the motivations behind the decision of the authors to undertake the sometimes arduous task of writing this book. An additional reason was the lack of texts that make use of the common theoretical underpinnings of generalized linear models (GLMs) as a *teaching* tool. So often one finds that introductory textbooks continue to present statistical techniques as disparate methods with little cohesion. In contrast we have begun with a brief exposition of the common conceptual framework and written the subsequent descriptions of the methods around this, making explicit the relationships between them. Our experience has been that students benefit from this unity and the insight which follows the extension of the model specification, criticism and interpretation techniques, learned with continuous data, to binary and multi-category data.

In keeping with the attempt to integrate modern statistics into social science research we have chosen to replace certain archaic terminology with current statistical equivalents. Thus, the terms explanatory and response variable are used instead of independent and dependent variable. Similarly, we have encouraged the use of the terms categorical variable, unordered or ordered, and continuous variable which more neatly map onto the GLM framework than the traditional classifications of variables into nominal, ordinal, interval

and ratio scales. The terminology used in this book has been standardized
to follow that used in McCullagh and Nelder (1989) and Agresti (1990), two
definitive books on the methods described here.

The data sets used in the present book were developed during the teaching of these methods over a number of years, most are hypothetical and are
designed to illustrate the range of techniques covered. It is hoped that the
use of made-up sets will encourage readers to experiment with the data — to
change distributions and add variables, examining the effects upon the model
fit. References are provided for examples with real-life data sets.

We have tried to make the chapters as software-independent as possible, so
that the book can be used with a wide variety of statistical software packages.
For this reason, the commands for two packages we have used for illustration
are confined to an appendix at the end of each chapter. SPSS for Windows
was chosen because of its friendly interface and widespread availability, whilst
GLIM was selected because of its sophisticated model specification syntax and
its integrated presentation of generalized linear modelling methods.

The material covered in the book has been taught as a course at Glasgow
University where it was presented to post-graduate students and researchers
(1994–1998). Each chapter can be taught in two 2-hour sessions, making a
complete course of ten 2-hour sessions viable. All data sets and GLIM code
are reproduced in the book and can also be obtained from the StatLib site on
the World Wide Web at: `http://lib/stat/cmu.edu/datasets/`.

We would like to express our thanks to the anonymous reviewers for Sage
Publications who gave many helpful comments on our earlier drafts. We would
also like to express our gratitude to those who have provided a number of
excellent courses in categorical methods and GLMs, particularly Richard B.
Davies, Damon M. Berridge, and Mick Green of Lancaster University, and
Ian Diamond of Southampton University. Murray Aitkin kindly sent pre-
publication copies of his article and macros for hierarchical modelling in GLIM,
and James K. Lindsey obtained a copy for us of his unfortunately out of print
text on the Analysis of Stochastic Processes using GLIM (1992).

This book was typeset by the authors using LaTeX and a debt of gratitude is
owed to Donald Knuth, the creator of TeX (Knuth, 1984), Leslie Lamport who
built this into the LaTeX document preparation system (Lamport, 1994), and
to the many contributors who freely give their time and expertise to support
this package.

Chapter 1

Introduction

For many years the social sciences have been characterized by a restricted approach to the application of statistical methods. These have emphasized the use of analyses based on the assumptions of the parametric family of statistics, particularly for multivariate data. Where methods have been used making less restrictive assumptions, these have typically been limited to data with only two variables, e.g., the non-parametric techniques described by Siegel and Castellan (1988). There has also been an emphasis on hypothesis testing using the convention of statistical significance at the $P \leq 0.05$ level as a criterion for the inclusion of a variable in one's theoretical framework. This approach to 'scientific truth' is detrimental in that it restricts the analysis which can be applied to the data, and does not distinguish between *statistical* and *substantive* significance. The distinction between the two is important as significance in one does not necessarily indicate significance in the other. Statistical significance indicates whether a particular result is likely to have arisen by chance (the criterion of 0.05 being a convenient convention), whereas substantive significance indicates the practical importance of a given variable or set of variables in the field of interest.

In contrast to this approach to data analysis a suite of statistical techniques have been developed, which have been applied mainly in the biological and medical fields, and offer multiple-variable techniques for dealing with data that do not meet all the requirements of traditional parametric statistics, such as binary and frequency data. Alongside this wider development of statistics has been an emphasis on *model building* rather than on mere *hypothesis testing* with greater use of confidence intervals to enable the predictive utility of models to be estimated in addition to their statistical significance. One important consequence of these developments has been the unification of traditional parametric techniques with methods for data which depart from linear parametric data assumptions through the conceptual framework provided by *Generalized Linear Models* (GLMs). This unified view has allowed us to organize this book around variations of a single theme — that by examining the properties of a data set, one can choose from a range of GLMs to develop a model of the data that offers both parsimony of explanation and a measure of the model's utility for prediction purposes. Thus, two common goals of science, the explanation and prediction of phenomena, may be successfully developed within the social sciences.

Whilst some of the statistical methods we shall describe have been developed within the framework of quantitative sociology, e.g., Goodman (1970; 1979), Bishop, Fienberg and Holland (1975), and Clogg (1982), it is our opinion that the widespread application of this approach to data from the social sciences is long overdue. In presenting this statistical framework, it has been assumed that the reader has completed an undergraduate course in statistics and is familiar with the concepts of linear regression, analysis of variance (ANOVA), and the analysis of contingency tables using the Pearson X^2 statistic.

1.1   Generalized Linear Models

The term Generalized Linear Model, refers to a family of statistical models that extend the linear parametric methods such as ordinary least-squares (OLS) regression and analysis of variance, to data types where the response variable is discrete, skewed, and/or non-linearly related to the explanatory variables. GLMs seek to explain variation in a response variable of interest in terms of one or more explanatory variables. The GLM modelling scheme was originally developed by Nelder and Wedderburn (1972) and extended in McCullagh and Nelder (1989) and can be summarized as having three components, a random component, a systematic component and a function which links the two.

1. **The random component** is the probability distribution assumed to underlie the response variable. The basic assumption is that a given data set is a random sample of independent observations, though variations exist to take into account observations that are not independent.

2. **The systematic component** is the fixed structure of the explanatory variables, usually characterized by a linear function.

3. **The link function** maps the systematic component onto the random component. This function can be one of *identity* for Normally distributed random components, or one of a number of non-linear links when the random component is not Normally distributed.

The terms 'multivariate' and 'multiple' regression are sometimes used interchangeably, which is unfortunate, since they have different meanings. 'Multiple' regression refers to an analysis with a single response variable and several explanatory variables, and is a univariate statistical technique. Whilst, a 'multivariate' statistical test refers to an analysis with more than one response variable and possibly additional explanatory variables (Ryan, 1997). A GLM can be considered as univariate with multiple explanatory variables, or truly multivariate, depending on the form of the model (McCullagh and Nelder, 1989).

1.1.1   The Random Component

Observations of a response variable are considered to represent the outcomes of a random variable (the response variable is the random component of the model). This random variable can be conceived as having a mean value with variation about this mean having an associated probability distribution. Examples of such distributions are the Normal, Poisson, Binomial and Multinomial distributions, each of which is characteristic of a different type of response variable (for example, a continuous or a dichotomous variable). These probability distributions, and their relationships to different types of response variables are given lucid discussions by Lindsey (1995), and Agresti (1996) and will not, therefore, be described in detail here. On the basis of the data type of the response variable, together with graphical plots, one makes an assumption about the random component of the model, assuming a given probability structure for the model. This is quite straightforward, since there are common prescriptions for different data types, such as continuous, binary, and frequency data, which offer a good starting point in an analysis.

1.1.2   The Systematic Component

Measurements of explanatory variables are used to model variation in the response variable — they allow us to estimate the means of the random variable assumed to underlie our response variable, with the additional variation assumed to be error following our chosen probability distribution. The explanatory variables are assumed to have a fixed structure and this is known as the *systematic component* of variation in our response variable. This makes explicit the assumption that the values of the explanatory variables are 'fixed' or known with little or no measurement error. The systematic component describes the linear structure of the explanatory variables and is shown in Equation 1.1, which is a multiple-variable form of the simple linear equation $y = \alpha + \beta x$.

$$\eta_i = \alpha + \beta_1 x_1 + \beta_2 x_2, \dots, \beta_j x_j \tag{1.1}$$

where η is the linear predictor,

$x_1, x_2, \dots, x_j$ are the explanatory variables,

$\beta_1, \beta_2, \dots, \beta_j$ are coefficients,

and α is the value of η when the x variables are all equal to zero.

The notion of a linear predictor allows the classical approaches to the estimation of parameters in a linear model, for example, those found in ordinary least-squares regression and analysis of variance, to be generalized to a wider range of models. Thus, concepts such as factorial designs, additivity between explanatory variables and interaction terms, can all be applied in the generalized context.

1.1.3   The Link Function

Since the relationship between the random and systematic components is not always a direct one, a link function needs to be included. The link function specifies the relationship between the linear model and the random component, thereby converting the η_i values to μ_i, the expected values of y.

$$g(\mu_i) = \eta_i \qquad (1.2)$$

where g is the link function,

μ_i represents the random component,

and η_i represents the linear component.

The nature of the function g is determined by a consideration of the data type, possibly in conjunction with graphical plots of the sample data. In this manner one converts the linear predictor into a series of expected values corresponding to the original response variable. The values of μ are calculated, using computer software, from maximum likelihood estimates of the model parameters. This is a computationally intensive procedure which derives the model parameters on the basis of the most probable ones, given the present sample and the known probability distribution of the random component.

The major link functions dealt with in this book are the identity, logit and log links. The identity link, commonly used in OLS regression, maps the systematic component directly onto the random component. The calculated parameters for the systematic component are therefore directly interpretable as fitted values of the random component — the relationship between the two is linear. The logit link, commonly used in logistic regression, maps the log odds of the random component onto the systematic component. The relationship between the random and systematic components is not linear, but once the logit link is applied, this relationship is rendered linear and the calculated parameters for the model can be appropriately interpreted. The log link, commonly used in loglinear analyses, maps the log of the random component onto the systematic component. The name 'loglinear' makes explicit the use of the log function to obtain a linear relationship. Using these three link functions, a wide variety of data can be modelled.

1.2   Data Formats

Data are typically analysed in the form of a *data matrix*. This is a table of data
in which the rows represent the individual cases, or groups in the study, and
the columns each represent a *variate*, that is a measurement on an explanatory
or response variable. An explanatory variable is also known as a *covariate* and
we use both of these terms interchangeably in the present book. Table 1.1
presents hypothetical data for an experiment looking at questionnaire ratings
of hostility following the playing of a violent versus a non-violent computer
game, across subjects of both gender. The first column is the Subject number.
The next two columns present the explanatory variables of Computer Game
(1=Non-violent, 2=Violent) and Gender (1=Female, 2=Male), whilst the final
column gives the corresponding Hostility rating, our response variable, out of
a maximum score of 100.

Table 1.1: Hypothetical Investigation of the Effect of Violent Computer Games
upon Subsequent Ratings of Hostility — Individual Cases

Subject	Game	Gender	Hostility	Subject	Game	Gender	Hostility
1	1	1	50	20	2	1	57
2	1	1	53	21	2	1	64
3	1	1	60	22	2	1	85
4	1	1	53	23	2	1	76
5	1	1	48	24	2	1	73
6	1	1	53	25	2	1	58
7	1	1	45	26	2	1	45
8	1	1	46	27	2	1	49
9	1	1	42	28	2	1	36
10	1	2	85	29	2	2	81
11	1	2	27	30	2	2	36
12	1	2	44	31	2	2	50
13	1	2	58	32	2	2	55
14	1	2	48	33	2	2	52
15	1	2	55	34	2	2	89
16	1	2	68	35	2	2	79
17	1	2	50	36	2	2	70
18	1	2	73	37	2	2	87
19	1	2	41	38	2	2	42

For grouped data the columns may represent mean values of the variates,
with an additional column indicating the count of the number of cases in the
group. Table 1.2 presents the same data averaged across each combination
of the explanatory variables. In this case, column one gives the level of the
Computer Game, whilst column two gives the Gender of the subjects. The
third column, the response variable, now consists of the Mean Hostility scores

for the group. The final column is the count of how many subjects were in each group, which allows us to weight the analysis appropriately.

Table 1.2: Hypothetical Investigation of the Effect of Violent Computer Games upon Subsequent Ratings of Hostility — Grouped Data

Computer Game	Gender	Mean Hostility	Count
1	1	50.00	9
1	2	54.90	10
2	1	60.33	9
2	2	64.10	10

We sometimes present grouped data in the form of contingency tables, with the levels of the response variable as the columns of the table and those of the explanatory variable as the rows, which can make any patterns in the data more easily visible.

Variables fall into two classes, the *response* variables, traditionally termed dependent variables, and the *explanatory* variates, traditionally called stimulus, predictor, or (somewhat misleadingly) independent variables. Both may consist of *quantitative* measurements, which are numerical and measured usually on a continuous scale, or *qualitative* measurements, which are non-numerical, categorical, and consist of a number of *levels*. Qualitative variables are termed *factors*, following the traditional analysis of variance framework, and include experimental and treatment variables used to describe the blocks of an experimental procedure, as well as categorical measurements of non-experimental explanatory variates. This terminology applies equally to describing the response variate. Ordinal data can be adapted into either form, and we consider the appropriateness of treating them as continuous or discrete in the relevant sections of the book.

1.3   Standard Statistical Analyses within the GLM Framework

The common statistical techniques used in the social sciences which are contained within the GLM framework are summarized in Table 1.3. As can be seen, a wide range of models can be fitted as GLMs, allowing many social science problems to be tackled within a single general approach to statistical modelling. This makes for more straightforward comparisons between different analyses as well as aiding the understanding of the techniques adopted, since they are all instances of linear models, generalized through the application of appropriate link functions, to different types of response variables. In addition to those already indicated, GLMs can be developed for other models such as

Table 1.3: Common Statistical Techniques within the GLM Framework

Statistical Analysis	Response Variable	Explanatory Variable	Link Function	Distribution
OLS Regression	Continuous	Continuous	Identity	Normal
ANOVA	Continuous	Factors	Identity	Normal
ANCOVA	Continuous	Mixed	Identity	Normal
Loglinear	Count	Factors	Log	Poisson
Logistic Regression	Proportion	Mixed	Logit	Binomial

probit models, multinomial response models and some commonly used models for survival data.

1.4 Goodness-of-fit Measures and Model-Building

Once a link function has been chosen, a computer software package can be used to explore a number of models which vary the systematic component, by adding or deleting explanatory variables and their interaction effects. One aim in developing statistical models is to obtain a balance between parsimony of explanation and a good-fitting model. Thus, simple models are preferable to more complex ones, providing one does not trade off too much accuracy in describing the data. A typical strategy is to compare two models that are *nested* within one another, e.g., a main effects only model compared to a model with the main effects plus one two-way interaction of interest. In such cases the linear structure of the first model is contained within that of the second more complex linear model. The more complex model will always explain more of the variability in the response variable than the simpler nested one (the extra term will explain at least one case), the question is whether the more complex model is sufficiently better to make its inclusion worthwhile. Statistical criteria will be described in the relevant chapters to facilitate this decision making.

By including as many parameters as there are cases in our sample, a complex model which fits the data perfectly can be derived. However, this gains us little, since the haphazard nature of the random variability present in the data is now present in our theoretical model, which is cumbersome and overly complex. By eliminating insignificant parameters we begin to smooth the data, describing it more succinctly, and improve the predictions we can make about other samples of data concerning the topic of research. McCullagh and Nelder (1989) use the term *scope* to refer to the range of conditions under which a model makes reliable predictions. An overly complex model has a poor scope because it cannot accommodate the inevitable variations between samples, i.e., different samples will result in different models. A 'good' model provides a balance between goodness-of-fit of the present data sample, parsimony, and scope. To some extent the process of model fitting remains a mixture of common checks for the fit of a model, together with some intuition about parameters to include or leave out in the process of generating models for examination. Following Box and Jenkins (1976), McCullagh and Nelder suggest three components to fitting a model:

1. The selection of models to be evaluated.

2. The estimation of the model parameters.

3. The use of the parameters to make predictions about future values.

This is not a unidirectional procedure, since one may follow false leads and blind alleys as one introduces additional terms in the model, or tries eliminating other terms, in the successive comparison of relatively more and less complex models.

The parameters of the systematic component of a generalized linear model can be estimated using a standard algorithm, e.g., iteratively re-weighted least-squares (described in Francis, Green and Payne, 1994). This standard method of calculating the parameter estimates, together with a common goodness-of-fit test, allows GLMs to be examined as a single extended class as opposed to a disparate set of unrelated techniques. The goodness-of-fit criterion used in GLMs is known as the scaled *deviance* and is shown in Equation 1.3.

$$D^* = -2\log(L_c/L_f) \tag{1.3}$$

where D^* is the scaled deviance,

L_f is the maximum likelihood that can be obtained with an exact fit of the expected values to the actual data,

and L_c is the maximum likelihood of the fitted values of the current model.

A model with as many terms as observations will result in a perfect fit of the observed data, and produce a scaled deviance of zero, since it will generate equal values of L_f and L_c. In obtaining an optimal set of parameter estimates for a particular model, the software minimizes the deviance. The units of the scaled deviance will depend on the particular link function in use, but equate to the traditional units used in a particular analysis. Thus, the identity link in OLS regression equates to the minimization of the least-squares, whilst a log link in loglinear modelling gives us a deviance in units of G^2 and a logit link in logistic regression gives a deviance in units of $-2LL$. This incorporation of the traditional measures used in model fitting within the overall concept of minimizing the deviance is a nice feature of the way in which linear models have been extended into generalized linear models. This unified approach to testing the goodness-of-fit of a model by examining the scaled deviance, which depends on the ratio of the likelihood of a perfect model to the tested model, is known as the *Likelihood Ratio* test.

The simplest model consists of the *null* model, and contains only one parameter, the mean of all the observed values. The most complex model is the *full* model that has one parameter per observation, with all the means corresponding to the data exactly — each derived from only one data point. We can characterize these two extremes by saying that the null model assigns all the variation to the random component with none to the systematic component, whilst the full model assigns all the variation to the systematic component, with none to the random component. The former is useless for explanation and prediction, whilst the latter is too cumbersome for explanation and too brittle for prediction to other samples from the same research area. The full model gives us our baseline against which to compare models with an intermediate number of parameters. Those models which show insignificant differences to the fit of the full model are regarded as good-fitting models, providing a useful increase in the parsimony of explanation and scope of prediction without leading to a significant reduction in the model fit.

In generalizing the linear model away from the assumption of Normal errors we lose the exact distributional theory available for the Normal distribution. Thus, the raw deviances themselves lack a large sample approximation that can be used to directly evaluate precise significance levels. Instead, one compares the *difference* in scaled deviances of nested models. The difference in the deviances can be evaluated in terms of statistical significance and the strategy is to try and find the simpler model that is not significantly different in its deviance from a more complex model from which it is a sub-branch. In summary, the emphasis is less on evaluating the absolute deviance as a measure of the goodness-of-fit of a model, instead we compare the reduction in deviance of two nested models.

1.5   The Analysis of Deviance

Analysis of variance is a common technique for investigating factorial explanatory variables and interactions amongst them, with data having Normal errors and constant variance. It is typically used for investigating orthogonal, i.e., uncorrelated, explanatory variables such as those which arise in factorial experimental designs with some kind of random allocation of subjects to the experimental conditions. In addition to these instances, generalized linear models also allow the inclusion of terms in a model that are non-orthogonal, as well as random components which depart from a Normal error distribution, e.g., binary or frequency response variables.

ANOVA can be seen as a series of model fits, each of which adds a further term to the model. Thus, with two explanatory variables, x_1 and x_2 we can proceed by starting with the null model consisting of just the intercept and then proceed by fitting a single main effect, e.g., x_1, then both main effects $x_1 + x_2$, and finally the interaction model $x_1 + x_2 + x_1 \times x_2$.

When the variables are coded in the same way, a GLM with an identity link gives the same goodness-of-fit statistics as ANOVA, but with the advantage of parameter estimates for how much the response variable changes for each term in the model, together with confidence intervals. This correspondence follows from the way in which ANOVA can be carried out in OLS Regression and is given further discussion in the concluding chapter.

The sequence in which the explanatory variables are entered into the analysis does not matter when the variables are orthogonal, however in extending the analysis to non-orthogonal variables, the sequence in which the terms are added becomes important. In such a case a number of model sequences may need to be investigated. This is a common problem in OLS regression where explanatory variables that have arisen from some naturalistic observation or survey method are often correlated. This is in contrast to factorial experimental designs where orthogonality is a consequence of the manner of allocation of subjects to conditions.

In analysis of covariance (ANCOVA) one examines models with explanatory variables that are a mixture of factors and continuous variates and this also has an equivalent representation in terms of OLS regression. Because of their flexibility, we place the emphasis on regression methods, bearing in mind that ANOVA and ANCOVA can be analysed as special instances of OLS regression. In generalized linear models these concepts can be applied directly to extended family of error distributions. The available link functions allow us to accommodate non-Normal error distributions, such that the additive and linear systematic component can generate expected values on the response variable's original scale of measurement. By using the generalized measure of discrepancy, the deviance, we can follow the techniques derived from ANOVA and ANCOVA and generate *analysis of deviance* tables of goodness-of-fit corresponding to the successive addition of terms to the model. Since the sequence of entry of the model terms becomes important when non-orthogonality of the explanatory variates is present, several strategies have been proposed for successive model fits, some of which are automated algorithms, these are described in some detail in the chapter on OLS regression.

1.6 Assumptions of GLMs

1.6.1 Properties of Scales and Corresponding Transformations

In choosing a model to fit real-world data within a linear framework, a variable may be entered as Y, $\log Y$, $1/Y$, etc., and the question arises as to what is the 'best' scale to work with. In ordinary least-squares regression a good scale is held to combine Normality, constant variance, and additivity of the systematic effects. This is a mathematical idealization — in practice we cannot rely upon a particular empirically derived scale having these three features at the same time. McCullagh and Nelder (1989) give the example of data consisting of frequency counts, which typically display a Poisson distribution for the response errors, with the systematic effects being multiplicative in combination. In order to convert such a scale for use in an ordinary least-squares framework a series of transformations are possible that each optimize one of the assumptions. Thus, $Y^{2/3}$ gives a good approximation of Normality, $Y^{1/2}$ approximates constant variance, whilst $\log Y$ produces additivity of the systematic effects — no one transformation produces a scale with all of the desired properties for OLS regression.

Generalized linear models simplify the problem to some degree. Since Normality and constant variance are no longer required in the generalized framework, one needs to know only the way in which the variance is a function of the mean. The methods for checking these assumptions are outlined in Chapter 2 on data screening, and in examples given in the main chapters for each method. Additivity of effects can be generated by the use of a link function in which the expected responses of the model acquire additivity, the fitted values being an approximation of the actual data obtained on the original scale. Such a link function can also be applied to a transformed Y scale, if for example, a separate transformation of the Y variable provides a better fit of the model.

It has been shown since the time of Gauss, that whilst Normality of the distribution of response errors is desirable in an OLS regression, estimates using least-squares depend more on the assumptions of independence and constant variance than on Normality. This applies in a wider sense to GLMs in that the presence of an assumed distributional form of the error for the response variable, such as Normal, binomial, Poisson, exponential, or gamma distributions, is less important than the independence of observations and the assumed relationship of the mean to the variance. This is useful since, as we have seen above, one rarely finds that all the distributional assumptions are obtained simultaneously.

1.6.2   Overdispersion and the Variance Function

In the case of response variables with Normal errors the variance is independent of the mean — this is a property of the Normal distribution — however, for some GLM error distributions, such as the binomial and Poisson distributions, the variance is actually a function of the mean. In such cases the assumption of this variance function may be at odds with the data. The most common departure is that of *overdispersion* which means that the variance of the response variable is greater than that predicted by the theoretical variance of the assumed distributional form, known as the nominal variance. Overdispersion is quite common and the most frequent mechanism by which it arises is clustering, thus in studies of public health, factors such as geographical region, neighbourhood, family etc., all constitute clusters of explanatory variates. Overdispersion can be conceived as a degree of 'attraction' between the cases, in the sense that measures of the response variables from individuals within a cluster are more similar than cases across clusters. Underdispersion occurs when there is a degree of 'repulsion' between cases on some measure, e.g., the spatial location of territorial animals such as foxes. The degree of over/underdispersion can be ascertained empirically and adjustments to the statistical analysis will be described. However, misleading conclusions can arise when the departure from nominal variance is due to the omission of an important explanatory variable from a model. Further discussion of this is given in Chapter 2 on data screening.

1.6.3   Non-linearity and the Link Function

GLMs allow the traditional linear modelling approach to be extended to a class of non-linear response variates by means of a link function and the option of an additional variance function. Some cases of non-linearity of the explanatory variates are dealt with by means of data transformations, but some cases are less tractable, being intrinsically non-linear in nature. In this book we limit ourselves to cases of non-linearity that can be rendered linear by means of a link function or data transformation, though McCullagh and Nelder (1989) demonstrate how some cases of intrinsic non-linearity may be dealt with. We suggest that researchers try and model the data using the techniques outlined in this book as a starting point. Failure to obtain a good fitting model when a complex systematic trend is apparent would then suggest the application of a more specialized non-linear technique. A number of developments of the GLM framework described in the present book are outlined, together with additional references, in the concluding chapter.

1.6.4   Independent Measurement

Generalized linear models assume that measurements are independent of one another, or at a minimum, uncorrelated. A more general version of this assumption is that the measured cases are independent in blocks whose size is fixed and known, for example in a factorial experimental design, where the manipulated variables fall into discrete levels. This appears to rule out spatial processes or time-series data which show autocorrelations, but McCullagh and Nelder (1989) do provide examples of how GLMs can be extended to deal with such data, as well as split-plot designs which have two error terms (a between-whole-plot variance, and a within-whole-plot variance).

1.6.5 Extrapolating Beyond the Measured Range of Variates

As pointed out in Section 1.4, a given set of data may have several good-fitting models which approximate the observed measurement range of each variable well. However, one should be cautious in generalizing beyond the measured range since the behaviour of the model outside the region of observation will be dependent upon choosing the right model and, especially, the appropriateness of the link function. For example, there are physical limits upon the range of stimuli which may be perceived by an organism, whilst its body places constraints upon the range of behavioural measures available, such as the rate of response, or a measure of anxiety such as the galvanic skin response. Such limits offer boundaries to the measured variables and imply that some form of non-linearity is required in our model. Generalizing from a narrow range of measurements to wider, more extreme, levels may result in a breakdown of the fitted model.

Note that this kind of extrapolation is necessary in the modelling of infrequent events, e.g., investigating the carcinogenic properties of a substance, the 'safe' dosage of an anti-depressant drug, or the reliability of a manufactured component. Other applications of GLMs to industrial quality control include models in which one is trying to select a combination of factor levels that maintains the mean of the response variable at some predetermined value whilst keeping the product variation at a minimum or within a set tolerance. In all such cases the occurrence of the undesirable condition is rare in real life, so one uses high doses of a drug or tests a component under extreme physical conditions, and then tries to make predictions about likely effects under more normal conditions. Expert knowledge from specialists in the subject domain may be able to provide some insight into when such extrapolations may be reasonable on the basis of existing knowledge about the phenomenon, however, ultimately all such inferences must be made cautiously.

1.7 Summary

In the course of this book we aim to illustrate to the reader the model building approach to analysing social science data, with its emphasis on parsimony of explanation and scope of prediction — a move away from the significance testing approach in the confirmation of hypotheses. This departure from a binary approach to determining 'scientific truth' brings with it the recognition that there may be more than one good-fitting model that describes a data set, which may make some researchers uncomfortable. However, it carries with it the promise of social sciences based on substantive significance, rather than simple statistical significance. As with the natural sciences, the goal of an analysis becomes one of both explanation and prediction.

The unification of a number of traditional statistical techniques within the concept of generalized linear models, provides us with a single conceptual framework within which we are able to present the techniques in this book. This has the advantages of promoting an understanding of why the different techniques are used, with a departure from a 'cookbook' approach to choosing statistical methods. It also means that appropriate techniques can be presented for binary and frequency data with multiple variables, that have traditionally been analysed using bivariate non-parametric techniques, whilst extensions of these methods to deal with ordinal data are also provided. Through the use of link functions between the random component of the response variable, and the model's linear systematic component, the need for distributional assumptions such as Normality and constant variance are removed, instead the emphasis moves to the assumed relationship of the mean to the variance. This provides greater flexibility since one rarely obtains data which meet all of the distributional assumptions simultaneously.

Chapter 2

Data Screening

The models described in this book are all instances of generalized linear models for they assume that the explanatory variables, weighted by their model parameters, combine in an additive fashion to form the linear predictor. This linear predictor is related to the response variable by means of a link function. As discussed in the introduction, the link function is chosen to optimize the fit of the model and depends upon the distributional assumptions of the response variable. For example, continuous response variables assume Normal errors, binary response variables assume binomial errors, and frequency response variables assume Poisson errors. Each of these error distributions has an associated link function, thus Normal errors use an identity link — the linear predictor itself, binomial errors use a logit link, and Poisson errors use a logarithmic link. These link functions transform the values of the linear predictor to the assumed distributional form of the response variable. Thus, in a GLM the *fitted* values are transformed into the non-linear form of the response variable. The corresponding goodness-of-fit statistics are then calculated upon the transformed fitted values and compared to the response variable on its original scale to determine how well the model fits the observed data. In comparison, traditional solutions using OLS regression emphasize transformation of the response variable itself — altering the values of the original measurements to better approximate the assumptions of the linear model. The advantages and disadvantages of both approaches will be discussed.

In contrast to such use of a link function with the response variable, where there is non-linearity in the relationship between the linear predictor of the response variable and one of the *explanatory* variables, the remedy is to transform the values of the explanatory variable. The same applies to violations in the distributional assumptions of the explanatory variable. This chapter emphasizes the examination and transformation of the explanatory variables, as required to meet the assumptions of a given GLM, since the choice of link function for the distributional assumptions of a response variable has been outlined in the introductory chapter. Occasionally we present instances where one might wish to directly transform the raw scores of the response variable, rather than use a link function.

In addition to checking for distributional assumptions and transforming to accommodate these, it is also important to identify outliers as these can exert a disproportionate influence on the model. The following are some techniques (of which many are available) which can be used to screen and transform data in order to get the most out of the statistical techniques.

2.1   Levels of Measurement

Most readers will be familiar with the notion of different levels of measurement from introductory statistical courses, and this distinction will be retained in this text, though with some modification. Categorical variables are measured on scales that consist of a set of discrete categories, they may be nominal, consisting only of qualitative differences such as religious affiliation, or they may be ordinal, where the data are discrete but can be ranked in order e.g., 'high alcohol consumption', 'moderate alcohol consumption', 'low alcohol consumption', and 'abstain from alcohol'. Continuous variables lie on some continuously varying numerical scale, for example an interval scale assumes that not just the rank of two cases can be stated, but also the numerical distance between them on the scale, e.g., body temperature in °Centigrade. Ratio data have the added property of an absolute zero point of measurement, e.g., the mass of a person's body or temperature measured in °Kelvin.

Traditionally there has been a distinction drawn between linear parametric statistics, that assume at least an interval level of measurement, along with Normality, linearity, and constant variances, and non-parametric statistics that only require ordinal or nominal data, and make far fewer assumptions about the data. Many researchers, attracted by the advantages of model building, have applied parametric linear models to ordinal data, relying on the robustness of the tests under certain conditions. The drawback has been that methods assuming Normal errors are best restricted to continuous variables, and can result in inferences of a dubious nature when the number of levels of a variable is small, e.g., four or five ordered categories, and the distance between the levels unknown. In recent years the model building approach has been extended to categorical data, with the development of logistic regression and loglinear methods, and these are discussed in this book.

One point of note is that some discrete variables can be treated as continuous, when many values are possible, such as 'year of birth', whilst others, such as number of live grand-parents, or number of garages in a house, may be better treated as ordinal in nature due to the greatly restricted range of values which they can take on. Many psychological scales derive their scores from a combination of a series of simple ordinal or nominal scales, e.g., Likert scales (strongly disagree – strongly agree), or the assignation of correct/incorrect to multiple choice answers. Since the final scores can take on a wide range of discrete values, it is often acceptable practise to treat them as continuous variables, use Normal error methods, providing one screens the data for violations of assumptions before carrying out the statistical analysis. However, where the data are drawn directly from a simple score result, rather than in combination with a series of other scores, a categorical statistical analysis may be more suitable, particularly since categorical methods such as loglinear and logistic regression methods allow a model building approach to the analysis of data. These issues are outlined in more detail below, in the chapters covering the individual techniques.

Ordinal data can be assigned numerical scores and treated as continuous in nature, or variants of categorical statistical models can be developed that make use of the extra information in the ranks. In each case, it is recommended that the researcher carry out a sensitivity analysis, by trying different schemes for numerically coding the same ordinal variables, and see if the models generated by a particular statistical method are robust across the different numerical codings. The use of GLMs in this case is a pragmatic approach — a reliable model need not lead one to make *quantitative* assertions based on the measurement scales and code assignments used. We can simply conclude that a particular GLM provides a useful description of any associations present in the data set. In addition, if the data were randomly sampled from the original subject population, then we can make predictions from the various levels of the explanatory variables in the model, together with confidence intervals for our predictions.

When a researcher considers the use of a particular statistical technique it is important that the assumptions of the test be met, if results of the analysis are to be meaningful. One starting point in ensuring that assumptions of a test are met is to begin with a screening of the data. This refers to an examination of the data set for errors in data entry, outliers, and for data with assumed Normal errors, constant variance and linearity.

2.2 Data Accuracy

An initial examination of the data should begin with a look at the range of the variables, using summary statistics such as the mean and standard deviation. With categorical variables a check should be made to see if the coded values are out of range, and whether missing values are correctly coded. Many statistical packages offer a 'descriptives' option that allows one to make quick examination of these points.

2.3 Reliable Correlations

Since GLMs examine patterns of correlation, or covariance, among variables it is important that they are accurately calculated. Inflated correlations amongst explanatory variables can result when composite variables are constructed from a number of individual items, and some items are reused across more than one explanatory variable. An instance of this would be when subscales obtained from a factor analysis are included in a subsequent model along with the over-all composite score, e.g., entering scores on several separate ability subscales together with an overall I.Q. score into an OLS regression analysis. In contrast, correlations can also be very low when the sample is restricted, e.g., a correlation between verbal ability and amount of television viewed would be restricted in a sample of graduate students in English Language. Since the range of verbal ability is narrow, it is constrained such that it cannot correlate highly with another variable. Tabachnick and Fidell (1996) provide a correction formula for estimating the correlation in a non-restricted sample, if one can estimate the standard deviation of the measure in the non-restricted sample. Correlations can also be underestimated when one variable is dichotomous and most of its values (80–90%) fall into one of the categories.

If the means of the variables for a given sample are very large numbers and the standard deviations very small, then computer programs can produce correlation matrices whose values are too small. One can check for this by ensuring that a variable's coefficient of variation (calculated as the standard deviation/mean) is less than 0.0001. If a sample fails this test, then one could try subtracting a large constant from every score of the variable with large numbers and then calculating the correlations. Removing a constant from each score does not alter the real value of r, but does eliminate the problem posed by the finite precision of computer software packages.

2.4   Missing Data

The problems caused by having a few randomly missing data points are usually not important and many statistical packages delete cases with missing values, by default. However, a substantial number of non-random missing values can have serious consequences. They can affect the inferences drawn about variables in the sample data, and the generalizability of the results to a population. The systematic refusal of respondents to answer a particular type of question in a survey can seriously distort the obtained results. In one remedial procedure, group means obtained from the available data are used in place of missing values before proceeding with the main analysis, e.g., a mean value for males on a particular measure is used to replace any missing values for males on that measure. However, this can produce bias in the parameter estimates. More sophisticated methods involve modelling the missing values, and the reader is referred to Aitken, Anderson, Francis and Hinde (1989) for a discussion of this topic.

If the sample data set is small, then it is recommended that the reader repeat the analysis with and without the estimated missing values. If the results are markedly different, then one will need to look further into why this is the case and which data set better represents the real population.

2.5   Outliers

When extreme values occur on one variable or a combination of variables, these data points are termed outliers. Statistical analyses can be distorted and unduly influenced by the presence of the outliers. Outliers may be cases with an extreme value on one variable, e.g., a person weighing 158kg (350lb) in a sample of 20 people, or they can occur across multiple combinations of explanatory variables, i.e., cases with an extreme combination of two or more scores, such as a 55-year-old woman who is pregnant. Such a case is not an outlier on either of the single dimensions, age or pregnancy, but the unusual combination of the two makes the observation an outlier. Outliers are points that lie far from the majority of observations and can exert an undue influence on the slope of the obtained regression model. For this reason they warrant careful examination. Figure 2.1 illustrates the influential effect of an extreme outlier upon a fitted linear model.

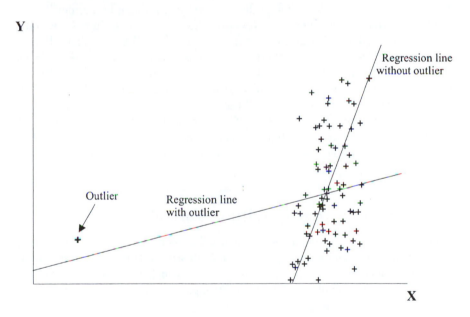

Figure 2.1: The effect of an outlier on a regression analysis

There are a number of reasons for the presence of outliers — data may have been incorrectly entered, missing value indicators may not have been set correctly in the analysis software (thus being read as actual values), the outlier may not be from the intended sample population, e.g., the person may be a member of support staff, such as a technician, in a study of academics. The case may in fact be from the intended population, but has extreme values greater than those expected for the assumed distribution. In the latter instance, the case may be used, but the value on that variable changed in some systematic way so that the case no longer distorts the analysis. The elimination or alteration of outlier scores is considered below.

Variables which are dichotomous are classed as outliers when there is a very uneven split in the frequency of each category, typically a 90–10% split. This uneven distribution leads to underestimation of correlation coefficients between these variables and others, with those scores in the smaller category having a greater proportional effect than those in the larger category.

2.5.1   Outliers on a Single Variable

For assumed Normal errors, outliers are cases with standard scores (i.e., z scores) in excess of ±3.00 on at least one variable. Some statistics packages allow one to represent the data as standard scores, allowing the identification of outliers on a single dimension to be carried out in a simple manner.

One can also use graphical methods to check for outliers in each variable and methods include histograms, box plots, and Normal probability plots. A box plot is a less common method that represents the data as a box drawn around the median, with cases falling far from the box counting as outliers. Normal probability plots are typically used to examine the distribution of the data for Normality and are discussed below. Outlying points will show up by being far from others in the plot. Before one deals with outliers in a single variable, it is recommended that one checks to see if they are also outliers across multiple variables, after which one can decide the best course of action.

2.5.2   Outliers Across Multiple Variables

These are cases where the pattern of scores across two or more variables produces an unusual combination, Figure 2.2 illustrates this diagrammatically. The region outside the ellipse indicates points which are outliers across the combination of two explanatory variables, e.g., adult body weight compared to daily energy expenditure. The number of possible combinations precludes one from screening for outliers from multiple explanatory variables by hand, however there are statistical and graphical methods available.

The statistical method involves fitting a model and examining Leverage values and Cook's distances for each case. These give a numerical indication of cases which have unusual combinations of explanatory variables and that have an unduly large effect on a regression model. Leverage values and Cook's distances are typically plotted against the case number to allow easy identification of extreme cases, but they can also be plotted against a variable to see if any relevant systematic trends are apparent in the data.

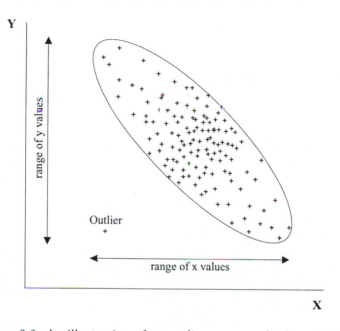

Figure 2.2: An illustration of an outlier across multiple variables

2.5.3 Identifying Outliers

Leverage Values

The Leverage statistic is useful for identifying outliers from multiple explanatory variables. The statistic is derived by comparing the distance of the value
of a case from the means of all of the independent variables. Cases with leverage values greater than that given in Equation 2.1 are possible outliers and
should be viewed with suspicion.

$$\text{cutoff} = 2p/n \tag{2.1}$$

where p is the number of model parameters including the intercept,
and n is the number of cases.

Table 2.1 presents hypothetical data from 150 generated observations with
Normal errors, which will be used for the purpose of illustration in Figures
2.3a–f. Figure 2.3e shows the leverage values for the set of data with Normal
errors, the horizontal cutoff line is calculated from the above formula, $2 \times
2/150 = 0.027$. From this it appears there are no outliers.

Table 2.1: Data Set with Normal Errors

X	Y	X	Y	X	Y	X	Y
74	422.903	132	756.281	65	400.113	144	809.993
137	825.184	77	355.968	26	54.545	33	277.713
102	542.211	44	143.740	50	398.950	113	546.454
134	827.150	43	298.701	98	704.613	48	347.757
18	374.837	139	754.011	59	292.620	121	420.121
111	677.230	56	92.664	90	616.877	29	278.186
3	87.196	124	472.401	22	3.948	84	383.100
103	612.331	9	79.188	68	208.100	125	788.379
127	646.358	36	172.479	4	114.524	107	788.623
110	772.305	146	849.198	83	552.137	16	113.616
133	929.739	128	771.050	52	307.536	54	212.241
109	841.624	131	655.151	100	599.460	7	−72.836
51	202.608	32	−39.891	69	452.041	30	29.631
6	52.520	79	317.326	38	259.617	21	190.062
92	602.520	64	499.028	147	919.436	82	216.507
5	−89.828	108	492.898	120	694.223	118	660.484
12	138.562	47	263.136	70	449.374	25	104.351
97	584.221	61	260.754	119	765.210	129	825.854
122	664.196	149	1000.000	106	654.319	142	835.634
27	68.508	86	492.262	63	409.051	17	88.793
42	133.618	45	312.095	95	475.666	80	318.227
71	408.097	88	501.509	20	120.415	91	543.712
138	749.393	93	518.186	34	235.633	145	560.112
14	99.037	78	363.998	81	473.737	35	110.953
73	631.965	66	398.536	49	263.600	55	328.767
23	81.141	13	130.815	148	657.768	96	666.745
89	549.172	101	613.184	76	240.108	67	287.565
37	54.724	60	334.205	104	407.754	53	308.182
117	671.125	1	165.847	140	816.654	41	470.287
11	78.681	15	111.668	105	455.376	10	−142.707
114	826.370	46	373.869	75	448.370	123	748.744
135	466.819	112	679.528	8	58.048	28	269.729
99	627.457	62	360.359	2	113.024	94	558.473
141	870.286	130	817.366	31	272.925	24	289.161
39	308.867	40	302.709	72	373.525	57	241.726
143	638.486	136	743.646	87	376.316	19	109.443
126	556.015	115	578.964	58	347.994	116	492.809
85	326.658	150	893.670				

Cook's Distance

This is a statistic which measures the change in all of the regression coefficients that results from the removal of a case from the analysis. The value of Cook's distance is obtained from the residuals (described in Section 2.6) taken together

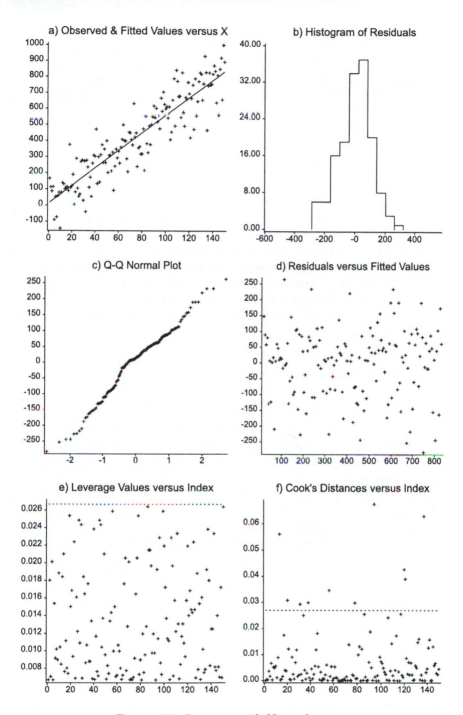

Figure 2.3: Data set with Normal errors

with the leverage values. The cases with the largest values of Cook's distance are those whose removal would change the coefficients the most. Cook and Weisberg (1982) generally consider a Cook's distance of greater than 1 to be *large*, indicating that one should take a closer look at the corresponding cases. However, we have found this to be far too conservative and recommend using a cut-point calculated from Equation 2.2 (see Swan and Scallan, 1995).

$$\text{cutoff} = \frac{4}{n-p} \qquad\qquad (2.2)$$

Using this more sensitive cutoff as a guideline, one should then examine the change in the model fit with and without a suspect case. This is to see if the observation makes a significant difference to the fit of the model. An example of Cook's distances for data with Normal errors is shown in Figure 2.3f. The cutoff line occurs at $4/(150 - 2) = 0.027$ and we see 10 cases that may significantly alter the model fit. Starting with the case with the largest Cook's distance one could then try omitting each of these cases and compare the fits of the models with and without the data point.

2.5.4   Dealing with Outliers

If the variable is dichotomous, with a 90–10% split or worse, one may simply delete the variable. Alternatively, Tabachnick and Fidell (1996) describe a procedure in which the obtained correlation is divided by the maximum that could be achieved given this split in the variables. The effect of this is to allow the full possible range of correlation values up to 1.0, rather than the smaller maximum value due to the uneven split.

Having checked that the data are accurately recorded, and missing value codes correctly indicated to the computer package, one can then decide on the most appropriate course of action for dealing with remaining outliers. When a single variable is responsible for most of the outliers it can be eliminated if it is highly correlated with other variables that do not have such a number of outliers. This is possible because there is always a portion of residual variance for correlated variables, therefore an outlier can occur on one of the variables and not the others, even though the variables are highly associated. If an extreme case is not part of the population from which the sample was intended, it can be deleted since one is usually interested in generalizations to the original population, rather than that from which the aberrant case came.

When outliers remain that are considered to have come from the intended population then two options remain for reducing their influence. One can assume that the cases are part of a non-Normal distribution and transform the variable to reduce their impact, this procedure is described below. Alternatively one can change the score of the outlying case so that it is less deviant — typically one gives the case a new score so that it is one raw score more or less than the next extreme value on a particular variable. In using a modified value for the case the analysis takes into account its direction away from the mean, without disproportionately influencing the fitted model.

One sometimes finds that, when a few cases that have been identified as outliers are removed, then other cases become extreme relative to the rest of the data or group. Thus, it is recommended that one screens for outliers from multiple explanatory variables several times, until no further outliers are found. After identifying the variables which the outliers belong to, one can then reflect upon which variable combinations the results may not generalize to — since one could then remove them from the analysis, or reduce their influence by modifying their scores.

With any such modifications to the data set it is recommended that the reader then report all alterations to the extreme values, together with the reasons for the changes, when describing the results of the analysis.

2.6 Using Residuals to Check for Violations of Assumptions

The analysis of the fit of the model involves an examination of the data graphically, together with the residuals. This involves generating a model from which predictions are compared with the observed data to provide a table of residuals. The residuals provide us with diagnostic information that can be used to look for violations of assumptions. We shall outline some of the common residuals before going on to how they are used, along with other graphical methods, to check the assumptions and fit of a model. Residuals are what are left over once a model has been fitted to the data — the difference between observed and predicted values. If the assumptions for a simple linear model are met, the residuals should have the following properties:

1. They should show no obvious pattern when plotted against the predicted values.

2. They should be roughly Normally distributed.

3. Their variance should be constant for all values of the explanatory variables.

4. Successive residuals should be independent, indicating that the value of one observation is not linked or dependent in some way upon the value of the next observation.

In order for appropriate inferences to be drawn from the results of a statistical test it is necessary to check that the data to be analysed meet the assumptions of the test. Here we will present a broad approach to preparing data with an emphasis on OLS regression models, since these have a narrower range of assumptions, followed by a consideration of diagnostics for logistic regression and loglinear models.

2.6.1   Ordinary Residuals

This is the simplest form of residual and is defined as the observed value of each case minus the fitted value from the model. *Ordinary residuals* have the disadvantage that they do not allow for the fact that the fitted values are estimated from the observed values and, hence, are correlated with them.

2.6.2   Standardized Residuals

These do take into account the correlation between observed and fitted values. When comparing the size of residuals it is often easier if they are re-scaled so that they have a mean of 0 and a standard deviation of 1. For data with Normal errors these are calculated by dividing the ordinary residuals by the estimated standard deviation of the residuals, and are known as *standardized residuals*.

2.6.3   Studentized Residuals

In standardized residuals, all of the observed residuals are divided by a constant, the estimated standard deviation of the residuals. However, the variability of the predicted values is not equal at all points, rather, it changes with the values of the independent variables. When an independent variable lies close to the mean there is a smaller variability for the predicted values, than for more extreme values of the independent variable. *Studentized residuals* allow for this changing variability and are calculated by dividing the observed residual by an estimate of the standard deviation *at that point*.

2.7   Assumptions

2.7.1   Normality

In OLS regression and related techniques such as ANOVA and ANCOVA there is the assumption that each variable and all linear combinations of the variables are Normally distributed. However, it is not always practical to test this directly due to the large number of tests required to examine all linear combinations of all variables. Instead, one examines single variables for Normality, and uses transformations, where appropriate, to obtain Normality for each variable. Through an examination of the linearity and variances of variables, together with the residuals, one can obtain further information about whether the assumption of Normality across the *combinations* of explanatory variables is likely to be met.

Statistical tests can be used in two ways, one is as a descriptive tool for summarizing the relationship between explanatory and response variables, the other way is in making inferences from the sample to the population from which the data were obtained, i.e., the likelihood of a type I error, and associated confidence intervals for the fitted values. In OLS regression statistical inference is weakened when departures occur from Normality of errors, constant variance, and additivity of effects. Even when used for solely descriptive purposes the analysis is improved if the statistical assumptions are met, since a better model fit is usually obtained.

Skewness is the degree of symmetry of the variable, and kurtosis is a measure of the relationship between the peak and the tails of the distribution. A Normal distribution has values of skewness and kurtosis that are zero. Statistical tests are available for assessing the significance of departures from Normality using measures of skewness and kurtosis, however, these are sensitive to the size of the sample and do not indicate how one might transform the variable to become Normal. In this chapter we will discuss graphical methods of identifying non-Normal distributions and the Box–Cox method of dealing with skewed errors, as this suggests appropriate transformations to render skewed data Normal (see Section 2.8.1).

One graphical method to investigate Normality is to examine a frequency histogram for each variable. Whilst such a strategy can identify departures from Normality in a single variable, it cannot identify departures which are the result of combinations of explanatory variables in the model. Therefore it is more useful to fit a provisional model first and then examine a histogram of the residuals. We illustrate this approach for a model with a single explanatory variable, but the extension to multiple explanatory variables is straightforward. A hypothetical data set with Normal errors was presented in Table 2.1, and we begin by fitting a simple linear model, $y = \alpha + \beta_1 x_1$. In Figure 2.3a we plotted the observed data (represented using the symbol +) and fitted values (represented as a straight line) for the response variable on the Y-axis against the explanatory variable on the X-axis. The model seems to provide a reasonable visual fit, and a statistical goodness-of-fit test can be carried out. A simple examination of Normality is obtained by plotting a histogram of the residuals from the model fit, this is illustrated in Figure 2.3b using ordinary residuals, and the departure from absolute Normality is about what we would expect for the sample of 150 cases drawn from a population with Normal errors. In using a histogram, one is looking for a symmetrical distribution with a single peak. Note that small data sets from a Normally distributed population don't necessarily look Normal, but if there are many outliers, or if the curve is obviously asymmetrical, then this brings the Normality assumption into doubt.

More useful than the frequency histogram are Normal probability plots, sometimes known as *quantile-quantile* plots, or Q-Q plots. In these plots a diagonal line drawn from lower left to upper right represents the expected values for a Normal distribution. If the actual distribution of the sample forms a diagonal, then we can conclude that this particular variable is Normally distributed. Departures from Normality result in a movement of the curve away from the diagonal of Normality. Figure 2.3c shows a Normal probability plot for our example data set, and any departure from a perfect diagonal is about what one would expect for this sample size. Outliers appear in the Normal probability plot as points that lie far from the rest of the cases. In Sections 2.8.1 and 2.8.2 we provide illustrations of similar data which are highly skewed in one case, and curvilinear in the second case.

If the plots of the residuals lie close to the line expected for a Normal distribution, then one does not need to examine the individual variables for Normality. Where departures from Normality are found in the residuals, then it is recommended that transformations be applied to the original variables, or an alternative link function be chosen, these options are discussed below. In practise, we find that a Normal probability plot is often more useful in assessing Normality of errors than a histogram, though it is worth looking at both graphs.

2.7.2 Constant Variance

One assumption for data with Normal errors is that the variance of one variable is about the same at each level of a second variable. This is known as *homoscedasticity*, whilst different levels of variance are termed *heteroscedasticity*. In the remainder of this text we shall use the more straightforward terms and refer to homoscedasticity as 'constant variance' and heteroscedasticity as 'non-constant variance'. For a single explanatory variable one can evaluate this through the use of a scatterplot. Returning to Figure 2.3a we see that the spread of observed values of the response variable, for each level of the explanatory variable, is similar — there is no systematic change in variability. With multiple explanatory variables one can check for constancy of variance by examining the residuals of the fitted model. A plot of the residuals versus the fitted values should lie in a horizontal band if the model is a good approximation and the variance is constant. This is illustrated in Figure 2.3d.

Non-constant variance can be the result of non-Normality of a particular variable, or as a result of a non-linear relationship between two variables. Thus, the non-constancy of variance can be reduced or eliminated as one proceeds to transform variables to obtain Normality of errors, and linearity between pairs of variables. Note that correcting for non-constancy of variance need not be the same procedure as for Normality, e.g., for frequency data which typically have Poisson errors a transformation of $y^{1/2}$ approximates constant variance, $y^{2/3}$ approximates Normality, whilst using $\log y$ gives us additivity in the systematic effects (McCullagh and Nelder, 1989). The problem of conflicting results from such procedures was one of the reasons that GLMs were developed in the first place — using a link function between the linear predictor and the fitted values to correct one problem, allows the option of applying a separate transformation to the observed values of the response variable.

If following such procedures there is still a degree of heteroscedasticity, this reduces the predictability of the data by a linear model. However, we can still proceed with an analysis, albeit a weakened one.

2.7.3   Linearity

Many phenomena can be usefully modelled with linear models, which may often provide a useful starting point in the absence of a quantitative theory relating a group of variables. A linear model is one in which the relations between variables are of the form of a straight line. For example, in Equation 2.3, which is the more general form of the simple linear equation $y = \alpha + \beta_1 x_1$, but for multiple explanatory variables.

$$y = \alpha + \beta_1 x_1 + \beta_2 x_2 \qquad (2.3)$$

    where y is an additive function of two explanatory variables,

    x_1 and x_2 are explanatory variables,

    β_1 and β_2 are regression coefficients,

    and α is the value of y when the x variables are at zero.

With non-linear functions, the relationship between y and the explanatory variables x_1 and x_2, is described by a curve. When one tries to generate a linear model with an OLS regression, a poor fit may be obtained since many points of the original data will lie above or below the line of best fit (refer to Section 3.2 for an example of this). However, some non-linear functions can still be dealt with using linear models, whilst others require alternative techniques developed specifically for modelling non-linear relationships. Consider a phenomenon in which the following relationship occurs:

$$y = \alpha + \beta_1 x_1 + \beta_2 x_2^2$$

In this case y is a linear function of x_1 plus (x_2 squared). By taking the measurements of x_2 and applying a square transformation to them, one can then develop a linear model of the transformed x_2 variable that provides a very good fit, and allows one to obtain estimates of the parameters α, β_1 and β_2. Many such transformations can be applied to a variable which has a non-linear relationship to y. The important thing is that the transformed explanatory variable then has a linear relationship to y, i.e., given:

$$y = \alpha + \beta_1 x_1 + \beta_2 F(x_2)$$

where F is a transformation applied to the variable x_2,

the transformation F can be applied to the original x_2 measurements. One can now generate a linear model of the form:

$$y = \alpha + \beta_1 x_1 + \beta_2 x_2'$$

where x_2' represents the variable x_2 after transformation.

For example, a multiple linear regression of the three variables would allow one to make predictions about the value of the response variable, y, given a particular combination of the explanatory variables, x_1 and x_2'.

Some non-linear relationships are not transformable to allow the use of a linear model, these are referred to as *intrinsically* non-linear and require alternative methods of analysis, such as non-linear regression. One example of an equation which is intrinsically non-linear is:

$$y = C_0^\alpha + C_1^{\beta_1 x_1} + C_2^{\beta_2 x_2}. \tag{2.4}$$

In this case there is no appropriate transformation that can linearize the terms of the equation to allow their use in developing a linear model.

GLMs are based upon a linear model between the explanatory variables and the linear predictor therefore any systematic non-linear relationship will be ignored or distorted, unless dealt with in the link function of the model, or by transformation of the observed values of a variable. As illustrated, non-linear relationships can sometimes be rendered linear if appropriate transformations are applied to the variables, prior to the statistical analysis. This transformation can then be incorporated in a statement of the resulting model between the variables, where it is meaningful to do so. A useful method for approximating curvilinear relationships between the response variable and explanatory variables is outlined in Section 2.8.2.

One can examine the data for non-linearity, either by means of scatterplots between pairs of variables, or through a plot of the residuals. The reader is once more referred to Figures 2.3a and 2.3d. In examining residuals, one plots the residuals against the fitted values from the model, and non-linearity appears as a systematic departure from the line of predicted values (an imaginary horizontal line drawn from zero on the Y-axis). By computing a series of plots of the residuals against each explanatory variable, one may more easily identify any non-linearity arising due to a particular explanatory variable.

2.7.4   Independence

Independence means that one observation bears no relation to the value of any other observation — they are not linked or dependent in any way, this is an important assumption of many GLMs. To evaluate this assumption additional information about the order in which the original observations were made is needed (this may not be present in a data set obtained from a survey, or public domain source). One then plots Studentized residuals against the order of the observations. No trend will produce a horizontal line, whilst a dependency will be shown by an upward or downward trend.

As a quick statistical examination of independence one can run a Durbin–Watson test on the Studentized residuals, versus the order of observation. If the observed value is within the range 1.5–2.5 then there is no cause for concern. This procedure is outlined in more detail in Section 2.12.

Although GLMs assume that residuals are independent, a systematic trend may be incorporated as part of the model and the reader is referred to Draper and Smith (1981) for an example of how to build a model with serial correlations present in the data.

2.8   Transformation and Curvilinear Models

The transformation of variables by some mathematical function is the traditional remedy for violations of Normality, linearity and constant variance. This can result in some complex linear models, particularly if one transformation is applied after another. For example, learning that one predictor of school performance is the $\log(\sqrt{(\text{parental income})})$ may provide us with a useful explanatory variable, but the theoretical implications of the function relating parental income to the other variables in the model may be unclear. In addition, optimizing one aspect, such as constant variance, may have side-effects on another, such as reducing additivity of the effects. Therefore, proponents of GLMs such as McCullagh and Nelder (1989) emphasize changing the link function of a model (see Section 2.7.2). One might feel the data suggest that the variance of a sample is in fact *proportional* to the mean, in which case a gamma error distribution is assumed and a reciprocal link function used. In this way one is able to change the relationship between the linear predictor of the model and the fitted values, but leave the observed scale of measurement untouched, which is desirable. Unfortunately, most statistics packages only implement a limited range of the facilities desirable for GLMs, such as a narrow choice of link functions, and the user may be *forced* to resort to transforming their observations. For this reason we include data transformation in this chapter, in addition to making contact with past treatments in OLS regression which are still a part of common practise.

Most statistical packages can be used to carry out a number of data transformations, including taking the inverse, logarithm, and the square root of the data set. With positively skewed data one can apply the transformation directly, if the skew is mild, then the square root is applied, if it is more severe, then a logarithmic transformation is applied. With very severe departures from Normality, one can try taking reciprocals of the observed variable, particularly when the distribution is positively accelerating. A constant is added if any of the values are negative or zero, since problems may arise when trying to apply transformations to minus numbers or zero values, e.g., $\sqrt{-1}$. Note that if the data are negatively skewed, one needs to reflect the variable so that it is the correct way round for the transformation, otherwise the skew will be increased, rather than decreased. This is simply done by adding 1 to the largest value to obtain a constant, k, and then applying the transformation to $(k - x)$, e.g., $\log(k - x)$, instead of $\log(x)$. Graphical illustrations of such transformations are provided in Tabachnick and Fidell (1996). A more flexible approach to these heuristics for data transformation is the Box–Cox family of transformations outlined the next section which shows the effect of correcting for a severe skew.

Failing all this, a remedial procedure involves splitting the data into two categories. The choice of a cut-point should result in two categories with a similar number of observations, avoiding the distorting effect of the 90–10% split discussed earlier. Since one loses information by dichotomizing a continuous variable, a less severe alternative for reducing a variable is to convert it into ordinal categories and score it with the mean value of each rank. By this means it can be entered into a model making fewer assumptions, such as the loglinear models described in Chapter 5.

2.8.1   Box–Cox Transformation with Skewed Errors

We now demonstrate a useful correction for data with non-constant variance and skewed distributions. This involves the calculation of a suitable transformation for the response variable from the power family of transformations. Table 2.2 shows a hypothetical data set with a severe skew.

Table 2.2: Data Set with Skewed Errors

X	Y	X	Y	X	Y	X	Y
38	$1.842e-07$	103	$4.043e+00$	86	$2.029e+01$	56	$3.292e-02$
45	$1.184e-03$	66	$2.322e-01$	58	$1.760e-01$	20	$-3.451e-06$
12	$1.219e-05$	41	$-7.505e-10$	90	$3.723e-01$	35	$5.602e-04$
2	$-5.070e-07$	96	$4.734e+01$	3	$-1.039e-07$	141	$1.609e+02$
146	$5.003e+02$	116	$9.215e+00$	113	$1.774e+01$	49	$5.572e-01$
22	$-1.051e-11$	63	$4.795e-01$	107	$1.013e+01$	100	$8.227e+00$
19	$1.033e-08$	55	$5.188e-03$	28	$1.067e-09$	129	$1.435e+02$
52	$7.985e-01$	143	$2.216e+02$	105	$5.576e+01$	26	$1.398e-06$
109	$1.669e+01$	44	$1.149e-08$	106	$3.490e+00$	127	$2.303e+02$
98	$8.163e+00$	91	$8.637e+00$	147	$2.068e+02$	83	$5.897e+00$
64	$9.350e-01$	59	$1.787e-02$	70	$4.752e+00$	75	$1.930e+00$

continued on next page . . .

... continued from previous page

X	Y	X	Y	X	Y	X	Y
131	$4.816e+01$	21	$7.294e-10$	24	$4.093e-07$	25	$1.846e-03$
51	$1.436e-01$	99	$1.813e+00$	120	$1.693e+01$	27	$8.087e-06$
16	$-9.719e-08$	11	$2.305e-05$	73	$7.861e-07$	82	$1.693e+01$
7	$-1.891e-07$	29	$1.252e-07$	33	$1.793e-03$	85	$1.722e+00$
115	$7.706e+01$	148	$2.447e+02$	60	$1.290e-02$	39	$5.005e-09$
134	$1.586e+01$	97	$1.112e+01$	136	$3.832e+01$	74	$7.151e-01$
14	$5.796e-04$	139	$1.012e+02$	8	$1.502e-04$	67	$6.334e-01$
13	$2.282e-05$	114	$9.944e+01$	95	$5.816e+00$	89	$5.567e+00$
23	$9.196e-09$	81	$3.012e-01$	149	$2.562e+02$	46	$7.266e-04$
135	$3.108e+02$	32	$1.339e-03$	17	$2.848e-11$	84	$4.677e+00$
53	$2.541e-01$	88	$2.305e-01$	144	$3.638e+02$	130	$4.362e+01$
142	$8.655e+00$	42	$2.996e-14$	150	$9.781e+02$	50	$1.299e-03$
125	$5.251e+00$	30	$3.849e-02$	104	$1.108e+00$	31	$3.160e-03$
76	$7.502e+00$	101	$6.893e+00$	5	$3.916e-03$	102	$7.729e+01$
118	$1.978e+00$	124	$1.690e+02$	117	$2.037e+01$	62	$9.248e-03$
77	$4.336e-01$	79	$8.468e-02$	138	$6.062e+01$	94	$7.040e+00$
15	$8.616e-19$	10	$3.980e-07$	87	$1.492e+00$	145	$3.680e+02$
57	$1.985e-03$	1	$-3.058e-06$	92	$3.632e-01$	9	$-5.065e-16$
37	$2.026e-05$	65	$2.865e-05$	140	$1.674e+02$	112	$2.256e+01$
47	$1.586e-05$	93	$1.468e+00$	36	$7.849e-05$	111	$5.161e+00$
126	$4.269e+01$	128	$4.361e+01$	34	$2.375e-04$	110	$2.124e+01$
4	$3.975e-05$	119	$5.742e+02$	123	$2.628e+02$	18	$-6.647e-11$
132	$7.628e+01$	121	$3.015e-01$	78	$2.313e-02$	6	$-1.341e-06$
108	$1.344e+00$	80	$6.364e-01$	43	$3.986e-03$	137	$2.050e+02$
68	$7.215e-01$	61	$4.873e-02$	72	$2.170e-01$	54	$4.594e-02$
40	$7.417e-03$	122	$1.000e+03$	48	$5.677e-09$	71	$4.602e-01$
133	$2.193e+02$	69	$2.838e-02$					

Figures 2.4a–f illustrate the data set with the response variable fitted by the same linear model and single explanatory variable, as in Figures 2.3a–f. In this case the data are highly skewed, as evidenced by the histogram of residuals in Figure 2.4b and the Normal probability plot of Figure 2.4c. The rapid increase in the spread of the observed values in Figure 2.4a and the residuals in Figure 2.4d both indicate non-constancy of variance. The fitted line of Figure 2.4a is a poor fit and appears to be influenced by several outlying values on the right of the graph. Confirmation of the presence of outliers is suggested by the isolated larger Cook's distances of two of the values in Figure 2.4f.

To help remedy the skew, we begin by grouping an explanatory variable into several regions, e.g., 10 cut-points, this allows us to calculate the mean and standard deviation of the response variable in each region of the explanatory variable. One then plots the logarithms of the standard deviations of the response variable against the logarithm of the means, excluding any intervals with single observations, since they have zero standard deviation and give us no useful information. If we obtain a straight line trend, then the slope, b, of this

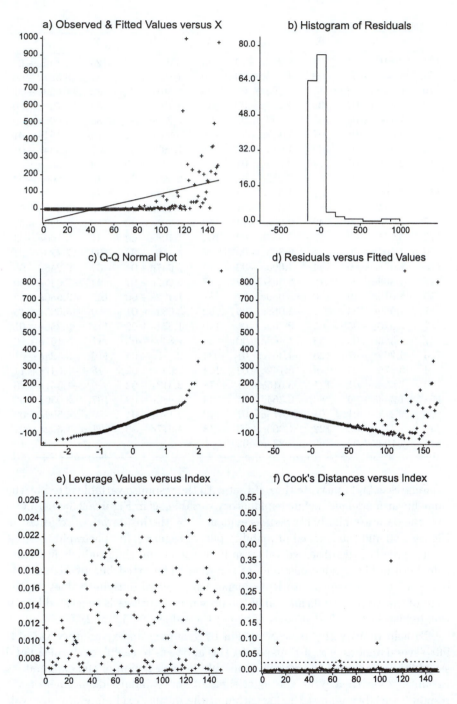

Figure 2.4: Data set with skewed errors

line indicates the need to transform the original response variable by raising
it to the power of $1 - b$. When $b = 1$ we simply need to take the logarithm of
the response variable to stabilize the variance. The slope is readily calculated
using OLS regression described in Chapter 3 — one regresses log (mean of y)
against log (sd of y), treated as the response variable, whilst weighting out the
single observations. The slope of the fitted line provides us with the value of
b. For this example we obtain $b = 0.9$ which indicates that a transformation
of $y^{1-0.9}$, i.e., $y^{0.1}$, will stabilize the variance and enable a better model fit.
One then can go back to the original model and fit the original continuous
explanatory variable to the transformed response variable, checking for any
improvement in the fit of the model.

Figures 2.5a–f show the same data set after the application of the transformation. In this case the data now show much improved variance properties,
Figures 2.5a and 2.5d, and now approximate Normality, Figures 2.5b and 2.5c.
As a consequence, the fitted line for the simple linear model now appears to
be a good fit, Figure 2.5a, and the Cook's distances of the two outlying points
has been reduced considerably suggesting fewer problems in this area, Figure
2.5f.

When using multiple combinations of explanatory variables in a model this
approach is not so straightforward, though one could look at the successive
values of b which are obtained from regressing log (mean y) against log (sd
y) for each explanatory variable alone. The range of values of b, will provide
suggestions of a transformation of the response variable that will help stabilize
the variance across the combination of the explanatory variables. The more
common technique is to determine the power transformations iteratively (Box
and Cox, 1964), comparing the change in the goodness-of-fit of the model over
increasing values of the power transformation. This technique is not available as a standard technique in many statistical packages, though one could
always work through successive power parameters, manually transforming the
response variable and refitting the model each time, and looking at which
power transformation produced the best goodness-of-fit statistic.

2.8.2   Fitting Models to Curvilinear Data Trends

In this example we illustrate a simple technique for dealing with curvilinear
relationships between the response variable and a given explanatory variable.
In Table 2.3 we see a data set where there is strong suggestion of a curvilinear
relationship, this is examined graphically in Figures 2.6a–f. Whilst the properties of Normality and variance seem acceptable, there is a clear systematic
deviation from the straight line fit of the simple linear model, shown in Figure
2.6a and more clearly in the plot of the residuals in Figure 2.6d.

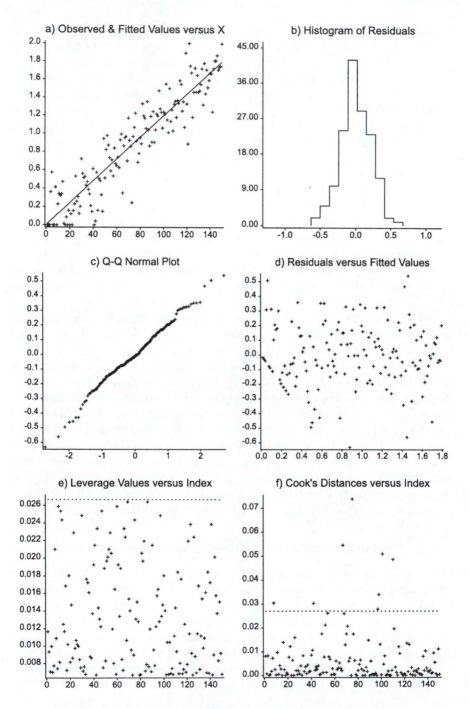

Figure 2.5: Data set with skewed errors after transformation

Table 2.3: Data Set with Curvilinearity

X	Y	X	Y	X	Y	X	Y
72	249.791	95	458.003	137	789.201	127	575.926
38	62.499	92	326.565	30	107.124	19	−42.791
98	495.886	25	22.454	131	832.988	119	612.524
24	−75.754	73	271.064	146	1000.000	135	782.881
15	78.427	53	223.204	34	26.382	28	−108.173
74	356.636	22	−263.659	4	−44.500	116	844.963
2	−187.926	147	892.882	60	238.450	97	440.371
7	−33.925	122	588.256	47	−239.124	134	676.827
63	181.206	132	603.366	64	119.303	124	715.990
120	368.288	100	609.033	61	158.941	112	456.618
75	−75.159	71	307.398	36	−4.636	106	654.291
11	182.174	143	835.975	113	526.128	31	107.996
84	532.086	82	393.234	150	781.897	130	889.754
108	521.793	104	589.643	129	644.314	43	−103.854
80	267.973	148	962.803	46	160.812	139	914.930
138	711.623	21	73.660	101	199.342	5	36.138
41	42.199	56	191.863	141	706.907	65	100.959
12	−172.026	114	577.091	10	−38.763	149	960.266
89	177.935	52	−35.354	50	63.446	13	157.332
16	−51.589	6	183.139	90	394.500	107	426.440
133	752.512	55	28.795	109	514.556	26	185.573
20	240.120	93	234.708	110	619.561	76	85.051
94	285.774	3	188.412	37	190.308	49	−7.449
42	162.236	123	444.898	145	849.341	14	12.001
40	−31.174	9	89.085	58	265.046	66	32.242
33	15.258	105	281.114	78	177.148	125	367.071
29	1.628	39	17.412	88	284.431	57	246.221
35	−4.459	81	329.056	51	−91.861	79	190.767
68	296.286	27	−45.469	128	782.892	86	409.721
32	−14.798	48	85.909	140	966.896	62	204.909
91	285.477	136	656.665	17	21.422	103	766.175
118	578.883	87	146.014	70	329.623	115	413.390
67	133.172	121	476.726	1	101.123	69	289.236
83	173.861	99	515.105	126	828.606	96	507.675
85	271.469	111	537.106	44	179.482	142	689.215
144	973.004	18	298.240	54	60.894	117	399.933
77	223.258	102	524.988	45	74.170	23	−6.419
59	440.566	8	35.675				

A simple remedy in such cases is to calculate a series of new variables, each one being a power function of our explanatory variable, i.e., x^2, x^3, x^4, etc. One then proceeds with a polynomial regression of the data, this consists of fitting *all* powers of x up to the one of interest, e.g., the cubic polynomial version would be:

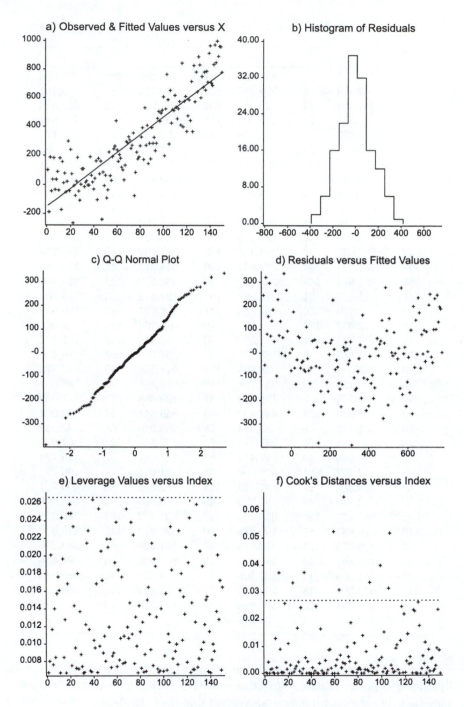

Figure 2.6: Data set with curvilinearity

$$Y = \alpha + \beta_1 x + \beta_2 x^2 + \beta_3 x^3.$$

For these data the β coefficient for x^3 provides no significant improvement in the model fit, compared to the quadratic model, thus x^3 can be dropped from the model, leaving us with the quadratic model:

$$y = \alpha + \beta_1 x + \beta_2 x^2.$$

Figures 2.7a–f show plots for the quadratic model. Figure 2.7a illustrates that there is now a much better correspondence between our fitted line and the observed data. Whilst the plot of the residuals in Figure 2.7d shows a more horizontal distribution of residuals versus the fitted values, indicating no systematic discrepancies in the model fit.

Series of polynomial terms for each explanatory variable can be entered into a model with multiple explanatory variables, and therefore they are quite versatile. However, a couple of words of caution are in order, firstly predictions outside the measured range of variables should be made with great caution since polynomial fits can rapidly deteriorate beyond these limits. Secondly, standard polynomials, like those so far discussed, generate parameter estimates that all change as each higher-order term is added, even when the new term is non-significant.

A better technique is to use polynomials with uncorrelated values of β, these are known as *orthogonal* polynomials. In OLS regression one simply fits all the terms of interest simultaneously since the parameter estimates will remain the same whether or not one chooses to include a higher-order term. Any non-significant higher order terms can then be omitted from the final model. This is illustrated in Table 2.4 in which orders of x up to the fifth power are presented along with their standard errors, obtained t values, and t values required for two-tailed significance at the 0.05 level. These are the results of simultaneously fitting the orthogonal polynomial model of

$$y = \alpha + \beta_1 x + \beta_2 x^2 + \beta_3 x^3 + \beta_4 x^4 + \beta_5 x^5.$$

At a glance, one can see from Table 2.4 that only the constant, x and x^2 terms are significant, therefore the simpler quadratic model can now be fitted to the data. It is unfortunate that not many statistical packages offer this facility.

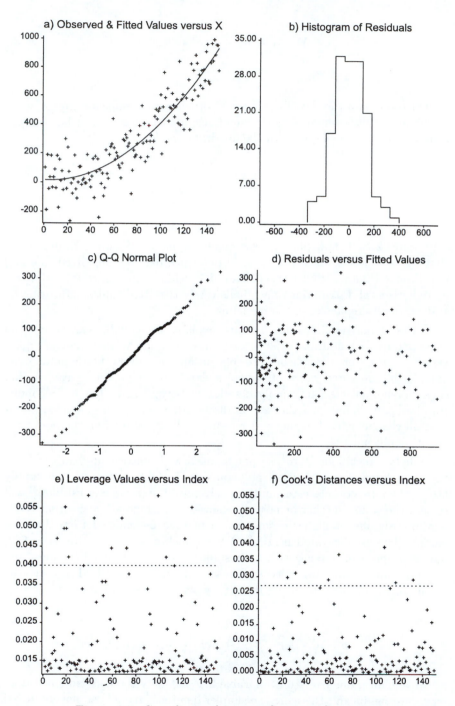

Figure 2.7: Curvilinear data set after transformation

Table 2.4: Parameter Estimates, Standard Errors, and t Values of Orthogonal Polynomial Terms Fitted to the Data Plotted in Figures 2.5a–f

	Estimate	s.e.	Obtained t Value	df	Required t Value
(constant)	0.317	0.010	31.000	144	±1.977
x	3.280	0.125	26.200	144	±1.977
x^2	0.899	0.125	7.177	144	±1.977
x^3	−0.142	0.125	−1.333	144	±1.977
x^4	0.094	0.125	0.752	144	±1.977
x^5	0.093	0.125	0.742	144	±1.977

2.9   Multicollinearity and Singularity

When the explanatory variables in a data set are highly correlated then we may have a problematic degree of what is termed *multicollinearity* amongst the variables. In the case where there is a perfect correlation we have *singularity*, this implies that one variable may have been used to obtain the values of a second variable, e.g., one may be a sub-scale used in the construction of the other. Correlations for pairs of explanatory variables can give rise to Multicollinearity and Singularity, and one should guard against including two variables with a correlation of over about 0.80, except in the case of factor analysis.

Multicollinearity and Singularity can also occur due to correlations amongst multiple combinations of explanatory variables, and one can check this by examining the squared multiple correlation (SMC) of a variable. Alternatively one can look at the *tolerance* which is defined in Equation 2.5.

$$\text{tolerance } \beta_i = 1 - R_i^2 \qquad (2.5)$$

where β_i is the regression coefficient for variable i,
and R_i^2 is the squared multiple correlation between x_i and the other explanatory variables.

Most computer programs set tolerance levels for the size of the SMC that is acceptable before a variable is included in the analysis. Variables that are greater than this level may be rejected from the analysis. Where multicollinearity or singularities are found, one would examine the original explanatory variables to try and understand the reason for this, and decide which variable can reasonably be removed from the analysis. Alternatively, one might find a method of combining them, e.g., factor analysis.

2.10   Diagnostics for Logistic Regression and Loglinear Models

As outlined in the introduction, logistic regression involves modelling a binary response variable using a logit link to the linear systematic component of the model. In logistic regression with a single explanatory variable, one can begin by dividing the explanatory variable into a series of intervals, e.g., 10 cut-points, and plotting a graph of the observed proportions of the binary response variable falling in each interval. Adding the fitted curve of the model will provide a visual inspection of how well a given model fits the observed data. However, when multiple explanatory variables are in the model, a plot of the residuals is more useful. Since the logit link function is non-linear, one plots the residuals against the *linear predictor*, rather than the fitted values. The linear predictor is obtained from a linear combination of the explanatory variables and can be used to check for linearity, and to examine how the variance diverges from the assumed form of the model. Ideally one is looking for a horizontal band of residuals in the manner of Figure 2.3d, but with the linear predictor plotted against the X-axis.

A curvilinear pattern in the residuals indicates a failure of the assumption of linearity, and plots of the residuals against each explanatory variable may indicate if this is due to a particular explanatory variable. One can then try and remedy this through the use of polynomial terms in the manner described above for data with Normal errors. However, if the vertical spread of the residuals increases (or decreases) with increasing values of the linear predictor, this indicates that the link function, or variance assumptions of the model are incorrect.

In loglinear models, combinations of the explanatory variables form cells in a multidimensional contingency table, and within each cell a frequency count indicates the number of observed instances found. Since the explanatory variables are categorical, the model diagnostics involve looking for numerical patterns of residuals across the table, suggesting how certain combinations of the explanatory variables deviate systematically from the fitted values of the model. Further details of this type of analysis are given in Chapter 5.

2.10.1   Under and Overdispersion

In OLS regression and other models assuming Normal errors the variance is assumed to be both constant and independent of the mean. However, in both logistic regression and loglinear modelling the assumed distributional properties of the response variable constrain the variance to be a fixed function of the mean. Logistic regression assumes binomial errors, therefore the variance is given by, $var(y) = \mu(1 - \mu)$, where μ is the mean of Y; whilst loglinear models assume Poisson errors, where $var(y) = \mu$. This property of the variance being a function of the mean allows us to check to see if the distributional assumptions of the model are correct. If the variance is greater than would be expected for the assumed distribution, then we have *overdispersion*.

Overdispersion can result from the underlying distribution of the population being different to that assumed, or it may be that an important explanatory variable has not been measured, and is therefore missing from the model. Overdispersed data can also arise because of non-random sampling, such as data being clustered into regional samples, university student populations, hospitals etc. The net result is that our model may be incorrect and the confidence intervals will be over optimistic. Overdispersion is examined by evaluating the measure of the goodness-of-fit of the model, i.e., the deviance, together with the residual degrees-of-freedom. To examine grouped data for the variance assumptions of logistic regression and loglinear models we use the following equation:

$$s = D/df \tag{2.6}$$

where s is a constant that can be used to correct the standard error of the model,

D is the deviance,

and df is the number of degrees-of-freedom of the model.

A value of $s = 1$ supports the assumed mean-variance relationship. When $s > 1$ the data are overdispersed, and when $s < 1$ the data display underdispersion. The latter suggests some form of repulsion in the original data generating mechanism, e.g., territorial behaviour leads to minimum distances between individuals or groups that are greater than the simple probability distribution would predict. A simple correction for over/underdispersion involves adjusting the standard errors from the original model fit using:

$$\text{adjusted standard error} = s.e. \times \sqrt{s}. \tag{2.7}$$

The adjusted standard error allows better estimates of confidence intervals for the fitted model to be obtained. However, if the over/underdispersion has arisen because an important variable has been missed out, then no amount of compensation will make the model correct, and one will have to go back and measure additional explanatory variables to try and find the source of the extra variability in the data. More discussion of corrections for over/underdispersion can be found in Aitken et al. (1989). A correction for use when modelling ungrouped binary data is presented in Collett (1991).

2.11   Summary and Recommendations on the Order of Screening Practices

An initial examination of the means and standard deviations, along with the minimum and maximum values allows one to spot any obvious mistakes when entering the data set. Having ascertained that the data entry seems accurate one can then begin to proceed with graphical and statistical examinations of the data set to check that the assumptions required for a planned test are viable. A general procedure for screening data is to begin by examining plots of the data for outliers, Normality, linearity across variables, and constant variances. On the basis of this graphical analysis one can determine if any obvious transformations of particular variables are necessary, carry out these transformations, and examine plots of the transformed variables. Once any gross violations have been dealt with, one can begin to examine the leverage values and Cook's distances of cases to look for any outliers and delete or recode any of these.

A check that the coefficient of variation of each variable (the standard deviation/mean) is less than 0.0001 will help guard against round-off errors generated by the limited precision of statistical software. Dichotomous variables should be examined for any very uneven splits, 90–10% splits or worse, and deletion or corrections to statistical calculations applied.

It is quite possible for a data set to contain variables that are non-Normal, as well as containing outliers. The question arises, as to whether one should transform the variables first and then deal with outliers, or vice versa. Since cases that are outliers in a skewed distribution are often brought closer to the mean when a transformation is applied that renders the distribution approximately Normal. Once a transformation has been applied there are generally fewer outliers in the new data set and so carrying out transformations prior to dealing with outliers is preferable. Since one may have to delete or change the scores of the outliers to reduce their exaggerated effect on the model generated by statistical analysis, fewer such changes are needed following variable transformation, which is desirable.

Some of these procedures can be carried out prior to the statistical analysis, however to check for outliers and Normality in multiple combinations of explanatory variables, one needs to fit the model and examine the residuals. This may involve a couple of runs as variables are transformed and outliers removed after each examination of the residuals. Where possible it is better to leave the variables on their original scale of measurement, and to improve the model fit by means of an altered link function or variance function. However, not many statistical packages offer such flexibility and the user may have to resort to the use of transformed variables.

Diagnostics for logistic regression will involve examination of the fitted model to the proportion data for the response variable, as well as an examination for linearity of the residuals when plotted against the linear predictor of the model. Plots of residuals against each explanatory variable can help reveal the source of any non-linearity.

Loglinear models involve contingency tables where combinations of the explanatory variables form cells in a multidimensional table, with a frequency count in each cell indicating the number of observed instances found. The categorical nature of variables leads us to look for systematic patterns of residuals across the table, suggesting how particular combinations of the explanatory variables deviate systematically from the fitted model.

The assumed relationship between the variance and the mean in logistic regression and loglinear models allows us to check for overdispersion. Where the observed variability in the data set is greater than would be predicted by the assumed distribution of the response variable, then one can make appropriate adjustments to the standard errors to give more realistic confidence intervals for the parameter estimates of the model.

The reader interested in a more detailed account of model diagnostics across the wide range of models available within the GLM framework is referred to McCullagh and Nelder (1989), in which they give a detailed discussion of the techniques available and illustrate the advantages of moving beyond the traditional parametric model with Normal errors. Agresti (1996) is a useful source for additional material on diagnostics for categorical data.

2.12   Statistical Software Commands

The data sets provided in this chapter have been generated using GLIM. Although the data was derived using a random number generator, the initial seed is constant for the programme and so identical data to those shown in the tables should be derived. Using a different seed, the numbers generated by the programme will not be identical to those in the tables, but will show the same overall patterns. Some SPSS and GLIM code is presented below to illustrate selected analyses described in this chapter.

2.12.1   SPSS

Detailed discussions of the SPSS procedures outlined in this section can be found in Norušis (1994) and in the appropriate SPSS manuals (see, for example, SPSS Inc., 1996a). All examples in this section are derived from the data presented in Table 2.1. The emphasis of these analyses is to reproduce the diagnostic graphs shown in Figures 2.3a to 2.3f using SPSS.

First input the data set in Table 2.1.

Detecting Outliers

When attempting to detect outliers it is sometimes useful to view the data as standard scores (i.e., z scores). A rule of thumb is that outliers on a single dimension have z values in excess of ± 3. Data can be represented as standard scores by using the commands:

Statistics   ▼
    Summarize   ▶
      Descriptives ...
        Variables(s): *input* x *and* y
        Save standardized values as variables: *check box*
      [OK]

For those variables chosen, new variables are created containing the corresponding z scores and are entered automatically into the spreadsheet. These are given the old variable name preceded with the letter 'z'. For the example above, two new variables 'zx' and 'zy' have been created.

One can also use graphical methods to check for outliers using histograms, box plots, and Normal probability plots. SPSS has a useful EXPLORE command that can be used to check for outliers graphically, and generate appropriate summary statistics. These are obtained using the commands:

Statistics   ▼
    Summarize   ▶
      Explore ...
        Dependent list: *input* x *and* y
        [Plots...]
          Normality plots with tests: *check box*
          Histogram: *check box*
        [Continue]
      [OK]

One can examine data for multivariate outliers numerically by examining distance statistics such as leverage values, and Cook's distances. They can be generated as part of a regression analysis using the following commands:

Statistics   ▼
    Regression   ▶
      Linear ...
        Dependent: *input* y
        Independent(s): *input* x
        [Save ...]
          Cook's: *check box*
          Leverage values: *check box*
        [Continue]
      [OK]

Cook's distances and leverage values are saved as new variables 'coo_1' and 'lev_1'. The cutoff point for leverage values is equal to $2p/n = 4/150 = 0.027$ (see Section 2.5). As we can see from the variable 'lev_1', no leverage values are above this value — the largest leverage value is 0.01974 (a simple method to check this is to sort the cases on the basis of scores on the variable 'lev_1' — extreme values will appear on either end of the scale). The cutoff point for Cook's distances is equal to $4/(n-p) = 4/(150-2) = 0.027$. As we can see from the variable 'coo_1', there are 10 Cook's distances above this value. The above analysis provides the same information as that provided in Figures 2.3e and 2.3f.

Generating Residuals

SPSS can generate a variety of residuals using the following commands:

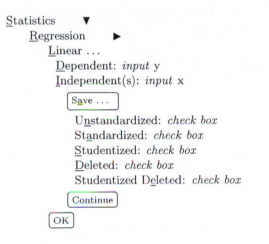

The residuals are saved to the data set as new variables. These variables can then be subjected to a variety of graphical and statistical analyses as described in the text.

Normality and Linearity

A quick check on Normality can be achieved by superimposing a Normal distribution over a frequency histogram for a variable. This is a useful graph when analysing residuals. The graph shown in Figure 2.3b can be obtained using the commands:

Graphs   ▼
    Histogram ...
      Variable: *input* x
      Display Normal curve: *check box*
    OK

More useful than the frequency histogram with a Normal distribution overlay, are Normal probability plots. Normal probability plots of the type shown in Figure 2.3c can be generated using the commands:

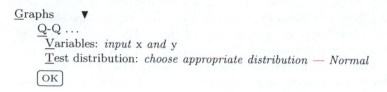

One can examine the data for non-linearity, either by means of scatterplots between pairs or groups of variables, or through plots of the residuals. Simple and matrix scatterplots can be simply generated in SPSS. For example, the plot shown in Figure 2.3a can be derived using the following procedure:

First, one has to compute the predicted values of y given the model $y = \alpha + \beta x$. This can be achieved using the commands:

Statistics   ▼
    Regression   ▶
      Linear ...
        Dependent: *input* y
        Independent(s): *input* x
          [Save ...]
            Predicted values: Unstandardized: *check box*
         [Continue]
       [OK]

The predicted values are saved as 'pre_1'. These can now be plotted using an overlay scatterplot:

Graphs   ▼
    Scatter ...
     Define: *overlay plot*
     [Define]
     input variables to be plotted
       y - x
       pre_1 - x
    [OK]

Checking for Independence of Residuals

As a quick statistical examination of independence one can run a Durbin–Watson test using the commands:

Statistics   ▼
   Regression   ▶
     Linear ...
       Dependent: *input* y
       Independent(s): *input* x
         &boxed; Statistics ...
          Durbin-Watson: *check box*
         Continue
      OK

If the observed value of the Durbin–Watson statistic is within the range 1.5–2.5 then there is no cause for concern. For the example above, the Durbin–Watson statistic is equal to 1.987, which is within accepted limits.

A plot of the residuals against the fitted values of the model can be used to investigate the independence of the residuals. Such a graph is shown in Figure 2.3d and can be obtained in SPSS using the commands:

Graphs   ▼
   Scatter ...
     Define: *simple plot*
     Define
       Y axis: res_1
       X axis: pre_1
      OK

Data Transformations

SPSS can be used to carry out a number of data transformations, including taking the inverse, logarithm, and the square root of the data set. It provides for a versatile range of data transformation techniques which are accessed with the commands:

Transform   ▼
   Compute ...
     Target Variable: *define new variable name*
       Numeric Expression: *define new variable using keypad and/or Functions*
     OK

2.12.2   GLIM

In order to run the GLIM examples presented below, type in the following command from within GLIM: $INPUT 'FILENAME.EXT'$, replacing FILENAME.EXT with that of each example file. To aid the reader, we have commented the commands extensively within each file. All macros which have been used are included at the end of this section.

Diagnostics for a Number of Data Sets

```
$page off $
$echo $
!       Input any macros that are needed.
$input %plc lev$
$input 'c:\glim4\examples\man.mac' hist $
$input 'screen.mac' $
!       Uncomment the gstyle command for monochrome figures when printing.
!       $gstyle 6 line 0 symbol 6 colour 1 $

!   Normal Errors
!   =============
$slen 150 $
!       Generate the error distribution
$calc x=%cu(1) $
$calc randkey=%sr(0) $
$sort x x randkey $
$calc yeq=2+3*x $
$calc error=60*%nd(%sr(0)) $
$calc y=(yeq+error)$
$nu ylarge $
$tab the y largest into ylarge $
$calc y = 1000*y/ylarge $
$yvar y $
!       Fit a simple linear model.
$fit x $
!       Display the parameter estimates.
$dis e $
!       Uncomment the following $open, $set and $close statements
!       to obtain a postscript file for high quality printout.
!                $open (status=new) 98='normerr.ps' $
!                $set device='POST' $
!       Call the macro to do graphical checks on the model fit.
$use checkgra $
!                $close 98 $set device='SCREEN' $
!
!   Skewed Errors
!   =============
!       Generate the error distribution
$calc x=%cu(1) $
$calc randkey=%sr(0) $
$sort x x randkey $
$calc yeq=2+3*x $
$calc error=60*%nd(%sr(0)) $
$calc y=(yeq+error)**9$
$nu ylarge $
$tab the y largest into ylarge $
$calc y = 1000*y/ylarge $
$yvar y $
$fit x $
!       Fit a simple linear model.
$dis e $
!                $open (status=new) 98='skewbef.ps' $
```

```
!                    $set device='POST' $
$use checkgra $
!                    $close 98 $set device='SCREEN' $
$num xsmall xlarge xstep x_grp $
!        Group the explanatory variable.
$tab the x largest into xlarge $
$tab the x smallest into xsmall $
$calc xstep=(xsmall+((xlarge-xsmall)/9))$
$assign xint=xsmall xstep ... xlarge $
!        The following is a fix to allow xlarge into the last interval
$calc xint(%len(xint))=xlarge+(xstep/1000000) $
$map x_gp= x intervals xint $
$tab the y mean;dev;weight for x_gp into mean;sd;n by xtable $
$cal w_sd=(n>1) $
!        Any sd's of 0 will cause a warning in the following statement:
$calc lm=%log(mean) : lsd=%log(sd) $
$cal w10=n-1 $
$weight w10 $
$yvar lsd $
!        Calculate the value of the slope for use in the transformation.
$fit lm $
$dis e $
$ext %pe $
$pr 'Slope of log mean vs log sd  for y is ' %pe $
$calc %p=1-%pe(2) $
$yvar y $
$fit x $
$num ysmall $
!        If powers is a real number, place variable in brackets:
!        y=(y)**(1-0.7753) $
$pr 'Transformation of y to y**' %p $
!        Transform the response variable.
$calc ytran=(y)**(%p) $
$calc y=ytran $
$yvar y $
!        Fit the model to the transformed response variable.
$fit x $
$dis e $
!                    $open (status=new) 98='skewaft.ps' $
!                    $set device='POST' $
$use checkgra $
!                    $close 98 $set device='SCREEN' $
!
!    Curvilinearity
!    ==============
!        Generate the error distribution
$calc x=%cu(1) $
$calc randkey=%sr(0) $
$sort x x randkey $
$calc x2=x*x $
$calc yeq=2+3*x+4*(x**2) $
!$calc error=4000*%nd(%sr(0)) $
$calc error=12000*%nd(%sr(0)) $
```

```
$calc y= yeq+error      $
$nu ylarge $
$tab the y largest into ylarge $
$calc y = 1000*y/ylarge $
$yvar y $
!       Fit a simple linear model.
$fit x $
$dis e $
!               $open (status=new) 98='crvlinbef.ps' $
!               $set device='POST' $
$use checkgra $
!               $close 98 $set device='SCREEN' $
!       Fit an orthogonal polynomial of X^5.
$fit x<5> $
$dis e $
!       Try the fit with an orthogonal polynomial of X^2.
$fit x<2>
$dis e $
!               $open (status=new) 98='crvlinaft.ps' $
!               $set device='POST' $
$use checkgra $
!               $close 98 $set device='SCREEN' $
$return
```

GLIM Macros for Data Screening

```
$mac grapause no $endmac $


!       Title for Histogram
$mac histitle b) Histogram of Residuals $end $
$mac h_optns t=histitle pause=no refresh=no   $end $

$mac (local= xf,yf,res,nqs,index,size)checkgra $
!       Plot fitted line and observed values versus an explanatary
!       variable.
$calc xf=x $
$predict (s=-1) x=xf $
$cal yf=%pfv $
$layout 0.17,0.67 0.5,1 $
$sort srty y x $
$sort srtyf yf x $
$sort srtx x $
$sort srtxf xf x $
$cal size=1.5 $
$gra (title='a) Observed & Fitted Values versus X' pause=no) srty/size;srtyf
        srtx;srtxf 6,10 $
!       Examination of residuals
!       Histogram of residuals
$var hwt $cal hwt=1 $num hpen=10 $
$num ressmall reslarge resstep $
$tab the %rs largest into reslarge $
$tab the %rs smallest into ressmall $
$calc resstep=(ressmall+((reslarge-ressmall)/9))$
```

```
$assign ix=ressmall resstep ... reslarge $
$layout 0.5,0.67 0.83,1 $
$use ghist %rs ix hwt hpen h_optns $
!        Normal plot
$sort res %rs $
$cal nqs=%nd((%gl(%nu,1)-0.5)/%nu) $
$layout 0.17,0.34 0.5,0.65 $
$gra (refresh=no title='c) Q-Q Normal Plot' pause=no) res/size nqs 6 $
!        Plot of residuals versus fitted values
$layout 0.5,0.34 0.83,0.65 $
$gra (refresh=no title='d) Residuals versus Fitted Values' pause=no)
         %rs/size %fv 6 $
!        Plot leverage values and Cook's distances
$extract %lv %cd $
$cal index=%ind(%lv) $
$layout 0.17,0 0.5,0.32 $
$var cutoff $
$calc cutoff=2*%pl/%sl $
$num maxval minval maxyaxis minyaxis$
$tab the %lv largest into maxval $tab the %lv smallest into minval $
$calc maxyaxis=%if(maxval>cutoff(1),maxval,cutoff(1))*1.0125 $
$calc minyaxis=%if(minval<cutoff(1),minval,cutoff(1))*0.9875 $
$gra (refresh=no ylim=minyaxis,maxyaxis
         title='e) Leverage Values versus Index' pause=no)
         %lv/size,cutoff  index 6,11 $
$cal index=%ind(%cd) $
$layout 0.5,0 0.83,0.32 $
$calc cutoff=4/(%sl-%pl) $
$tab the %cd largest into maxval $tab the %cd smallest into minval $
$calc maxyaxis=%if(maxval>cutoff(1),maxval,cutoff(1))*1.0125 $
$calc minyaxis=%if(minval<cutoff(1),minval,cutoff(1))*0.9875 $
$gra (refresh=no ylim=minyaxis,maxyaxis
         title='f) Cook''s Distances versus Index')
         %cd/size,cutoff index 6,11 $
$del xf yf res nqs index $
$endmac $

$return $
```

Chapter 3

Ordinary Least-Squares Regression

Ordinary least-squares (OLS) regression is one of the most popular statistical techniques used in the social sciences. It is used to predict values of a continuous response variable using one or more explanatory variables and can also identify the strength of the relationships between these variables (these two goals of regression are often referred to as prediction and explanation).

OLS regression assumes that all variables entered into the analysis are continuous and the regression procedure attaches importance to actual values. Response variables, i.e., those variables which are being modelled, must be continuous and be recorded on at least an interval scale if they are to be modelled using OLS regression[1]. Response variables which cannot be assumed to be continuous may be more appropriately analysed using other generalized linear modelling techniques discussed in this book, such as logistic regression (for variables which are dichotomous) or loglinear analysis (for categorical variables in the form of frequency counts). Though explanatory variables are also required to be continuous, dichotomous data can legitimately be used in a regression model. This is particularly useful as it makes it possible to include multi-category ordered and unordered categorical explanatory variables in a regression model provided that they are appropriately coded into a number of dichotomous 'dummy' categories.

OLS regression is a generalized linear modelling technique, which, as the name suggests, models linear relationships. The three components of generalized linear models for OLS regression are a random component for the response variable, which is assumed to be Normally distributed, a systematic component representing the fixed values of the explanatory variables in terms of a linear

---

[1] Although a continuous scale is assumed, OLS regression is often used to model ordered categorical data when there are a relatively large number of levels and an underlying continuous distribution can be assumed.

function, and finally, a link function which maps the systematic component onto the random component. In OLS regression, this is simply an identity link which means that the fitted value of the response variable is the same as the linear predictor arising from the systematic component. This might appear to be quite restrictive since a number of the relationships one might wish to model are likely to be non-linear. It is possible, however, to model non-linear relationships using OLS regression if appropriate transformations are applied to one or more of the variables which render the relationships linear.

OLS regression is a powerful technique for modelling continuous data, particularly when it is used in conjunction with dummy variable coding and data transformation. This chapter discusses in some depth its application to different types of data, which are related both linearly and non-linearly, and demonstrates how models can be constructed for explanatory and predictive purposes.

3.1 Simple OLS Regression

A description of simple linear regression, where there is just a single explanatory variable, serves as an introduction to the more complex technique of multiple regression where a number of explanatory variables can be entered into a model simultaneously. Simple regression is used to model the relationship between a continuous response variable y and an explanatory variable x.

3.1.1 The Regression Equation

For this discussion we will deal with a simple example of OLS regression where both the response and explanatory variables are continuous. A direct linear relationship between two such variables can be expressed in the form of an equation which identifies a straight line.

$$y = \alpha + \beta x \tag{3.1}$$

where α is the intercept of the line on the y axis,
and β is the slope of the line.

Equation 3.1 describes a direct linear relationship between x and y where the value of y can be precisely calculated from the value of x. The slope of the line can be described as the change in y which is associated with a unit change in x. For example, as x increases from 4 to 5 (a unit change), y increases by the value of β, the slope of the line. The slope of the line is also known as the *regression coefficient* and shows the effect that the explanatory variable has on the response variable. Figure 3.1 depicts the regression line for two variables which are perfectly linearly related and shows the regression coefficient, β, and the intercept, α.

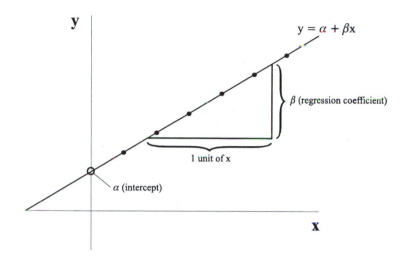

Figure 3.1: An OLS regression model depicting a perfect linear relationship

In the social sciences, however, perfect relationships of the type shown in Figure 3.1 are the exception rather than the rule, as relationships are rarely direct and measurement rarely error-free. The best we can hope to do is to calculate a line of *best-fit* to approximately describe the relationship between variables x and y. For OLS regression, the most common method for calculating this line is to use the least-squares procedure which minimizes the sum of the squared deviations (also known as the error, or residual) of each data point from the line (for a full description of the least-square technique refer to an introductory statistics book such as Crawshaw and Chambers, 1984 or Hays, 1994). Equation 3.2 defines a line of best-fit ($y = \alpha + \beta x$) and includes a term which indicates the degree to which data points deviate from this line.

$$y = \alpha + \beta x + \varepsilon \qquad (3.2)$$

where ε represents the error.

The deviation, or error, is often represented as the difference between the observed value of y and the value of y predicted from the model ($\hat{y}$). The term $y - \hat{y}$ provides a measure of deviation, or, put another way, the amount of error when y is predicted using the regression model. It should be noted that the term 'error', as it is used here, does not indicate that any mistake has been made, it simply indicates that the relationship between the variables is not exact.

The interpretation of the parameters α and β in Equation 3.2 are slightly different to those provided for Equation 3.1. α now represents the *average* value of y when $x = 0$, whilst β represents the *average* change in y which is associated with a unit change in x. Figure 3.2 shows the parameters α and β for a line of best-fit which models the relationship between two imperfectly related variables. The reader will note that the equation of the line does not include an error term since these are not explicitly estimated in regression models (error terms are, however, used in the construction of confidence and prediction intervals and in the calculation of goodness-of-fit statistics).

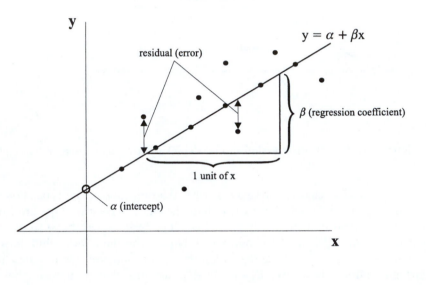

Figure 3.2: Line of best-fit

Using equations 3.1 and 3.2 it appears that one can predict the value of y, or at least the average value of y, for any given value of x. Whilst this is true mathematically, it is often unwise to predict values of a variable which are outside of the range of the observations. Ryan, 1997, distinguishes between *prediction*, where values of y are predicted within the observed range of the explanatory values, and *extrapolation*, where values of y are 'predicted' outside of the range of explanatory variables. For example, if a sample contained values of an explanatory variable that were between 0 and 25, it may not be appropriate to predict (extrapolate) the value of the response variable when the explanatory is equal to, say 60, as we do not know that our model will hold for such an extreme value.

Even though OLS regression is a linear modelling technique it can be used to accurately model non-linear relationships provided that one or both of the variables are transformed so that the relationship between them approximates to a straight line. Non-linear relationships which can be transformed to linear ones have been referred to as intrinsically or transformably linear. Failure to transform a non-linear relationship will not prevent an OLS regression model being fitted to the data, but will result in a degraded analysis and adversely affect the model fit. A complete example of how an OLS regression model can be applied to non-linear data is provided in Section 3.2.

3.1.2   Confidence Intervals for β

Although the value of β indicates the change in y which is associated with a unit change in x, its absolute magnitude does not indicate the 'strength' of the relationship between the variables. Consider the data presented in Table 3.1 and the accompanying scatterplots in Figure 3.3, for the three variables Y, X_1 and X_2.

Table 3.1: Data for Two Simple Regression Models

Y	X_1	X_2
0.52	10.50	11.09
2.09	13.19	12.91
4.52	16.62	14.09
1.93	14.94	15.29
0.63	12.17	16.15
4.52	16.85	17.06
2.52	16.35	18.34
5.19	18.34	18.72
4.02	18.40	19.03
8.21	23.21	20.07
4.77	21.30	21.87
7.97	23.81	22.27
8.24	25.02	23.98
7.01	22.68	24.19
8.92	26.28	24.75

The OLS regression line for the model $Y = \alpha + \beta X_1$ is identical (to 2 decimal places) to that for the model $Y = \alpha + \beta X_2$, even though the two scatterplots differ in the degree to which the data points are dispersed about the lines of best-fit. The relationship between Y and X_1 appears to be 'stronger' than the relationship between Y and X_2 (that is, β can be more precisely estimated), even though the value of β is the same in both cases. A useful exercise for determining the utility of the estimate of β is to identify the limits within

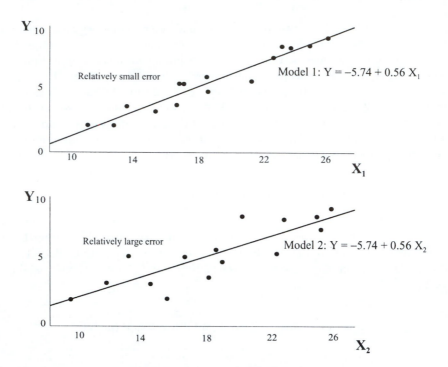

Figure 3.3: Two simple regression models with different degrees of error

which repeated samples can be expected to fall. These limits, or confidence intervals as they are commonly called, can be calculated using Equation 3.3.

$$\text{confidence interval for } \beta = \hat{\beta} \pm t_{\alpha/2,n-k-1}(\text{s.e. } \hat{\beta}) \qquad (3.3)$$

where $\hat{\beta}$ is the estimated value of β,

$t_{\alpha/2,n-k-1}$ is the value of t given the confidence interval $\alpha/2$ and degrees-of-freedom $n-k-1$,

n is the number of cases used to construct the model,

k is the number of terms in the model (not including the constant),

and s.e. $\hat{\beta}$ is the standard error of $\hat{\beta}$.

The 'hat' symbol which appears above β indicates that this parameter is estimated. The term $t_{\alpha/2,n-k-1}$ provides the value of t for the confidence interval, $\alpha/2$ (for example, a 95% two-tailed interval), with $n-k-1$ degrees-of-freedom. It should be noted that k indicates the number of *terms* in the model and not the number of *explanatory variables*. Although for this example, the number of terms in the model is equivalent to the number of explanatory variables, this isn't always the case since categorical variables may be represented using more than one term (see Section 3.3.7). It should also be noted that n refers to the number of cases used to construct the model and not the number of cases observed for a particular variable (cases with missing values for a particular variable are often completely removed from the analysis). The value of t can be derived using software or from statistical tables which provide critical values of the t distribution. For example, the value of t for a 95% two-tailed confidence interval with 19 degrees-of-freedom (that is, 21 observations and 1 term in the model) is equal to 2.093. Since the large sample (above about 30) approximation of t for 95% two-tailed confidence intervals is 1.96, Equation 3.3 can be simplified to Equation 3.4.

$$\text{confidence interval for } \beta = \hat{\beta} \pm 1.96(\text{s.e. } \hat{\beta}) \tag{3.4}$$

where 1.96 is the large sample approximation of t for a two-tailed, 95% confidence interval.

Table 3.2: Statistics for the Regression Models Shown in Figure 3.3

	Coefficient	s.e.	t	P	95% CIs Upper	95% CIs Lower
Model 1						
X_1	0.562	0.041	13.813	0.000	0.474	0.650
(constant)	−5.738	0.782	−7.335	0.000	−7.428	−4.048
Model 2						
X_2	0.562	0.100	5.612	0.000	0.345	0.778
(constant)	−5.738	1.911	−3.002	0.010	−9.867	−1.609

Model 1: $Y = \alpha + \beta X_1$
Model 2: $Y = \alpha + \beta X_2$

The coefficients for variables X_1 and X_2 in Table 3.2 provide the values of β (the slope of the line of best-fit) whilst the coefficients for the constants provide the values of α (the intercept of the line of best-fit on the Y-axis). Although identical regression equations are derived for both models ($Y = -5.738 + 0.562X$), Model 1 has a smaller standard error associated with the estimate of β and consequently has a smaller confidence interval. For Model 1, we can say with 95% confidence that for each unit increase in X_1, Y is expected to increase somewhere between 0.474 and 0.650 (a range of 0.176). For Model 2, each unit increase in X_2 is expected to increase the value of Y somewhere between 0.345 and 0.778 (a range of 0.433). Clearly, a more accurate estimate of Y can be obtained using X_1 than can be obtained using X_2. These values were calculated using software (see Section 3.6), but could also have been calculated manually (as this is a relatively small sample we will use Equation 3.3 rather than Equation 3.4). For example, the confidence intervals for β which are associated with X_1 can be calculated as

$$
\begin{aligned}
\text{95\% two-tailed CIs for } \beta &= \hat{\beta} \pm [t_{n-k-1}(\text{s.e. } \beta)] \\
&= 0.562 \pm [t_{13} \times 0.041] \\
&= 0.562 \pm [2.16 \times 0.041] \\
&= 0.473, 0.651
\end{aligned}
$$

which, allowing for rounding error, is the same result as that obtained using software (see Table 3.2).

Using these intervals, it is a simple matter to determine whether a significant linear relationship exists between the response and explanatory variables. Confidence intervals for β which include zero indicate no significant linear relationship as a unit change in x is associated with no change in y (x is therefore independent of y). For example, as neither of the confidence intervals for X_1 or X_2 include zero (see Table 3.2) both variables can be said to be significantly linearly related to the response variable at the 95% level. In OLS regression, the hypothesis that there is no linear relationship between the variables (i.e., that the slope of the line of best-fit is equal to zero) can be explicitly tested using the t statistic, which is calculated by dividing the regression coefficient by the standard error. The significance of t_{n-k-1} can be determined using software or statistical tables. As a rough guide, the regression coefficient should be at least twice the value of the standard error for a statistically significant result.

3.1.3   Confidence Intervals for Fitted y

The fitted value for the response variable is the estimate of its *mean* value for a given value of the explanatory variable. Similar to the case of β, it is possible to construct confidence intervals for this mean fitted value. For large samples (n greater than about 30), 95% confidence intervals for fitted y can be calculated using Equation 3.5.

$$\text{confidence interval for fitted } y = \hat{y} \pm 1.96\sqrt{s_{\hat{y}}^2} \qquad (3.5)$$

where $\hat{y}$ is the fitted value of y,

1.96 is the large sample approximation of t for a two-tailed 95% confidence interval,

and $s_{\hat{y}}^2$ is the standard error of the mean prediction.

Figure 3.4 shows two regression models which have been fitted to the data presented in Table 3.1 along with the confidence intervals for fitted y. It is obvious from the graph that these intervals are not parallel, but are in fact curved. This is because fitted y can be more accurately predicted when x is close to its mean value. The size of the confidence interval depends on the distance of x from $\bar{x}$. The confidence intervals for fitted y given a number of different values of the variables X_1 and X_2 are provided in Table 3.3.

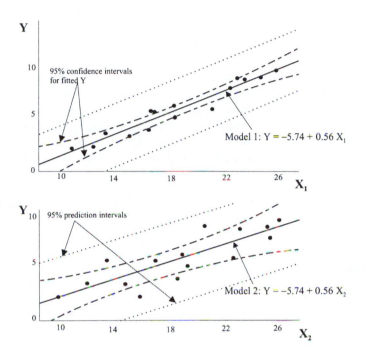

Figure 3.4: Confidence and prediction intervals for two regression models

3.1.4 Prediction Intervals

Equation 3.5 can be extended to allow probability statements to be made about the likely values of *individual* cases of the response variable given a certain value of the explanatory variable. This interval is not called a *confidence interval* since y is a random variable and not a parameter (Aitkin, Anderson, Francis & Hinde, 1989). The equation for this prediction interval has an extra term since the additional variation in the random variable needs to be allowed for. Ninety-five percent two-tailed prediction intervals for large samples can be calculated using Equation 3.6:

$$\text{prediction interval for } y = \hat{y} \pm 1.96\sqrt{s^2 + s_{\hat{y}}^2} \tag{3.6}$$

where s^2 is the standard error of the estimate,

and $s_{\hat{y}}^2$ is the standard error of the mean prediction.

Figure 3.4 shows the prediction intervals calculated for two regression models. Similar to the confidence intervals for fitted y, these intervals are curved with values of y predicted more accurately when x is close to its mean value. The manual calculation of the expression $\sqrt{s^2 + s_{\hat{y}}^2}$ is quite involved and will not, therefore, be demonstrated here (see Ryan, 1997 and Norušis, 1994, for examples of how prediction intervals can be calculated manually). It is, however, unnecessary to manually compute prediction intervals for y as these can be generated using statistical software (see Section 3.6). Prediction intervals for Y, given a number of different values of X (some of which are included in the data in Table 3.1, and some of which are not), are provided in Table 3.3.

Table 3.3: Confidence and Prediction Intervals for Two Regression Models

Value of X	Fitted Value of Y	95% CIs		95% PIs	
		Upper	Lower	Upper	Lower
Model 1					
10.50	0.162	−0.666	0.989	−1.646	1.969
18.34	4.567	4.150	4.982	2.907	6.226
31.87	12.168	9.941	12.070	9.078	12.933
Model 2					
7.30	−1.638	−4.249	0.972	−5.955	2.678
18.34	4.561	3.671	5.451	1.009	8.113
24.75	8.161	6.572	9.750	4.373	11.948

Model 1: $Y = \alpha + \beta X_1$

Model 2: $Y = \alpha + \beta X_2$

The interpretation of the intervals shown in Table 3.3 is similar to the interpretation of the confidence intervals for β which were discussed earlier. For example, when X_1 has a value of 10.5, the mean value of Y is predicted to lie between −0.666 and 0.989, and an individual case between −1.646 and 1.969. When X_1 and X_2 are both 18.34, the fitted values for Y are similar (the regression equations are nearly identical) but there are differences in the confidence and prediction intervals for the two models. Model 1 predicts a narrower range of values for Y and suggests that X_1 is a more useful variable than X_2 for predicting mean and individual values of Y. From Table 3.3 it is easy to see that the prediction intervals are curved, as the optimal predictions are achieved when x is close to its mean value (the difference between the upper and lower prediction intervals are smaller for less extreme values of x). It is also clear that the confidence intervals for the mean value of y are narrower than the prediction intervals for individual values of y.

To summarize, one uses *confidence intervals* for fitted y when making statements about the predicted mean value of the response variable in further samples, whilst *prediction intervals* are used when predicting the value of a single case of the response variable.

3.1.5   Goodness-of-fit Measures

Confidence and prediction intervals provide an indication of the usefulness of a regression model, but do not provide an easily interpretable goodness-of-fit measure (that is, how well the regression model fits the data). Two statistics are discussed here, R^2, which provides some descriptive information about the model fit, and the F statistic, which provides a measure of significance.

The R^2 Statistic

R^2 provides descriptive information about the model fit and is calculated using Equation 3.7 which compares observed values of y with those predicted from the model. R^2 for a simple regression, where there is a single explanatory variable, is known as the coefficient of determination.

$$R^2 = \frac{\sum(\hat{y} - \bar{y})^2}{\sum(y - \bar{y})^2} \tag{3.7}$$

where y is the observed value of y,
$\hat{y}$ is the value of y predicted from the model,
and $\bar{y}$ is the mean value of y.

In Equation 3.7, if $\hat{y}$ and y are the same (that is, the model perfectly predicts y), the numerator and the denominator assume identical values and $R^2 = 1$. If, on the other hand, the model provides no clues as to the value of y, then $\hat{y} = \bar{y}$ (that is, the predicted value of y remains constant and the explanatory variable therefore plays no part in determining the value of the response variable) and the expression $(\hat{y} - \bar{y})^2 = 0$, which in turn leads to an R^2 value of 0. Values of R^2 therefore range from 0, which indicates no linear relationship, to 1, which indicates a perfect linear relationship.

R^2 is commonly interpreted as the percentage of the variability in y that is explained by x when it is used to predict y. In general terms, it provides an indication of how well the model fits the data. For simple regression,

R^2 indicates the strength of the linear relationship between x and y. For example, if a simple regression model has an R^2 value of 0.748 one can conclude that 74.8% of the variability in the response variable is accounted for by the explanatory variable. It should be noted, however, that although R^2 is widely used and accepted as a measure of model fit, it has a tendency to increase as the slope of the regression line increases and is not, therefore, a completely unbiased measure (see Barrett, 1974). Even with this limitation, R^2 is a useful statistic and is used extensively in this chapter to provide an easily understood estimate of model fit.

The F Statistic

Whilst R^2 provides an indication of the explanatory power of a model, it does not indicate the level of significance (that is, how likely it was that the R^2 value had been obtained by chance). To do this we need to test the hypothesis that the regression coefficient, β, equals zero. A test of this hypothesis is provided by the F test which can be calculated using the R^2 statistic, or, more appropriately, directly from the measure of deviance. Equation 3.8 (see Afifi and Clark, 1996 and Berry and Feldman, 1993) shows how F can be calculated from R^2.

$$F_{k,n-k-1} = \frac{R^2/k}{(1 - R^2)/(n - k - 1)} \tag{3.8}$$

where R^2 is the coefficient of determination,

n is the number of cases used to construct the model,

and k is the number of terms in the model (not including the constant).

If the value of F is not significant, the null hypothesis of no linear relationship between x and y is accepted. If, on the other hand, the value of F is significant the null hypothesis is rejected and the hypothesis that there is a significant linear relationship between x and y is accepted. You will note that for the simple case, the F test is equivalent to the t test since both evaluate the relationship $\beta = 0$. In fact, $\sqrt{F} = t$.

A more useful method of testing the hypothesis $\beta = 0$, is to derive the value of F from the residual sum of squares statistic (RSS), which is the deviance for a GLM with an identity link. RSS is the sum of the squared differences between the observed and predicted values of y, i.e., $(\sum(y - \hat{y})^2)$, and gives a measure of how much the observed data differ from predictions from the model. Equation 3.9 overleaf shows the general formula for calculating the value of F from the deviance measure RSS (see Afifi and Clark, 1996 and Francis, Greene and Payne, 1994).

This equation compares the amount of deviance in the null model ($y = \alpha$) with the amount of deviance in the model $y = \alpha + \beta x$. If the explanatory

$$F_{(df_{null}-df_{model}),df_{model}} = \frac{RSS_{null} - RSS_{model}}{(df_{null} - df_{model})(RSS_{model}/df_{model})} \qquad (3.9)$$

where 'null' indicates the model $y = \alpha$,

'model' indicates the model $y = \alpha + \beta x$,

RSS is the residual sum of squares for the designated model,

and df is the degrees-of-freedom for the designated model.

variable does not enable a significantly better prediction to be made, RSS_{null} and RSS_{model} will have similar values and the value of F will tend to be small. If, on the other hand, the explanatory variable has a large effect on the model, the expression $RSS_{null} - RSS_{model}$ will assume a relatively large value and F will also tend to be large. Although Equations 3.8 and 3.9 can both be used to calculate F, the latter is more useful as it is more general and enables not only the significance of the entire model to be determined, but through the computation of a *partial-F* statistic, enables the significance of individual and groups of variables to be assessed. This is particularly useful in multiple OLS regression and is discussed further in Section 3.3.5.

Table 3.4: Goodness-of-fit Measures for Two Regression Models

	Coefficient	R^2	t	F	P
Model 1					
X_1	0.562	0.936	13.813	190.80	0.000
Model 2					
X_2	0.562	0.708	5.612	31.34	0.000

Model 1: $Y = \alpha + \beta X_1$

Model 2: $Y = \alpha + \beta X_2$

Table 3.4 shows a number of statistics which assess the model fit of the two regression models computed for the 15 cases in Table 3.1. These values have been calculated from software, but could also have been calculated manually. For example, using Equation 3.8 the value of F for model 1 can be calculated from R^2 as $0.936/[0.064/(15–1–1)]$, which equals 190.134 (allowing for rounding error, this is the same result as that obtained using software). F can also be derived using Equation 3.9. Given $RSS_{null} = 112.715$ and $RSS_{model} = 7.190$, the value of F is equal to $(112.715 - 7.190)/(7.190/13)$, which equals 190.796 (the calculation of F from RSS statistics is demonstrated in Section 3.6). Given that the general form of equation for calculating F is more useful (and also easier to understand), this book will standardize on the use of Equation 3.9 to calculate the F statistic.

3.2   A Worked Example of Simple Regression

Table 3.5: The Cost and Sound Quality of Music Systems

Cost (£)	Quality	Cost (£)	Quality	Cost (£)	Quality
35	5	180	49	502	78
39	7	186	51	550	78
40	34	190	60	595	75
48	9	195	48	655	76
50	32	200	72	660	79
55	15	205	69	690	82
58	42	210	71	775	78
79	30	246	63	842	84
97	43	254	72	910	76
100	30	300	69	1000	79
100	18	335	64	1050	81
149	41	350	65	1099	82
150	61	415	82	1200	79
156	43	430	71	1225	75
175	40	448	73	1300	88

Table 3.5 contains hypothetical data showing the cost (£ sterling) and sound quality of 45 different music systems of varied price. Sound quality is recorded on a continuous scale and represents scores provided by a group of raters (the higher the score the better the sound reproduction).

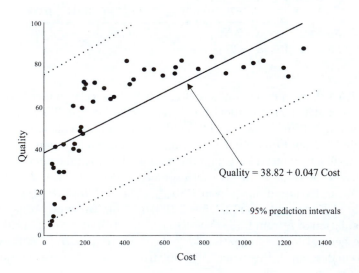

Figure 3.5: Relationship between rated quality and cost of music systems

The scatterplot in Figure 3.5 displays the relationship between Cost and Quality for the music systems included in the study and shows that this relationship does not appear to be linear. There is a relatively large increase in sound quality between systems costing £50 to £300, but after this, for a given increase in the cost of the system, the increase in sound quality is much less dramatic. There appears to be a relationship between Cost and Quality which conforms broadly to a 'law of diminishing returns'. A simple OLS regression analysis of the data in Table 3.5 gives the model shown in Equation 3.10.

$$\text{Quality} = 38.820 + 0.047\,\text{Cost} \qquad (3.10)$$

Quality and Cost are significantly linearly related ($F_{1,43} = 53.25; P < 0.0005$) with an R^2 value of 0.553. Even though this is a highly significant result, the regression line does not appear to describe the relationship between Quality and Cost particularly well. It is obvious that a non-linear relationship is being described using a linear model (see Figure 3.5). In an attempt to improve this model, transformations were applied to the variables using some of the techniques described in Chapter 2. Cost was transformed using a natural log, whilst Quality was squared (see Equation 3.11). These transformations were chosen solely for the purpose of improving the model fit and resulted in a relationship between the variables which more closely approximated a straight-line (see Figure 3.6).

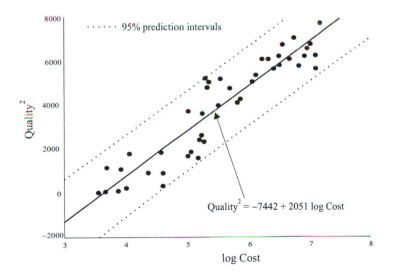

Figure 3.6: Relationship between Quality^2 and log Cost

$$\text{Quality}^2 = -7442.02 + 2051.20\,\text{log Cost} \qquad (3.11)$$

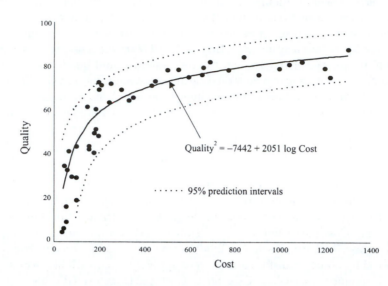

Figure 3.7: The transformed model

Table 3.6 shows clearly that the transformed model provides a higher value of R^2 and a more significant linear relationship between the variables than does the untransformed model. Redrawing Figure 3.6 using the original axes (Cost and Quality) demonstrates clearly that the transformed model provides a closer approximation to the data.

Table 3.6: Two Models Predicting Sound Quality

System Cost	Predicted Sound Quality	95% 2-tailed PIs Lower	95% 2-tailed PIs Upper	PI Range
Model 1				
£100	43.53	10.72	76.33	65.61
£385	56.94	24.39	89.49	65.10
£1200	95.30	61.18	129.43	68.25
Model 2				
£100	44.77	13.49	61.86	48.37
£385	69.06	54.40	81.11	26.71
£1200	84.27	72.48	94.60	22.12

Model 1: Quality = 38.82 + 0.047 Cost
$F_{1,43} = 53.25$, $P < 0.0005$, $R^2 = 0.55$

Model 2: Quality^2 = −7442 + 2051.2 log Cost
$F_{1,43} = 266.96$, $P < 0.0005$, $R^2 = 0.86$

The prediction intervals for the transformed model are narrower making it a more useful model for predicting sound quality. The differences between the two models are shown in Table 3.6 which shows estimates for the sound quality of systems priced at £100, £385 and £1200 (all within the range of those sampled) which have been calculated using the transformed and untransformed models described above. Of particular note are the narrower prediction intervals associated with the transformed model which enables more accurate predictions to be made.

3.3   Multiple OLS Regression

Multiple regression is a technique which can be used to investigate the relationship between a response variable and more than one explanatory variable. As with simple regression, it can be used to both identify significant relationships (explanation) and predict values of the response variable (prediction). The ability to analyse the effect of multiple variables is particularly useful in the social sciences as it is usually the case that more than one source of information is required to make adequate predictions. For example, wage may be dependent upon a number of factors including gender, education, ethnicity and experience, all of which have to be accounted for if wage is to be successfully modelled.

Although it is possible to investigate the relationship between a response variable and a number of explanatory variables using multiple simple regressions, this method is not appropriate if the explanatory variables are interrelated. Multiple simple regressions do not take into account relationships between explanatory variables and as a result can provide a misleading picture of the data. This can be illustrated with the help of a hypothetical example where a particular company employs on the basis of educational achievement and not on the basis of gender[2]. If this company recruits in a region where males and females do not have equal access to education, it is likely that a simple regression model predicting wage from gender will show a significant relationship between the two. In this case, the relationship is not due to discrimination by the company on the basis of gender, but is due to a bias in the provision of education which results in greater access to schools and colleges for males. Males tend to be more highly educated and, consequently, better paid. The relationship between gender and wage is a consequence of the relationship between gender and education; a relationship which is not accounted for using simple regression analyses.

Figure 3.8 shows a graphical representation of the relationship between wage, education and gender. These variables are represented by circles with

---

[2]Although we have so far dealt exclusively with continuous data, this example introduces the use of discontinuous data in regression. The variables 'gender' and 'educational achievement' are not continuous but can still be included in a regression model provided that they have been appropriately coded (see Section 3.3.7).

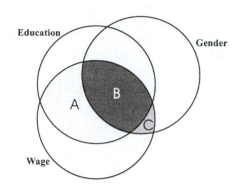

Simple regressions:

Wage = α + β Education

Area = A + B: R^2 = 0.76

Wage = α + β Gender

Area = B + C: R^2 = 0.47

Multivariate regression:

Wage = α + β_1 Education + β_2 Gender

Area = A + B + C: R^2 = 0.79

Figure 3.8: Relationship between wage levels, education, and gender

overlapping areas indicating the degree of correlation (this can be viewed as equivalent to the R^2 measure). The regression model Wage = $\alpha + \beta$ Education, has a model fit equivalent to areas A and B, and the regression model Wage = $\alpha + \beta$ Gender has a model fit equivalent to areas B and C. Since the R^2 values of both models include the area B, we cannot simply combine them to provide a figure for the overall R^2 when wage is predicted using both explanatory variables. For example, combining the two R^2 values for the simple regression models gives an overall R^2 of 1.23 (equivalent to areas A+B+B+C), which suggests that over 100% of the variance in the response variable can be explained by the two explanatory variables. The extent to which wages can be predicted by both explanatory variables needs to be determined using a multiple regression model which takes account of both variables simultaneously and provides an overall R^2 value equivalent to the area A+B+C (which is equal to 0.79 in the example above).

Using multiple regression, one can calculate the effect that each explanatory variable has on the response variable whilst controlling for other variables in the model. In the example above, the effect of education on wage is calculated whilst gender is held constant and the effect of gender on wage is calculated whilst education is held constant. The regression coefficients indicate the unique contribution made by each explanatory variable. In this case, the unique contributions of education and gender to predicting wage correspond to areas A and C respectively. It is clear from Figure 3.8 that gender has a relatively small effect on wage once its relationship with education has been taken into account.

3.3.1   The Regression Equation

Multiple OLS regression aims to arrive at an equation which describes the relationship between a continuous response variable and a number of explanatory variables. The multiple regression equation is almost identical to the simple regression equation except that it accounts for more than one explanatory variable. The general form of the equation is:

$$y = \alpha + \beta_1 x_1 + \beta_2 x_2 + \beta_3 x_3 + \ldots + \beta_k x_k \qquad (3.12)$$

where α is the average value of y when each $x = 0$,
x_1 to x_k are the values of k different explanatory variables,
and β_1 to β_k are partial regression coefficients.

In Equation 3.12, β represents the average change in y which is expected to result from a change of one unit in x *when all other variables are held constant*. For example, if β_4 equals 1.98, y increases by an average of 1.98 each time x_4 increases by 1. Similarly, if β_2 equals -37.1, y decreases by 37.1 for each unit increase in x_2. The partial regression coefficient β identifies the effect that x has on y independent of other variables in the model (that is, it identifies the unique contribution made by x in determining y). It should be noted that partial regression coefficients, β_k, are dependent upon the units in which variables are measured and cannot therefore be used directly to compare the relative importance of terms in a model — one must use confidence intervals for the coefficients, or significance tests for this purpose.

Interactions and Curvilinearity

Equation 3.12 assumes that the effects of the explanatory variables are additive. That is, the response variable is determined by so much of x_1, plus so much of x_2, plus so much of x_3, etc. This regression model assumes that the effect of any single explanatory variable remains the same across the range of other explanatory variables. The model, as it stands in equation 3.12, does not account for interactions between explanatory variables. It is, however, relatively easy to include interaction terms by including terms which are the product of the explanatory variables that are interacting (for example, an interaction between x_1 and x_2 can be represented in a model by including the term $x_1 \times x_2$). Equation 3.13 shows a regression model containing terms for two explanatory variables and an interaction between them. The 'main effect' of each variable is given by the terms $\beta_1 x_1$ and $\beta_2 x_2$, whilst the interaction between them is represented by the term $\beta_3 x_1 x_2$.

$$y = \alpha + \beta_1 x_1 + \beta_2 x_2 + \beta_3 x_1 x_2 \qquad (3.13)$$

The regression coefficient β_3 indicates the change in y which is expected to occur as a result of a unit change in $x_1 \times x_2$, whilst controlling for the other terms in the model. Although this definition is quite straightforward, it can be difficult to meaningfully interpret interactions (y is dependent on the product of x_1 and x_2). Interpreting interactions generally becomes more difficult as more explanatory variables are included. Interactions can contain as many terms as there are explanatory variables in the model. For example, a regression model containing five explanatory variables (x_1 to x_5) can contain an interaction term which is the product of all five variables ($x_1 \times x_2 \times x_3 \times x_4 \times x_5$). In addition to this 5-way interaction term, the model can also contain a number of 4-way, 3-way and 2-way interactions. The number of interactions which can be included increases greatly with the number of explanatory variables and consequently makes the regression model considerably more complex.

It is important to check interactions and include in the model those which are significant, even if interpretation proves difficult (in practice, however, many interactions tend to be insignificant and can be left out of the model; see Lewis–Beck, 1993). Significant interactions need to be included as these affect the parameters which are calculated for the other terms in the model. For example, a regression model with two explanatory variables x_1 and x_2, shows a significant interaction. This interaction needs to be included in the model (by including the term $x_1 \times x_2$) as it has consequences for the parameters calculated for x_1 and x_2. In this case, to appropriately interpret the effect that x_1 or x_2 have on the response variable, the interaction term needs to be included. It should be noted that the appropriate coding and interpretation of these terms is quite complex and a full discussion is beyond the scope of this chapter. Detailed accounts of how to code and interpret interactions can be found in Chapter 5 as well as a number of other texts (see, for example, Lewis–Beck, 1993; Hardy, 1993 and Jaccard, Turrisi and Wan, 1990). A worked example of a multiple regression with an interaction term is provided in Section 3.4.

The usefulness of OLS regression as a modelling tool is further enhanced since, in addition to interaction terms, regression models can include terms for non-linear and quadratic relationships. These relationships can be dealt with in much the same way as interactions, with additional terms (for example, x^2 and x^3) being added to the model (see Chapter 2 for a discussion of these types of relationships).

3.3.2 Confidence Intervals for β

As with simple regression, confidence intervals can be calculated to indicate the range within which the partial regression coefficients are expected to fall a certain proportion of the time (for example, 95% or 99% of the time). Ninety-five percent two-tailed confidence intervals for β can be calculated using Equation 3.3, which, for large samples can be simplified to Equation 3.14.

$$\text{Confidence interval for } \beta = \hat{\beta} \pm 1.96(\text{s.e. } \hat{\beta}) \qquad (3.14)$$

The confidence intervals associated with partial regression coefficients are interpreted in much the same way as the confidence intervals for simple regression coefficients which were discussed in Section 3.1.2. The only difference is that other terms in the model are controlled for. A partial regression coefficient of zero indicates that there is no linear relationship between that regressor and the response variable after controlling for all other terms in the model. Similarly, a confidence interval which includes zero indicates that there is no significant linear relationship between that term and the response variable. The significance of the relationship between individual partial regression coefficients and the response variable can be formally tested using the t statistic (with $n - k - 1$ degrees of freedom) to evaluate the hypothesis $\beta = 0$. If β is significantly different to zero, it can be concluded that there is a linear relationship between the explanatory and the response variable[3].

3.3.3 Confidence Intervals for Fitted y

Confidence intervals for the mean value of fitted y can be calculated in an identical way to that used in simple regression. Ninety-five percent two-tailed confidence intervals for a large sample can be derived using Equation 3.15.

$$\text{confidence interval for fitted } y = \hat{y} \pm 1.96\sqrt{s_{\hat{y}}^2} \qquad (3.15)$$

3.3.4 Prediction Intervals

The technique for calculating prediction intervals in multiple regression is identical to that used in simple regression and for large samples can be derived using Equation 3.16.

---

[3]It is also possible to test the significance of a partial regression coefficient using an F test with k and $n - k - 1$ degrees-of-freedom (see Edwards, 1985, for a discussion of this).

$$\text{prediction interval for } y = \hat{y} \pm 1.96\sqrt{s^2 + s_{\hat{y}}^2}. \qquad (3.16)$$

As with simple OLS regression, the size of the confidence and prediction intervals depend on the distance of x_k from $\bar{x}_k$. The more extreme the values of x_k used to predict individual or mean values of y, the larger the intervals will be. Similar to OLS regression, the confidence intervals for the fitted values of the mean of y are narrower than the prediction intervals for individual values of y. A demonstration of the calculation and use of prediction intervals in a multiple regression model is shown in Section 3.4.

3.3.5   Goodness-of-fit Measures

The goodness-of-fit of multiple regression models can be assessed using the R^2 and F statistics in much the same way as in simple regression.

The R^2 and R_a^2 Statistics

The goodness-of-fit of a multiple regression model can be indicated by the R^2 statistic which shows the proportion of the response variable that can be explained by *all* terms (or regressors) included in the model (see Equation 3.7). The R^2 statistic calculated for a model containing multiple terms is commonly known as the coefficient of multiple determination and is widely used. However, it is not an ideal indicator of model fit since each term introduced into a model increases the value of R^2 even if it has *no* influence on y, as each term will 'account for' at least one case. R^2 therefore provides an optimistic measure of model fit which tends to 1.0 as the number of terms included in the model increases relative to the number of cases. When there are as many terms in the model as there are cases, R^2 will always equal 1.0, no matter what the relationship between the response and explanatory variables. One solution to this problem is to calculate an *adjusted* R^2 statistic (R_a^2) which takes into account the number of terms entered into the model and does not necessarily increase as more terms are added. Adjusted R^2 can be derived using equation 3.17.

$$R_a^2 = R^2 - \frac{k(1 - R^2)}{n - k - 1} \qquad (3.17)$$

where R^2 is the coefficient of multiple determination,

n is the number of cases used to construct the model,

and k is the number of terms in the model (not including the constant).

In a similar way to R^2, R_a^2 only provides a 'rough indication' of the model fit. In a discussion of the use of R_a^2, Draper & Smith (1981, page 92) conclude that it "might be useful as an initial gross indicator, but that is all". Given that neither statistic provides a 'perfect' measure of model fit, this book will use the more widely adopted R^2 statistic.

The F and Partial-F Statistics

An F test can be used to formally test the null hypothesis that there is no linear relationship between the response and all of the explanatory variables in the model (see Equation 3.18).

$$\beta_1 = \beta_2 = \beta_3 = \beta_4 =, \ldots, = \beta_k = 0 \tag{3.18}$$

where β_1 to β_k are partial regression coefficients,
and k is the number of terms in the model.

In multiple regression, the value of F can be calculated using Equation 3.9 in exactly the same way as was demonstrated for simple regression and provides a measure of overall model fit. This equation is, however, of limited use in multiple regression as it does not enable the significance of individual terms in the model to be assessed. Equation 3.19 shows a modification to Equation 3.9 that allows nested models (a nested model is one which is a subset of another) to be compared through the calculation of a partial-F statistic.

$$F_{(df_p - df_{p+q}), df_{p+q}} = \frac{\text{RSS}_p - \text{RSS}_{p+q}}{(df_p - df_{p+q})(\text{RSS}_{p+q}/df_{p+q})} \tag{3.19}$$

where 'p' indicates the smaller model,
'p+q' indicates the larger model,
RSS is the residual sum of squares for the designated model,
and df is the degrees-of-freedom for the designated model.

The partial-F statistic is important in OLS regression as it allows the significance of individual and groups of terms to be determined. For example, the unique effect that variable x_2 has on the model $y = \alpha + \beta_1 x_1 + \beta_2 x_2$ can be determined by comparing this model with the model $y = \alpha + \beta_1 x_1$. The difference in the model fit between the two, as determined by the partial-F statistic, indicates the effect that variable x_2 has on the response variable. Similarly, the effect that a group of terms has on the model fit can be determined by comparing a model which contains the group with a nested model which does not. For example, if a model containing three explanatory variables (a, b and

c) shows a significant three-way interaction, the regression model predicting y can be represented as:

$$y = \alpha + \beta_1 a + \beta_2 b + \beta_3 c + \beta_4 ab + \beta_5 ac + \beta_6 bc + \beta_7 abc.$$

If the terms containing variable a are not highly significant, and are not the-oretically crucial, it might be useful to remove all these parameters from the model (i.e., $\beta_1 a$, $\beta_4 ab$, $\beta_5 ac$ and $\beta_7 abc$). The effect on the model fit of remov-ing all parameters containing variable a can be determined using a partial-F test computed using the full model above and the nested model:

$$y = \alpha + \beta_1 b + \beta_2 c + \beta_3 bc.$$

The resulting partial-F value shows the unique effect that all four terms con-sidered together have on the model fit.

The partial-F statistic is used extensively in model selection and allows the process of model-building to be greatly simplified and accelerated. As it allows nested models to be compared, groups of terms can be assessed for significance which allows the significance of some or all terms which relate to one particular variable to be derived as well as the effect of, say, all two-way or three-way interactions (see Section 3.6 for an example of this in GLIM). In addition to this, partial-F allows the significance of categorical variables, which are represented as a number of separate terms, to be appropriately assessed. Given its importance in OLS regression, the use of the partial-F statistic is discussed in detail in Section 3.3.8 and demonstrated in Sections 3.4 and 3.6.

3.3.6   Multicollinearity

The technique of multiple regression allows more than one explanatory variable to be entered into a model. However, there are some considerations concern-ing which variables may be entered. Perhaps the most important of these is *multicollinearity*, a term used here to describe a situation where an explana-tory variable is related to one or more of the other explanatory variables in the model. If these relationships are perfect or very strong, the calculation of the regression model and the appropriate interpretation of the results can be affected. In the case where one explanatory variable can be precisely predicted from one or more of the other explanatory variables (perfect multicollinearity), the analysis fails as a regression equation cannot even be formulated. When a relationship is strong, but not perfect (high multicollinearity), the regression equation can be formulated, but the parameters may be unreliable. Parameters which are unreliable can change dramatically as a result of relatively minor changes in the data set with the addition or deletion of a small number of observations exerting a large influence on the regression equation and, subsequently, on the interpretation of the results.

The consequences of multicollinearity depend, to some degree, on the objectives of the analysis. If the goal is prediction, then multicollinearity need not present much of a problem, as it primarily affects the calculated importance of the explanatory variables. Even though the interpretation of the regression coefficients associated with the explanatory variables may be suspect, the response variable may still be able to be accurately predicted. However, if the goal is explanation (that is, the aim is to identify the strength of relationships between individual explanatory variables and the response variable), the presence of a high degree of multicollinearity poses a serious problem for the correct interpretation of the results. When conducting a multiple regression, one has to identify when multicollinearity is likely to present a problem and a strategy to deal with it must be decided upon.

Perfect Multicollinearity

Perfect multicollinearity occurs when an explanatory variable can be precisely predicted from other explanatory variables in the model. When this happens, the variable contributes no unique information to the model and is therefore redundant. The inclusion of one or more redundant explanatory variables in a regression model is problematic as it is not possible to determine the parameters associated with these variables and, consequently, a regression equation cannot even be formulated. This problem can be demonstrated by looking at a three-variable relationship, which can be represented algebraically as a plane $y = \alpha + \beta_1 x + \beta_2 z$ (the three variables are y, x and z). If one of these explanatory variables is redundant (say, $x = 5z$) then y can be described in terms of a single variable (x or z), which is represented algebraically as a line ($y = \alpha + \beta x$). The regression procedure attempts to calculate parameters for x and z, but since there is merely information about one of them, only one coefficient can be computed and the regression technique breaks down (for a detailed discussion of this see Berry and Feldman, 1993 and Maddala, 1992). In essence, when there is perfect multicollinearity, the regression parameters cannot be formulated as the multiple regression procedure attempts to fit an equation which has more dimensions than are present in the data.

In practice, perfect multicollinearity is not usually a problem as it is quite rare and can be readily detected. In fact, many statistical analysis packages automatically alert the user to its presence. A more serious problem for the analyst is the presence of high multicollinearity where a regression model can be formulated, but the parameters associated with some of the explanatory variables may be unreliable.

High Multicollinearity

When explanatory variables are highly (but not perfectly) related to one or more of the other explanatory variables in the model it becomes difficult to disentangle the separate effect of each variable. As a variable which shows a high degree of multicollinearity provides little unique information, the regression coefficient associated with it is also based on limited information and therefore tends to have a large standard error (for detailed discussions on this refer to Afifi and Clark, 1996 and Edwards, 1985). In such cases the regression parameters are unlikely to accurately reflect the impact that x_i has on y in the population.

The problems associated with high multicollinearity can be demonstrated using hypothetical data which shows the relationship between the number of college places offered to students and marks obtained in two compulsory subjects, English and Mathematics (see Table 3.7)[4].

Table 3.7: Exam Marks and Offers of College Places

Number of Colleges Offering Places	English (%)	Mathematics (%)
0	22.0	17.0
1	32.5	34.5
2	38.0	18.0
3	39.5	46.0
4	52.0	48.0
5	44.5	35.0
6	49.5	43.5
7	72.5	70.5
8	61.5	67.5
9	85.5	74.5
10	68.5	87.6

One would expect there to be a strong relationship between the number of college places a student is offered and the student's marks in English and Mathematics as the decision to offer a place at a college is based largely on the student's academic performance. One would also expect a student's mark in one subject to be strongly related to their mark in the other subject, as good students tend to score relatively highly in both. This three-variable relationship is shown in Figure 3.9 and the associated regression model in Equation 3.20 overleaf (for the simple purpose of demonstration this model does not include an interaction term). The model appears to provide a good prediction of the number of college places offered to a student as indicated by the F and R^2 statistics ($F_{2,8} = 32.520; P < 0.0005 : R^2 = 0.890$) which corresponds to area A + B + C, in Figure 3.9.

---

[4] For this example we will assume that all students applied to the same 10 colleges.

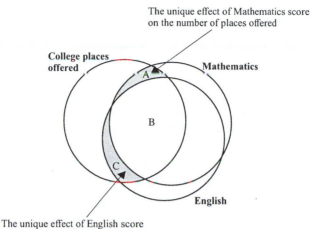

Figure 3.9: The relationship between exam marks and the number of college places offered

$$\text{College places offered} = -2.79 + 0.086\,\text{English} + 0.068\,\text{Mathematics} \quad (3.20)$$

From Figure 3.9 it can be seen that the *unique* contributions made by each of the explanatory variables to the number of college places offered is relatively small. When controlling for marks in Mathematics, marks in English only contribute a small amount to the model fit (area C). Similarly, when controlling for marks in English, marks in Mathematics only contribute a small amount to the model fit (area A). The results in Table 3.8 confirm this and show that the unique contribution of each of the explanatory variables when they are both entered into the model (Model 1) is not significant, as shown by the t statistics. It appears clear from the F and R^2 statistics that Model 1 provides a good fit, even though neither of the explanatory variables are significant. This, perhaps unexpected, result is due to the high degree of multicollinearity between the explanatory variables. Logically we might expect marks in both English and Mathematics to be strongly related to the number of college places offered as places are offered mainly on the basis of academic performance. This is what we find when simple regression models are calculated using single subjects to predict college places (Models 2 and 3). The resulting models fit almost as well as the model which uses both variables, but the regression parameters for the explanatory variables are now highly significant. We can see that the presence of multicollinearity has not really affected the predictive power of the model, but has serious implications for the interpretation of the importance of the explanatory variables.

Table 3.8: Modelling the Number of College Places Offered to Students

	Coefficient	s.e.	t	P
Model 1				
English	0.086	0.046	1.863	0.100
Mathematics	0.068	0.038	1.805	0.109
(constant)	−2.790	1.148	−2.431	0.041
Model 2				
English	0.161	0.023	7.028	0.000
(constant)	−3.276	1.248	−2.625	0.028
Model 3				
Mathematics	0.131	0.019	6.951	0.000
(constant)	−1.473	1.021	−1.443	0.183

Model 1: Places offered $= \alpha + \beta$ English $+ \beta$ Mathematics
$\quad F_{2,8} = 32.52, \ P < 0.0005, \ R^2 = 0.089$
Model 2: Places offered $= \alpha + \beta$ English
$\quad F_{1,9} = 49.394, \ P < 0.0005, \ R^2 = 0.846$
Model 3: Places offered $= \alpha + \beta$ Mathematics
$\quad F_{1,9} = 48.313, \ P < 0.0005, \ R^2 = 0.843$

Identifying Instances of Multicollinearity

Some instances of multicollinearity can be identified by inspecting pair-wise correlation coefficients. Relationships between explanatory variables which are of the order of about 0.8 or larger indicate a level of multicollinearity that *may* prove to be problematic[5]. In the above example, the correlation between English and Mathematics scores is 0.897 indicating that multicollinearity may be a problem for these data. Whilst this approach is quite adept at identifying problem relationships between pairs of explanatory variables, it cannot always identify those instances where a combination of more than one variable predicts another. These relationships can, however, be determined using R^2 values to show the degree to which each explanatory variable can be explained using the other explanatory variables in the model. As with pair-wise correlations, we cannot say with any certainty how high the value of R^2 must be before multicollinearity is viewed as a cause for concern, but typically, values of about 0.8

---

[5]0.8 is an arbitrary figure and is used here because it is commonly quoted in a number of texts. It should be noted, however, that correlations smaller than 0.8 can also cause problems for the regression procedure.

or higher are taken as being indicative of a degree of multicollinearity which may be problematic. In the example above, if we predict a student's Mathematics score using their English score we obtain a regression model with an R^2 value of 0.804, which indicates that a problematic level of multicollinearity may be present.

Calculating individual R^2 values for each explanatory variable in the model is a useful method of identifying instances of multicollinearity, but can be quite a lengthy process if there are a number of variables. It is, however, not necessary to manually compute these R^2 values as a number of analysis packages provide equivalent information through the 'tolerance' and 'variance inflation factor' (VIF) statistics shown in equations 3.22 and 3.21.

$$\text{Tolerance}(\beta_i) = 1 - R_i^2 \qquad (3.21)$$

where β_i is the regression coefficient for variable i,
and R_i^2 is the squared multiple correlation coefficient between x_i and the other explanatory variables.

$$\text{VIF}(\beta_i) = \frac{1}{\text{Tolerance}} \qquad (3.22)$$

We can see from equation 3.22 that an R^2 value of 0.8 will result in a VIF value of 5 and a tolerance value of 0.2. Any explanatory variables which have a VIF value of 5 or more, or a Tolerance of 0.2 or less, are therefore of interest as they show a degree of multicollinearity which could be problematic. Table 3.9 shows the regression analysis of the example data set with VIF and tolerance values of a high enough level to be of concern. It should be noted that as there are only two explanatory variables, the statistics for both variables are the same.

Table 3.9: VIF and Tolerance Statistics

	Coefficient	s.e.	t	P	Tolerance	VIF
English	0.086	0.046	1.863	0.100	0.196	5.099
Mathematics	0.068	0.038	1.805	0.109	0.196	5.099

Places offered $= \alpha + \beta_1$ English $+ \beta_2$ Mathematics
$F_{2,8} = 32.52$, $P < 0.0005$, $R^2 = 0.890$

The tolerance and VIF statistics are based on the R^2 measure and therefore assume that the data are continuous. It is, however, possible to use these statistics on discontinuous data provided that the variables have been coded appropriately (see Section 3.3.7). This greatly increases the usefulness of the techniques as it enables problematic relationships between all types of variables to be identified. It should be noted, however, that these statistics can only give a rough indication of which relationships may be problematic, they do not provide any proof that multicollinearity will be a problem, nor do they identify all instances of problematic relationships. The tolerance and VIF statistics merely provide a convenient method for identifying at least some of the relationship of concern.

Dealing with Multicollinearity

There are a number of ways in which multicollinearity can be reduced in a data set. These methods include:

1. Collect more data

   As multicollinearity is a problem which results from insufficient information in the sample, one solution is to increase the amount of information by collecting more data. As more data is collected and the sample size increases, the standard error tends to decrease which reduces the effect of multicollinearity (see Berry and Feldman, 1993). Although increasing the amount of data is an attractive option and one of the best methods to reduce multicollinearity (at least when the data set is relatively small), it is in many instances, not practical or possible, so other less attractive methods need to be considered.

2. Collapse variables

   One option to reduce the level of multicollinearity is to combine two or more explanatory variables which are highly correlated into a single composite variable. This approach is, however, only reasonable when the explanatory variables are indicators of the same underlying concept. For example, using the data in Table 3.7, it makes theoretical sense to combine the two explanatory variables (marks in English and Mathematics) into a single index of academic performance. This single index could simply be the sum of the two scores, or the average score for the two subjects. The use of a composite variable in the regression model enables one to assess the contribution made by academic performance to the number of college places offered, without the problem of a high degree of multicollinearity which existed between English and Mathematics scores.

   The process of combining variables into latent variables (or factors as they are sometimes called) is not always as straightforward as in the example shown above, where two variables were related in quite an obvious way and could be combined easily into a single index. If there are a number of variables which are inter-related, it might be appropriate to first identify any latent variables in the sample using factor analysis and then enter these into the regression model. The technique of factor analysis is discussed in detail in Chapter 6

3. Remove variables from the model

When it is not possible to collapse highly related explanatory variables into a composite variable, one may delete one or more variables to remove the effect of multicollinearity. This option, whilst being one of the easiest to accomplish practically, can be problematic if the variable measures some distinct theoretical concept which cannot be easily dismissed from the model. It should be noted that the removal of a relevant explanatory variable from a model can cause more serious problems than the presence of high multicollinearity (the removal of important variables may result in a model which is mis-specified, see Berry and Feldman, 1993). It is, therefore, generally unwise to remove explanatory variables from a regression equation merely on the grounds that they show a high degree of multicollinearity.

In general, the most reasonable method of dealing with multicollinearity is to collect more data and, where possible, collapse a number of variables into composite or latent variables, provided that they make theoretical sense. If no more data can be collected, the variables cannot be incorporated into a composite variable, and the highly related variables are deemed to be a necessary part of the model (and therefore cannot be removed), then one might just have to recognize its presence and live with its consequences (the consequence being that it is not possible to obtain reliable regression coefficients for all of the variables in the model).

3.3.7   Dummy Variable Coding Discontinuous Data

One of the requirements of OLS regression is that all variables entered into the model are measured on a continuous scale, a requirement which is, unfortunately, not met by all social science data. It is possible, however, to include dichotomous, or binary, data in a model since the OLS regression procedure treats this as continuous data which can only assume one of two values. The ability to include dichotomous data enables variables such as male–female, dead–alive, rich–poor, passed–failed, high–low etc., to be used as explanatory variables[6]. Multi-category categorical explanatory variables, such as drinking levels (high, medium and low), location (Europe, North America, South America, Africa), educational level (unqualified, high school, university), and

---

[6]For reasons which will become clear in the chapter on logistic regression, it is not appropriate to model a binary response variable using OLS regression.

different treatments (treatment 1, treatment 2, treatment 3, etc.) can also
be included if they are dichotomized. The ability to include dichotomous and
multi-category data in OLS regression models greatly increases the usefulness
of the technique. The process of transforming discontinuous data into a form
which can be entered into a regression model is called dummy coding. There
are a number of methods of dummy coding data, however, only two of the
more common methods, indicator and deviation coding, will be discussed in
detail here.

Indicator Coding

Indicator coding is perhaps the easiest dummy coding method as it involves
simply transforming data into a number of dichotomies. The dichotomy *must*
be coded 0 and 1 (either explicitly in the data set, or internally by software)
to indicate the presence or absence of a particular attribute. For example, in
the case of gender, if a code of 0 refers to 'not female', a code of 1 refers to
'female'. Alternatively, if a code of 1 refers to 'male', a code of 0 refers to 'not
male'[7]. It is not appropriate to code the data using other numbers, such as 1
and 2 (which is perhaps more intuitive for coding purposes) as the regression
procedure attaches a specific meaning to these numbers (the group coded 2
will be twice the value of the group coded 1). By using the values 0 and 1 we
are merely describing the presence or absence of a particular attribute, rather
than defining its level.

Table 3.10 shows a categorical variable (the different categories are designated by the letters A, B, C and D) which has been recoded into a series of
dichotomies. In the table, the original variable is represented as four separate dummy variables, each indicating the presence or absence of a particular
category. For example, dummy variable 1 only records whether or not the
original variable is equivalent to A, dummy variable 2 only records whether
or not the original variable is equivalent to B, and so on. The information
contained in the original variable is now represented by a number of discrete
dummy variables.

The use of dummy variables in an OLS regression model is not completely
straightforward because the inclusion of all of them at the same time leads to a
situation where perfect multicollinearity exists (refer to section 3.3.6). For example, dummy variable 4 in Table 3.10 can be perfectly predicted from dummy
variables 1, 2 and 3 and is therefore redundant. If any of the variables 1, 2 or
3 have the value of 1, then variable 4 necessarily takes the values of 0, and if
variables 1, 2 and 3 all have the value of 0, then variable 4 necessarily takes
the value of 1. In general, if we have j categories, a maximum of $j-1$ dummy
variables can be entered into a model. The dummy variable which is omitted
is called the reference category and is the category against which other dummy

---

[7]Of course, someone who is designated 'not female' will be 'male' which allows a comparison to be made between male and female, even though we have, technically speaking,
only coded for the presence of one of the categories.

Table 3.10: The Indicator Method of Dummy Variable Coding

Original	Dummy Variables			
Variable	1	2	3	4
A	1	0	0	0
B	0	1	0	0
C	0	0	1	0
D	0	0	0	1

variables are compared. This is also known as *aliasing* a variable. It should be noted that the choice of reference category is often quite arbitrary, although sometimes there will be reasons that a particular reference category is chosen. For example, when comparing a number of treatments for a particular illness, it might make sense to compare each with the standard treatment currently used to treat the disease (see Hardy, 1993, for a more in-depth discussion of reference category choice). The choice of reference category does not affect the model fit as this remains the same no matter which category is designated as the reference. Changing the reference category merely alters the way the differences are apportioned between the dummy variables. The setting of one level of a categorical variable to be the reference category is commonly called *aliasing*.

The use of dummy variables in OLS regression is demonstrated using data collected as part of a study of the quality of statements elicited from young children. Details of the data collection methods and overall design of the study can be found in Hutcheson, Baxter, Telfer and Warden, 1995. It should be noted that the original data set has been changed somewhat and that some variables have been added to enable certain analysis techniques to be demonstrated clearly. The data in Table 3.11 includes variables which record statement quality, the child's gender, age and maturity, how coherently they gave their evidence, the delay between witnessing the incident and recounting it, the location of the interview (the child's home, school, a formal interview room, and an interview room specially constructed for children), and whether or not the case proceeded to prosecution.

Table 3.11: The Quality of Children's Testimonies

Age	Gender	Location	Coherence	Maturity	Delay	Prosecute	Quality
5–6	male	3	3.81	3.62	45	no	34.11
5–6	female	2	1.63	1.61	27	yes	36.59
5–6	male	1	3.54	3.63	102	no	37.23
5–6	female	2	4.21	4.11	39	no	39.65
5–6	male	3	3.30	3.12	41	no	42.07
5–6	female	3	2.32	2.13	70	yes	44.91
5–6	female	4	4.51	4.31	72	no	45.23
5–6	female	2	3.18	3.08	41	no	47.53

continued on next page . . .

... continued from previous page

Age	Gender	Location	Coherence	Maturity	Delay	Prosecute	Quality
5–6	male	1	2.66	2.72	13	no	45.81
5–6	female	3	4.70	4.98	29	no	49.38
5–6	male	2	4.31	4.21	39	yes	49.53
5–6	female	3	3.46	3.54	47	no	47.51
5–6	female	2	3.42	3.33	31	yes	50.54
5–6	male	1	3.08	3.07	82	no	51.25
5–6	female	4	4.04	4.12	29	no	51.63
8–9	male	3	3.12	3.01	51	yes	52.02
5–6	female	3	3.23	3.08	78	no	52.39
5–6	male	1	2.63	2.62	81	no	54.49
8–9	male	3	3.02	3.00	71	no	54.64
5–6	female	2	3.62	3.53	43	no	55.27
8–9	male	1	1.54	1.21	55	yes	55.47
5–6	male	3	2.79	2.74	45	no	55.56
8–9	male	1	2.76	2.71	27	no	56.47
8–9	female	1	4.63	4.66	74	no	56.72
5–6	male	3	3.35	3.07	88	yes	57.07
5–6	female	1	2.63	2.82	29	no	57.76
8–9	female	2	2.77	2.71	56	yes	57.87
8–9	male	4	3.26	3.91	55	yes	58.33
5–6	male	1	2.99	2.87	75	no	58.73
5–6	male	3	3.59	3.09	61	no	58.84
8–9	female	2	2.43	2.39	76	yes	59.19
8–9	male	4	2.41	2.38	45	no	59.64
8–9	male	1	2.37	3.36	90	yes	59.86
8–9	male	2	3.92	3.98	92	no	59.97
5–6	male	3	3.63	3.72	44	no	60.81
5–6	female	1	2.30	2.21	45	yes	60.88
8–9	female	4	1.56	1.92	16	no	61.83
8–9	female	2	2.92	2.81	23	yes	61.98
8–9	female	3	4.11	1.72	63	yes	62.09
5–6	female	1	2.49	2.51	87	no	62.54
5–6	female	2	2.41	2.04	55	no	62.84
8–9	female	3	2.56	2.65	66	yes	63.38
8–9	male	1	1.95	2.03	8	yes	63.67
8–9	male	2	2.52	2.49	75	no	64.34
8–9	female	3	2.15	2.09	81	yes	64.37
5–6	male	4	2.78	2.79	9	yes	65.07
5–6	female	1	2.95	3.01	39	no	65.77
8–9	male	4	1.89	3.45	68	yes	65.93
8–9	female	3	3.62	3.56	26	yes	66.60
8–9	female	2	2.16	2.91	10	no	67.08
8–9	male	1	3.65	3.91	52	yes	68.33
8–9	male	4	2.32	2.33	19	yes	68.44
8–9	male	1	1.34	1.42	77	no	68.90
8–9	female	1	2.02	2.11	25	yes	69.59
8–9	male	4	1.76	1.72	86	no	69.89
5–6	female	4	1.78	1.77	45	yes	70.45
8–9	female	2	2.52	2.54	2	yes	70.71
8–9	male	4	1.83	1.73	29	yes	71.40
8–9	male	4	1.51	1.73	45	yes	71.83
8–9	female	3	3.08	2.08	14	no	72.30
5–6	female	4	1.03	0.98	25	yes	72.61
8–9	female	1	1.76	1.65	21	no	73.99
8–9	male	4	2.00	1.94	17	yes	74.18
8–9	male	4	2.90	2.94	19	yes	75.38
8–9	male	2	3.24	3.43	22	yes	76.01
8–9	male	2	2.90	2.87	14	no	76.28
5–6	female	4	3.11	3.01	26	yes	77.59
8–9	female	3	2.86	2.93	57	no	78.47
8–9	female	2	1.94	1.99	46	yes	80.67
8–9	male	4	1.89	1.87	15	yes	83.15

Table 3.12 shows the results of an OLS regression calculated on some of the data presented in Table 3.11. This analysis uses a selection of the available data and is only meant to provide an illustration of the use of dummy variable coding and not a full model of statement quality [8]. The response variable is the quality of statements elicited from children, whilst the explanatory variables are the delay in days from the incident to the interview and the location of the interview (the four different locations have been coded into three dummy variables with the special interview room acting as the reference category). The coefficients show the effect that each explanatory variable has on the response variable (each dummy variable can be considered as a separate explanatory variable). For example, the coefficient for the variable Delay shows that for each unit increase in the delay (an increase of 1 day), the quality of the statement elicited from a child decreases by an average of 0.099; a relationship that is not significant ($t_{65} = -1.897$; $P = 0.062$). When $j-1$ dummy variables are

Table 3.12: Modelling Statement Quality Using Delay and Location (indicator dummy-coded)

	Coefficient	s.e.	t	P
Delay	−0.099	0.052	−1.897	0.062
Location dummy variables				
Location-Home	−6.042	3.630	−1.664	0.101
Location-School	−7.042	3.550	−1.983	0.052
Location-Formal	−8.938	3.621	−2.469	0.016
(constant)	70.790	3.137	22.565	0.000

Model: Quality $= \alpha + \beta_1$Delay $+ \beta_2$Location-Home
$\qquad\qquad\qquad\qquad +\beta_3$Location-School $+ \beta_4$Location-Formal
$F_{4,65} = 3.455,\ P = 0.013,\ R^2 = 0.175$

included in the model (as they are here) each dummy variable indicates the effect of one of the locations compared to the reference category. For example, the parameters for the dummy variable Location-Home indicate that the quality of information elicited from children who are interviewed at home is 6.043 points less than the quality of information elicited from children who are interviewed in the special interview room (the reference category). The value of the t statistic suggests that this difference is not significant at the 0.05 level ($t_{65} = -1.664$; $P = 0.101$). Similarly, the parameters associated with the dummy variable Location-Formal indicate that the quality of information elicited from children who are interviewed in a formal interview room is 8.938 points less than those children interviewed in the special interview room, a difference which is significant at the 0.05 level ($t_{65} = -2.469$; $P = 0.016$).

---

[8] An analysis of the full data set is shown in Section 3.4.

The reason that the parameters for each of the dummy variables in Table 3.12 provides a comparison between the category coded 1 and the reference category is that the other location categories are controlled for. For example, although dummy variable Location-Home only indicates the presence or absence of a home interview, the parameters for this variable relate to the comparison between interviews conducted at home with the reference category, and not, as might be expected from the dummy variable coding, a comparison between interviews conducted at home and those conducted away from the home. This rather counter-intuitive meaning of the parameters comes about because when we include the other dummy variables in the model, these control for the other interview venues.

The regression coefficients associated with dummy variables only provide a comparison with the reference category when $j-1$ dummy variables are included in the model. If fewer than $j-1$ dummy variables are included, the interpretation of the parameters change. For example, if only the dummy variable Location-Home is included in the model, the parameters for this variable indicate the difference between an interview conducted at home and an interview conducted away from home. If dummy variables Location-Home and Location-School are the only ones to be included in the model, the parameters for Location-Home indicate the difference between interviews conducted at home to ones conducted in the formal and the special interview rooms (by including Location-School in the model, the effect of being interviewed at school has been controlled for). When interpreting the parameters associated with dummy variables one needs to check how many have been included in the model as this affects the interpretation of the regression parameters. This is quite an important point, particularly when automatic model selection procedures are used, since dummy variables are not always entered into the model as a group.

The choice of reference category does not affect the overall model fit as long as $j-1$ dummy variables are included in the model. This is demonstrated in Table 3.13 where models 1 and 2 show the parameters associated with $j-1$ dummy variables when different reference categories are used. The only difference between the models is that the effect of location is apportioned differently amongst the dummy variables. The model fit is, however, affected when dummy variables are removed, a result which is demonstrated by comparing models 1 and 2 with models 3 and 4.

Deviation Coding

When investigating the effect of a categorical variable, it is not always appropriate, or even desirable, to compare each dummy variable against a reference category as is the case with indicator coding. In such circumstances, deviation or effects coding may be used to compare each dummy variable to the group average (see Table 3.14).

Table 3.13: A Comparison of Four Models of Statement Quality Using Delay
and Location (dummy-coded using indicator method)

	Coefficient	s.e.	t	P
Model 1				
Delay	−0.099	0.052	−1.897	0.062
Location dummy variables				
Location-Home	−6.042	3.630	−1.664	0.101
Location-School	−7.042	3.550	−1.983	0.052
Location-Formal	−8.938	3.621	−2.469	0.016
(constant)	70.790	3.137	22.565	0.000
Model 2				
Delay	−0.099	0.052	−1.897	0.062
Location dummy variables				
Location-Home	2.896	3.444	0.841	0.404
Location-School	1.896	3.571	0.531	0.597
Location-Special	8.938	3.621	2.469	0.016
(constant)	61.852	3.738	16.547	0.000
Model 3				
Delay	−0.132	0.052	−2.539	0.014
Location dummy variables				
Location-Home	−1.125	3.150	−0.357	0.722
Location-School	−2.624	3.182	−0.824	0.413
(constant)	67.852	2.991	16.547	0.000
Model 4				
Delay	−0.129	0.052	−2.483	0.016
Location dummy variable				
Location-Home	−0.310	2.983	−0.104	0.918
(constant)	66.707	2.715	24.566	0.000

Model 1: $F_{4,65} = 3.455$, $P = 0.013$, $R^2 = 0.175$
Model 2: $F_{4,65} = 3.455$, $P = 0.013$, $R^2 = 0.175$
Model 3: $F_{3,66} = 2.391$, $P = 0.077$, $R^2 = 0.098$
Model 4: $F_{2,67} = 3.263$, $P = 0.044$, $R^2 = 0.089$

The coding scheme used for deviation coding is similar to that used for
indicator coding (see Table 3.10) except for the way in which the reference
category is identified. Using indicator coding, the reference category is always
coded 0, but in deviation coding the reference category is explicitly coded as
−1. Using the deviation coding method, the contrast indicated by each dummy
variable is between the group coded 1 and the reference group. For example,
in Table 3.14, the dummy variable Location-Home provides a contrast between

Table 3.14: Deviation Dummy Variable Coding of Location

	Dummy Variables		
Location of Interview	1	2	3
Child's Home	1	0	0
Child's School	0	1	0
Formal Interview Room	0	0	1
Special Interview Room	−1	−1	−1

interviews conducted at the child's home and those conducted in the special interview room, whilst the dummy variable Location-School provides a contrast between interviews conducted at the child's school and those conducted in the special interview room. When $j-1$ dummy variables are included in the model, the parameters associated with each dummy variable indicate a comparison between the group coded 1 and the average of all of the groups.

Table 3.15 shows a similar analysis to that shown in Table 3.12, however, this time the location variable has been dummy coded using the deviation coding method. Although the parameters associated with the variable 'delay' are identical in value and meaning to those in Table 3.12, the interpretation of the parameters associated with the dummy variables have changed. The parameters associated with the dummy variable Location-Home indicate the difference in the quality of interviews conducted in the child's home to the average quality of interviews from all of the interview venues. In this case we can say that interviews conducted at home are 0.537 of a point poorer than the average for all of the groups, a difference which is not significant ($t_{65} = -0.248; P = 0.805$). Similarly, the parameters associated Location-School show that those interviews conducted at the child's school are 1.536 points poorer than the average, a difference which is also not significant ($t_{65} = -0.703; P = 0.485$).

Using deviation coding, the comparison is between each dummy variable category and the average value. Therefore, the regression coefficients for the dummy variables remain constant no matter which category is chosen as the reference. This can be clearly seen in Table 3.15. In a similar fashion to indicator coding, we have to note how many dummy variables have been entered into the equation. As it is difficult to correctly interpret the regression coefficients when fewer than $j-1$ categories are entered into the model, it is recommended that when deviation coding is used, all $j-1$ categories are entered to ensure that the comparison is with the average of all groups and not a subset.

Tables 3.13 and 3.15 show similar models calculated using different dummy variable coding schemes. A quick inspection of these tables demonstrates that the type of dummy coding used does not affect the overall model fit, it merely affects the distribution of the differences between the dummy variables. Look-

Table 3.15: A Comparison of Four Models of Statement Quality Using Delay and Location (dummy-coded using deviation method)

	Coefficient	s.e.	t	P
Model 1				
Delay	−0.099	0.052	−1.897	0.062
Location				
Location-Home	−0.537	2.166	−0.248	0.805
Location-School	−1.536	2.184	−0.703	0.484
Location-Formal	−3.433	2.159	−1.590	0.117
(constant)	65.285	2.720	24.003	0.000
Model 2				
Delay	−0.099	0.052	−1.897	0.062
Location				
Location-Home	−0.537	2.166	−0.248	0.805
Location-School	−1.536	2.184	−0.703	0.484
Location-Special	5.506	2.226	2.474	0.016
(constant)	65.285	2.720	24.003	0.000

Model 1: $F_{4,65} = 3.455$, $P = 0.013$, $R^2 = 0.175$
Model 2: $F_{4,65} = 3.455$, $P = 0.013$, $R^2 = 0.175$

ing at models 1 and 2, where $j-1$ dummy variables have been included, we can see that the overall model fit remains the same, as do the parameters associated with the variable Delay. The only statistics to change are those associated with the dummy variables.

Dummy Coding Ordered Categorical Data

Explanatory variables with ordered categories can be input into regression models by utilizing dummy coding procedures, however, this often incurs a 'cost' as the dummy coding techniques presented above do not retain information about order. For example, in the case of a variable which codes for four levels of drinking behaviour (high, medium, low, and abstinent), if indicator or deviation coding is used, the individual categories are treated as being unrelated, even though this is clearly not the case. Using these coding methods, information about the order of the categories is lost and the analysis consequently loses some power.

In circumstances where it is important to take account of the ordered nature of the data (for instance, when the effect is relatively small) it is advisable to use a scoring method where this information is retained (for example, in integer coding, 1, 2, 3...). If a continuous variable has been collapsed, then the mean value of the original variable for each category can be used to score the ordered categories. A more detailed treatment of ordinality for both explanatory and response variables is given in Chapter 5.

3.3.8   Model Selection

Consider the two models presented in Table 3.16, which have been calculated using the data in Table 3.11 (for simplicity, only the main effects have been included in these models). Model 1 uses the variables Delay and Gender to model Quality, whilst the nested Model 2 only uses Delay. Although Model 1 has a larger R^2 value, which we would expect as it contains a greater number of terms, the F statistics show that the smaller model actually provides a more significant linear prediction of Quality. The inclusion of Gender in the model does not improve the prediction of Quality and can therefore be omitted without any significant loss of 'power'. Ideally, only those variables which contribute significantly to the prediction of the response variable should be retained. The removal of unimportant variables results in a simpler model which helps in interpretation and often provides a clearer insight into the way the response variable varies as a function of changes in the explanatory variables. In general, a good model should enable an accurate prediction to be made of the response variable, but only contain those explanatory variables which play a significant role.

Table 3.16: Model Selection

	Coefficient	s.e.	t	P
Model 1				
Delay	−0.133	0.051	−2.590	0.012
Gender	−1.108	2.578	−0.430	0.669
(constant)	67.372	3.144	21.429	0.000
Model 2				
Delay	−0.130	0.050	−2.571	0.012
(constant)	66.677	2.680	24.881	0.000

Model 1: Quality = 67.372 − 0.133(Delay) − 1.108(Gender)
$F_{2,67} = 3.358$, $P = 0.041$, $R^2 = 0.091$
Model 2: Quality = 66.677 − 0.130(Delay)
$F_{1,68} = 6.611$, $P = 0.012$, $R^2 = 0.089$

Criteria for Including and Removing Variables

Decisions about which variables may be entered or removed from a model can be made on the basis of the partial-F statistic. Using Equation 3.19, nested regression models can be compared to assess the effect that individual (or groups of) explanatory variables have on the response variable. For example, to assess the effect that Gender has on Quality (whilst controlling for Delay), one can compare the model Quality $= \alpha + \beta_1 \text{Delay} + \beta_2 \text{Gender}$ with the model Quality $= \alpha + \beta_1 \text{Delay}$. The value of partial-$F$ indicates the effect that Gender has on Quality when Delay is controlled for. To calculate partial-F, the residual sum of squares and the degrees of freedom for the two regression models need to be calculated. From software, these are computed to be:

$$\text{Quality} = \alpha + \beta_1 \text{Delay} + \beta_2 \text{Gender} \qquad RSS = 7648.585, \; df = 67$$
$$\text{Quality} = \alpha + \beta_1 \text{Delay} \qquad\qquad\qquad RSS = 7669.682, \; df = 68$$

which, when entered into Equation 3.19 gives the value of partial-F as

$$F_{68-67,68} = \frac{7669.682 - 7648.585}{(68 - 67)(7648.585/67)}$$

$$F_{1,68} = 0.1848; P = 0.669.$$

The effect that Gender has on the model is shown by the partial-F statistic. In this case, as the difference in the number of terms between the two models is equal to 1 the partial-F statistic is equivalent to the t statistic, which is commonly provided by software (in fact, $\sqrt{F} = t$). For the model above it can be seen that this is the case as $\sqrt{0.1848}$ does indeed equal 0.430 (see Table 3.16). The t statistic therefore shows the unique contribution of individual terms in the model and can be used to determine which terms may be retained or removed during the process of model-building. When more than one term is added or removed from a model in a single step, the partial-F statistic can be used to determine significance (an example of the use of t and partial-F values in model-building is provided in Section 3.6).

3.3.9   Automated Model Selection

Automated selection procedures can be used to make decisions about whether terms are included or excluded from a regression model on statistical grounds according to how much the variables contribute to predicting the response variable. Ideally, such decisions should be based on theoretical as well as statistical grounds, however, it is sometimes convenient to use automated procedures. Whilst such a technique of model-building is relatively quick and efficient at deriving a model which provides a good prediction of the response variable, it does not always provide a model which is adequate for explanatory purposes. Agresti makes the point that ...

Computerized variable selection procedures should be used with caution. When one considers a large number of terms for potential inclusion in a model, one or two of them that are not really important may look impressive simply due to chance. For instance, when all the true effects are weak, the largest sample effect may substantially overestimate its true effect. In addition, it often makes sense to include certain variables of special interest in a model and report their estimated effects even if they are not statistically significant at some level.

Agresti, 1996; p. 129.

An additional problem with automated variable selection procedures is that most software packages will not preserve the hierarchy of terms when interactions are examined. For example, a main effect may be removed from the model even though an interaction including that variable is included. This is problematic since to appropriately interpret an interaction one needs to include the main effects in the model. We recommend that if an automated model selection procedure is used, it should be used with caution, particularly when interactions are being considered, and only in conjunction with theoretical considerations about the most useful form of the model.

Even with these reservations, automated selection procedures are widely used. For this reason, three of the more common methods are discussed below, forward selection, backward deletion, and stepwise selection. It should be noted that none of these selection procedures is 'best' in any absolute sense. They merely identify subsets of variables which, for the sample, are good predictors of the response variable.

Forward Selection

The forward selection method of automated model-building selects terms to enter into the model singularly, on the basis of relative importance, as determined by the partial-F test. The first term to be entered into the model is the one which, if added, results in the most significant change in the value of F (as determined by the partial-F, or equivalent t statistics), provided that this meets an 'entry criterion' (for variable entry, this is usually set at $P < 0.05$). Once a term has been added to the model, the regression is recalculated and partial-F values obtained for all terms still to be considered for entering into the model. Of these terms, the one which would result in the most significant change to the F statistic is entered into the model (provided that it is above the criterion) and the regression recalculated. This procedure continues until all terms are either included in the model or until no more reach the required level of significance.

Backward Elimination

The backward elimination technique of model building is very similar to forward selection except that the starting model is one where all explanatory variables are entered and terms are then removed from the model sequentially. At each step in the process, the term which, if removed, results in the smallest significant change in the value of F (as denoted by the partial-F or t statistics), is removed from the model — provided that it has reached a 'removal criterion' (in backward elimination the removal criterion is usually set at $P = 0.1$). After each term is removed, the regression equation is recalculated and those terms left in the model are re-examined to see if any contribute less than the criterion level (as determined by partial-F). This process continues until all terms have been removed from the model, or until no more reach the criterion for removal.

Stepwise Selection

Stepwise selection is simply a combination of forward selection and backward elimination and is one of the most commonly used methods of automated variable selection. Stepwise selection builds a model in much the same way as in forward selection except that at each step, rather than just assessing which terms can be added to the model (using the forward selection procedure), those which are currently included are tested to see if any can be removed (using the backward elimination procedure). The advantage of this procedure is that those terms whose importance diminishes as additional terms are added can be removed.

Stepwise selection proceeds in the same way as forward selection until two terms have been entered into the model. At this point, both are examined to see if they still meet the criteria for retention. If either of them do not, the least significant one is removed and the regression recalculated. This process of removing terms continues until all are above the criterion for retention ($P < 0.1$). The model selection procedure then proceeds to test whether any of the terms currently not in the model reach the criterion for entry ($P < 0.05$). If any do reach the criterion, the most significant one is entered into the model and the regression is recalculated. The process is then repeated with all terms in the model checked for significance and if any are below the criterion for retention they are removed. This procedure of entering and removing terms continues until no more variables reach the entry criterion.

The automated model selection procedure for a number of software packages rely on the inputting of terms into the model individually. It should be noted that this can cause some problems for categorical variables which have been dummy coded, since these will often require to be treated as a group so that the regression parameters can be appropriately interpreted (see Section 3.6 for a demonstration of how categorical variables can be defined as a group using SPSS). As grouped terms often have to be dealt with using manual modelling procedures, the use of automated model selection procedures appears less attractive. Given this and earlier comments about automated selection techniques, they should be used with a degree of caution.

3.4   A Worked Example of Multiple Regression

This section shows a complete example of how OLS regression may be used to analyse a data set. It should be noted that this example is only designed to provide a demonstration of how the techniques described in this chapter may be used and does not provide 'the' correct way to analyse these data. The data to be analysed are the child witness data shown in Table 3.11 which have already been used for demonstration purposes earlier in this chapter. These data contain four continuous variables, Quality of statement, Coherence of evidence, Maturity of child, and the Delay between the child witnessing the incident and recounting it, three dichotomous variables, Age (5–6 and 8–9-year-olds), Gender and whether or not the cases led to a Prosecution[9], and one categorical variable, Location, which indicates where the interview was conducted (at the child's home, school, in a formal interview room, or in a room specially designed for children). All the dichotomous variables were dummy coded 0 and 1 with the code of 1 indicating 8–9-year-old and male children. Location was coded into three dummy variables using the indicator coding method with the formal interview room chosen as the reference category (this can be considered to be the 'standard' location of interviews and was therefore ideal to use as a reference category). For simplicity we will assume that none of the variables require transforming, that there are no outliers, and that the residuals do not give any cause for concern (see Chapter 2).

A useful first step in the analysis of these data is to determine if there are any associations between the explanatory variables which could give cause for concern. Table 3.17 shows that the variables Coherence and Maturity have VIF and tolerance values above recommended limits. It is quite easy to hypoth-esize why this might be the case for these data, for Coherence and Maturity are likely to be rated similarly since a child rated as being relatively mature is likely to have been perceived this way, at least partly as a result of the coher-ence of his or her evidence. A highly significant pair-wise correlation between these variables ($r = 0.91; P < 0.0005$) appears to confirm this view. This problematic association was 'solved' in this example by removing Maturity from the analysis as, of the two, this variable was perhaps the more difficult to rate accurately. The removal of Maturity from the model shown in Table 3.17, will not make a significant difference to the model fit ($t_{60} = -0.774; p = 0.442$) and once removed reduces the tolerance and VIF values for Coherence to more acceptable levels (on a recalculation of the initial statistics the tolerance and VIF values for Coherence are reduced to 0.743 and 1.346, respectively).

---

[9]Although this variable is not used in the present analysis, it is mentioned here as it is used in Chapter 4 to demonstrate logistic regression.

Table 3.17: Initial Statistics

	Coefficient	s.e.	t	P	Tolerance	VIF
Age	10.521	2.220	4.739	0.000	0.817	1.223
Coherence	−0.587	3.395	−0.173	0.863	0.129	7.754
Delay	−0.062	0.043	−1.441	0.155	0.847	1.181
Gender	2.116	2.162	0.979	0.331	0.856	1.169
Location dummy variables						
Location-Home	1.553	3.024	0.514	0.609	0.572	1.747
Location-School	0.277	2.993	0.092	0.927	0.607	1.647
Location-Formal	6.260	3.302	1.896	0.063	0.499	2.006
Maturity	−2.400	3.100	−0.774	.442	0.148	6.779
(constant)	63.109	6.038	10.452	0.000		

In order to demonstrate the use of an interaction term in OLS regression, one is constructed here and entered into the model. The interaction chosen here is that between Age and Coherence and is represented by the variable Age×Coh which is the product of Age and Coherence. Although there are many interaction terms which could have been entered, all of them are, however, insignificant. The interaction term Age×Coh is chosen merely to demonstrate how such a term may be included in an OLS regression model. Once all the variables to be considered for the model have been appropriately coded and any problematic levels of multicollinearity dealt with, insignificant terms may be removed from the model. For the purpose of demonstration, a stepwise selection procedure is used here to select a subset of terms to model Quality. A proposed model is shown in Table 3.18 and shows that Age, Coherence, Delay, and the three dummy variables representing Location have been retained in the model[10]. Using the t statistics, the contribution of each of the dummy variables to the model can be determined. The t statistics will not, however, provide the significance of Location overall. To do this we need to compute a partial-F statistic. The residual sum of squares statistic for the model which includes all of the location dummy variables is 4389.317 with 63 degrees-of-freedom and the nested model where the dummy variables are removed has a residual sum of squares equal to 4639.385 with 66 degrees-of-freedom. Entering these data into Equation 3.9 partial-F is computed as:

$$F_{66-63,63} = \frac{4639.385 - 4389.317}{(66 - 63)(4389.317/63)}$$

$$F_{3,63} = 1.196; P = 0.319.$$

---

[10]The three location dummy variables have been kept in the model as a group (i.e., $j-1$ variables) to enable comparison with the reference category.

Table 3.18: Model Selected Using Stepwise Selection

	Coefficient	s.e.	t	P
Variables included in the model				
Age	9.885	2.155	4.573	0.000
Coherence	−3.112	1.406	−2.214	0.030
Delay	−0.072	0.042	−1.701	0.094
Location dummy variables				
Location-Home	0.532	2.891	0.184	0.854
Location-School	0.053	2.902	0.018	0.986
Location-Special	4.880	3.087	1.581	0.119
(constant)	65.999	5.573	11.842	0.000
Variables not included in the model				
Gender	0.104		1.064	0.291
age*coh	0.425		1.301	0.198

$F_{6,63} = 9.631$, $P < 0.0005$, $R^2 = 0.478$

On this evidence, Location does not make a significant contribution to the model and can therefore be removed. The final model which contains only the variables Age, Coherence and Delay is shown in Table 3.19.

Table 3.19: Final Model

			95% CIs for β			
	Coefficient	s.e.	Lower	Upper	t	P
Age	9.862	2.152	5.566	14.157	4.583	0.000
Coherence	−3.786	1.319	−6.418	−1.153	−2.871	0.005
Delay	−0.086	0.041	−0.167	−0.006	−2.133	0.037
(constant)	69.878	4.550	60.794	78.963	15.358	0.000

$F_{3,66} = 17.905$, $P < 0.0005$, $R^2 = 0.449$

Once a final model has been derived, the regression parameters can be interpreted. From Table 3.19 it can be seen that as Age increases from 5–6 to 8–9 years (a unit increase) Quality improves by an average of 9.862 ($P < 0.0005$). Furthermore, we can say with 95% confidence that we can expect the improvement to be between 5.566 and 14.157. Compared to 5–6-year-old children, 8–9-year-olds are expected to provide statements which are at least 5.6% and at most 14.2% higher quality. Similarly, as the coherence score for the child increases by one unit, Quality decreases by an average of 3.786. As the initial coding scheme assigned low values to children who were coherent and high values to those who were incoherent, this result means that the children who are rated as more coherent provide higher quality statements. Similar interpretations of the regression coefficients and associated confidence intervals can be applied to Delay.

One can also calculate confidence intervals for the fitted values of mean Y and the prediction intervals. For example, a child aged 5–6 with a coherence rating of 3.81 and a delay of 45 days can be expected to provide a statement of quality 51.565. This result can be derived using software, or manually using the equation:

$$\text{Quality} = 69.878 + 9.862 \text{ Age} - 3.786 \text{ Coherence} - 0.086 \text{ Delay}.$$

From software, the confidence intervals for the fitted values of mean Y are 48.026 to 55.104, and the prediction intervals are 34.456 to 68.675. For a large sample of 5–6-year-old children with a coherence rating of 3.81 and a delay of 45 days (if such a sample could be found), one would expect the mean statement quality to be at least 48.026 and at most 55.104. An individual with the same characteristics one would expect to provide a statement with a quality of at least 34.456 and at most 68.675. The software commands to obtain these statistics can be viewed in Section 3.6.

This worked example has demonstrated how OLS regression might be used to analyse a selection of continuous, dichotomous and categorical variables. Problematic levels of multicollinearity were first identified and dealt with, interaction terms were computed and entered into the model (explicitly defining interaction terms in this way is a requirement of some, but not all software packages) and then an automatic selection process (stepwise) used in conjunction with manual modelling techniques (for categorical data) was used to derive a final model. In practice, it would also be wise to investigate the model residuals (see Chapter 2), but to save space in this example, these were assumed not to give any cause for concern. The SPSS and GLIM software commands for the above procedures are provided in Section 3.6.

3.5   Summary

OLS regression provides a model-building approach to the analysis of continuous data. It is a generalized linear model which directly maps the random component of a model (the continuous response variable) onto the systematic component (the explanatory variables expressed as a linear function). OLS regression explicitly models continuous variables and although it is most easily demonstrated using continuous explanatory variables, the application of dummy coding methods enables dichotomous and categorical explanatory variables to also be included in the model. By this means, OLS regression allows one to carry out analysis of variance and analysis of covariance which have traditionally been treated as separate techniques. This greatly increases the utility of the technique and has no doubt contributed to its popularity.

Since OLS regression is a form of generalized linear model, it shares much common ground with the related techniques of logistic regression and loglinear analysis, which are used to model dichotomous and categorical data. Due to the common theoretical underpinnings of these models, many of the methods discussed in this chapter can be applied to other generalized linear modelling techniques described in Chapters 4 and 5. The form and interpretation of the OLS regression equation, dummy variable coding and model-building have direct relevance to the techniques used in logistic regression and loglinear analysis and should be viewed as being complimentary to these chapters. The material in this chapter provides much of the information required to understand and utilize logistic regression and loglinear analysis and can therefore be regarded as an introduction to these techniques.

3.6   Statistical Software Commands

3.6.1   SPSS

Detailed discussions of the SPSS procedures outlined in this section can be found in Norušis (1994) and in the appropriate SPSS manuals (see, for example, SPSS Inc., 1996a).

Computing Regression Coefficients and Associated Confidence Intervals

Input the data from Table 3.1 in three columns, exactly as shown in the table. The regression coefficients and associated confidence intervals can be derived using the commands:

Statistics   ▼
    Regression   ►
        Linear . . .
            Dependent: *input Y*
            Independent(s): *input X_1 or X_2*

            | Statistics . . . |

                Regression Coefficients Estimates: *check box*
                Regression Coefficients Confidence intervals: *check box*

            | Continue |

        | OK |

Predicting Values of y and Associated Confidence and Prediction Intervals

Input the data from Table 3.1 in three columns, exactly as shown in the table. The following commands can be used to generate statistics relating to the response variable.

<u>S</u>tatistics ▼
    <u>R</u>egression ▶
        <u>L</u>inear ...
           <u>D</u>ependent: *input Y*
           <u>I</u>ndependent(s): *input X_1 or X_2*

             | S<u>a</u>ve ... |

                Predicted Values <u>U</u>nstandardized: *check box*
                Prediction Intervals M<u>e</u>an: *check box*
                Prediction Intervals <u>I</u>ndividual: *check box*

             | Continue |
       | OK |

Running the above regression model will create five new variables; the predicted value of Y (pre_1), the upper and lower confidence intervals for the fitted mean value of Y (lmci_1 and umci_1), and the upper and lower prediction intervals for individual values of Y (lici_1 and uici_1). You will note that predictions are only given for those points included in the data set. It is possible, however, to obtain predictions for Y given any value of the explanatory variable by inputting the value of X into the spreadsheet. For example, the prediction intervals for Y when X_1 is equal to 29.8 can be calculated by the following method:

- Enter a new case for variable X_1 and give it the value of 29.8 (i.e., add the value 29.8 onto the bottom of the column of values for X_1).

- **Do not** enter any value for the Y variable.

- Run the regression as above and the predicted values for all cases will be saved including the values for the new case.

This procedure works in SPSS as cases are removed from the analysis listwise. The data point added will, therefore, play no part in the calculation of the regression model, but the programme will nevertheless calculate a value of Y when X_1 is equal to 29.8. In this case, the predicted value of Y is 11.005, the prediction intervals are 9.08, 12.93, and the confidence intervals for y are 9.94, 12.07.

Calculating the Residual Sum of Squares (RSS) Statistics

The value of F for the models shown in Table 3.4 can be calculated using Equation 3.9. To do this manually, we need to compute the value of RSS for the null and final models using OLS regression (see above). For the model $Y = \alpha + x_1$, SPSS provides the statistics shown in Table 3.20.

Table 3.20: Statistics for Calculating F

	Sum of Squares	Degrees of Freedom	Mean Squares
Regression	105.525	1	105.525
Residual	7.190	13	0.553
Total	112.715	14	

From Table 3.20, $RSS_{null} = 112.715$ (the total deviance in the model) and $RSS_{final} = 7.190$ (the deviance in the model that includes the explanatory variable). $df_{null} = 14$ $(n - k - 1$, where $k = 0)$ and $df_{final} = 13$ $(n - k - 1$, where $k = 1)$. Inputting these values into Equation 3.9, the value of F can be calculated as:

$$F_{1,13} = \frac{112.715 - 7.190}{(7.190/13)} = 190.796$$

RSS statistics are also required for computing partial-F statistics when comparing nested models (see Equation 3.19). Table 3.21 shows how the RSS statistics were derived for the model shown in Table 3.18. To obtain these statistics, one needs to compute two regression models (see above), one model which includes the locations and one which does not.

From Table 3.21, $RSS_{p+q} = 4389.317$ (the deviance in the larger model) and $RSS_p = 4639.385$ (the deviance in the smaller model). $df_{p+q} = 63$ $(n - k - 1$, where $k = 6)$ and $df_p = 66$ $(n - k - 1$, where $k = 3)$. Inputting these values into Equation 3.19, the value of partial-F is calculated as:

$$F_{66-63,63} = \frac{4639.385 - 4389.317}{(66 - 63)(4389.317/63)}$$

$$F_{3,63} = 1.196$$

Calculating Tolerance and VIF Values

Enter the data from Table 3.7 into an SPSS spreadsheet. To calculate the tolerance and VIF statistics, use the commands:

Table 3.21: Statistics for Calculating Partial-F

	Sum of Squares	Degrees of Freedom	Mean Squares
The larger model (p+q)			
Regression	4025.988	6	670.998
Residual	4389.317	63	69.672
Total	8415.306	69	
The smaller model (p)			
Regression	3775.920	3	1258.640
Residual	4639.385	66	70.294
Total	8415.306	69	

Model p+q: $\alpha + \beta_1 \text{Age} + \beta_2 \text{Coherence} + \beta_3 \text{Delay} +$
$\beta_4 \text{Location}$ (3 dummy variables)

Model p: $\alpha + \beta_1 \text{Age} + \beta_2 \text{Coherence} + \beta_3 \text{Delay}$

Statistics   ▼
  Regression   ▶
    Linear ...
      Dependent: *input response variable*
      Independent(s): *input both explanatory variables*
       | Statistics ... |
        Collinearity diagnostics: *check box*
       | Continue |
     | OK |

Specific Code Relating to the Example in Section 3.4

Input the data from Table 3.11 into an SPSS spreadsheet. To define the dummy location variables, one can recode the location variable using the indicator coding method:

Transform   ▼
  Recode   ▶
    Into Different Variables ...
      Define the input and output variables
       Define | Old and New Values | (make each variable consist of 0 and 1)
      | Continue |
    | OK |

The interaction between the variables 'age' and 'coherence' can be defined using the commands:

Transform   ▼
    Compute . . .
        Define the Target Variable: as 'age*coh'
            Input the Numeric Expression: as 'age*coherenc'
        [OK]

The stepwise regression model shown in Table 3.18 can be computed using the commands:

Statistics   ▼
    Regression   ▶
        Linear . . .
            Dependent: *input* Quality
            Independent(s): *input* Age, Coherence,
                        Delay, Gender, *and* Age*Coh.
            select the regression Method: as **Stepwise**
            Select [Next]: *this allows the dummy variables to be entered as a group.*

            input the dummy variables Home, School *and* Special
            select the regression Method: as Enter
        [OK]

3.6.2   GLIM

In order to run the GLIM examples presented below, type in the following command from within GLIM: `$INPUT 'FILENAME.EXT' $`, replacing `FILENAME.EXT` with that of each example file. To aid the reader, we have commented the commands extensively within each file. All macros which have been used are included at the end of this section.

Computing Regression Coefficients and Associated Confidence and Prediction Intervals

```
$echo on $
!       Example from the data set in Table 3.1
!       First input any macros that we require.
$input %plc 80 NORMAC $ $echo on $
$input 'ols.mac' $
!       Read in the data set.
$slen  15 $
$data Y X1 X2 $
$read
0.52    10.50    11.09
2.09    13.19    12.91
etc.
etc.
7.01    22.68    24.19
8.92    26.28    24.75
```

```
$
!       Declare the response variable.
$yvar Y$
!       Fit the first model.
$fit X1 $
!       Display parameter estimates and standard errors.
$dis e $
!       Call macro to calculate a t-test and the 95%
!       Confidence Intervals for each parameter.
$use ttest $
!       Fit and examine the second model.
$fit X2 $
$dis e $
$use ttest $
!       Predict fitted values for all original values of the explanatory
!       variable, for the first model.
$fit X1 $
$predict X1=X1 $
!       Call macro to tabulate the fitted values, confidence intervals for
!       fitted Y, and the prediction intervals, with the original values of
!       the explanatory variable.
$look X1 $
$use cipiori $
!       Predict fitted value for a new value of the explanatory variable.
$predict X1=29.8 $
!       Call macro to display fitted value, confidence interval for
!       fitted Y, and the prediction interval, with a new value of
!       the explanatory variable.
$use cipinew $
!       Predict fitted values, 95% Confidence Intervals for Fitted Y,
!       and the Prediction Intervals, with all the original values of
!       the explanatory variable, for the second model.
$fit X2 $
$predict X2=X2 $
$look X2 $
$use cipiori $
!       Now calculate these for a new value of X2.
$predict X2=29.8 $
$use cipinew $
!       Calculate R-square and and F-test for the first model.
$fit X1 $
!       Call macro to calculate r-squared.
$use rsq $
!       Call macro to set rss and df for fitted model.
$use rssdf1 $
!       Remove the tested model term.
$fit -X1$
!       Call macro to set rss and df for reduced model.
$use rssdf2$
!       Call macro to calculate F-test.
$use ftest $
!       Calculate R-square and and F-test for the second model.
$fit X2 $
```

```
$use rsq $
$use rssdf1 $
$fit -X2 $
$use rssdf2 $
$use ftest $
$return $
```

Calculating Tolerance and VIF Values

```
$echo on $
!          Example from the data set in Table 3.7
!          First input any macros that we require.
$input %plc 80 NORMAC $ $echo on $
$input 'ols.mac' $
!          Read in the data set.
$slen   11 $
$data PLACES ENGLISH MATHS $
$read
0          22      17
1          32.5    34.5
etc.
etc.
9          85.5    74.5
10         68.5    87.6
$
!          Declare the response variable.
$yvar PLACES $
!          Fit the model to be tested.
$fit ENGLISH+MATHS $
!          Call macro to calculate r-squared.
$use rsq $
!          Display parameter estimates and standard errors.
$dis e $
!          Call macro to calculate a t-test of each parameter.
$use ttest $
!          Call macro to set rss and df for fitted model.
$use rssdf1 $
!          Remove the tested model terms.
$fit -(ENGLISH+MATHS) $
!          Call macro to set rss and df for reduced model.
$use rssdf2$
!          Call macro to calculate F-test.
$use ftest $
!          Fit the ENGLISH main effect model.
$fit ENGLISH
$use rsq $
$dis e $
$use ttest $
$use rssdf1 $
$fit -ENGLISH $
$use rssdf2 $
$use ftest $
!          Fit the MATHS main effect model.
```

```
$fit MATHS $
$use rsq $
$dis e $
$use ttest $
$use rssdf1 $
$fit -MATHS $
$use rssdf2 $
$use ftest $
!       Calculate VIF and Tolerance values for explanatory variables.
!       First calculate VIF and Tolerance for ENGLISH.
$yvar MATHS $
$fit ENGLISH $
$use tolvif $
!       Then calculate VIF and Tolerance for MATHS.
$yvar ENGLISH $
$fit MATHS $
$use tolvif $
$return $
```

Analysis of Child Witness Data Presented in Section 3.4.

```
$echo on $
!       Example from the data set in Table 3.11
!       First input any macros that we require.
$input %plc 80 NORMAC $ $echo on $
$input 'ols.mac' $
$slen  70 $
$factor age 2 gender 2 location 4 $
$data
AGE     GENDER  LOCATION
COHERENC        DELAY
MATURITY        QUALITY PROSECUT $
$read
1 1 3 3.81 45 3.62 34.11  0
1 2 2 1.63 27 1.61 36.59  0
    etc.
2 2 2 1.94 46 1.99 80.67  1
2 1 4 1.89 15 1.87 83.15  1
$
$yvar QUALITY $
!       Note that prosecut is a response variable used in the
!       Logistic Regression chapter, and is not used in this analysis.
!
!       Examine the two complete main effects models of Table 1.13.
!       Set reference category for LOCATION to level 4.
$factor location 4 (4) $
$fit DELAY+LOCATION
$use rsq $
$use ttest $
$use rssdf1 $
$fit -(DELAY+LOCATION) $
$use rssdf2 $
$use ftest $
```

```
!       Set reference catagory for LOCATION to level 3.
$factor location 4 (2) $
!       Fit and test the DELAY+LOCATION model
$fit DELAY+LOCATION
$use rsq $
$use ttest $
$use rssdf1 $
$fit -(DELAY+LOCATION) $
$use rssdf2 $
$use ftest $
!       Calculate VIF and Tolerance for each continuous explanatory
!       variable as in Table 1.20.
!       Note that the declaration of a factor as the response variable
!       is not supported with the macro viftol since GLIM uses internal
!       dummy coding of factors ---  a error message is given.
$yvar COHERENCE $
$fit AGE+DELAY+GENDER+LOCATION+MATURITY $
$use tolvif $
$yvar DELAY$
$fit AGE+COHERENCE+GENDER+LOCATION+MATURITY $
$use tolvif $
$yvar MATURITY $
$fit AGE+COHERENCE+DELAY+GENDER+LOCATION $
$use tolvif $
!       Check the correlation between MATURITY and COHERENCE
$yvar COHERENCE $
$fit MATURITY $
$use rsq $
!       Fit the full main effects model and try removing MATURITY.
$yvar QUALITY $
$factor location 4 (3) $
$fit AGE+GENDER+LOCATION+COHERENC+DELAY+MATURITY $
$use rsq $
$dis e $
$use ttest $
$use rssdf1 $
$fit -MATURITY $
$use rssdf2 $
$use ftest $
$use rsq $
$dis e $
$use ttest $
!       Fit model of Table 1.22.
$fit AGE+COHERENCE+LOCATION $
$use rsq $
$dis e $
$use ttest $
$use rssdf1 $
$fit -(AGE+COHERENCE+LOCATION) $
$use rssdf2 $
$use ftest $
!       Recode LOCATION into two levels with levels 1,2 and 4
!       combined to form the reference category.
```

```
$factor LOC2 2 $
$calc LOC2=%eq(LOCATION,4)+1$
!       Refit model using LOC2.
$fit AGE+COHERENCE+LOC2 $
$use rsq $
$dis e $
$use ttest $
$use rssdf1 $
$fit -(AGE+COHERENCE+LOC2) $
$use rssdf2 $
$use ftest $
!       Refit model of interest.
$fit AGE+COHERENCE+LOC2 $
!       Predict fitted value for a new value of each explanatory
!       variable. First example.
$predict AGE=1 COHERENCE=3.2 LOC2=1 $
!       Call macro to display fitted value, confidence interval for
!       fitted Y, and the prediction interval, with a new value of
!       the explanatory variable.
$use cipinew $
!       Predict fitted value for a new value of each explanatory
!       variable. Second example.
$predict AGE=2 COHERENCE=1.3 LOC2=2 $
$use cipinew $
!       A simultaneous test of all two-way interaction terms.
$fit (AGE+GENDER+LOCATION+COHERENC+DELAY+MATURITY)**2$
$use rsq $
$use rssdf1$
$fit AGE+GENDER+LOCATION+COHERENC+DELAY+MATURITY $
$use rsq $
$use rssdf2$ $use ftest $
$return $
```

GLIM Macros for OLS Regression

```
!       Macros for use in OLS Regression Chapter.
$mac tolvif
$num tol vif $
!       Outputs tolerance and VIF values.
$use rsq $
$calc tol=1-%r $
$calc vif=1/tol $
$pr 'Tolerance ='tol' and VIF ='vif ;$
$endmac $
$mac ttest
!       Produces a table of t, P-values, and CI's
!       for the model parameters.
$num td95 $
$extract %pe %se $
$calc t=%pe/%se : pt=2*(1-%tp(%abs(t),%df)) $
$calc td95=%td(0.975,%df) $
$calc pelo=%pe-(td95*%se) $
$calc pehi=%pe+(td95*%se) $
```

```
$acc 4 3 $ $look %pe %se t pt pelo pehi $ $pr $ $acc $
$delete t pt pelo pehi $
$endmac $
$num rss1 rss2 df1 df2 df21 s2 ss21 ms21 f p $
$mac rssdf1 $assign rss1=%dv: df1=%df: s2=%sc $ $endmac $
$mac rssdf2 $assign rss2=%dv: df2=%df $ $endmac $
$mac ftest
!        Calculates F-test
$calc ss21=rss2-rss1: df21=df2-df1 $
$calc ms21=ss21/df21: f=ms21/s2 $
$calc p= 1-%fp(f, df21, df1) $
$pr 'F  ='f' with 'df21', 'df1' df and P ='p ;$
$endmac $
$mac cipiori
!        Calculate and tabulate fitted values, confidence intervals
!        for fitted Y, and the prediction intervals,
!        with the original values of the explanatory variables.
$calc td95=%td(.975,%df) $
$calc cifylo=%pfv-td95*%sqrt(%pvl): cifyhi=%pfv+td95*%sqrt(%pvl)$
$calc pilo=%pfv-td95*%sqrt(%sc+%pvl): pihi=%pfv+td95*%sqrt(%sc+%pvl)$
$acc 4 3$ $look %pfv cifylo cifyhi pilo pihi$ $pr $ $acc $
$endmac $
$mac cipinew
!        Calculate and display fitted value, confidence interval for
!        fitted Y, and the prediction interval, with a new value of
!        the explanatory variable.
$num cifynewlo cifynewhi pinewlo pinewhi  $
$calc td95=%td(.975,%df) $
$calc cifynewlo=%pfv-td95*%sqrt(%pvl): cifynewhi=%pfv+td95*%sqrt(%pvl)$
$calc pinewlo=%pfv-td95*%sqrt(%sc+%pvl): pinewhi=%pfv+td95*%sqrt(%sc+%pvl)$
$pr 'Fitted value = '%pfv' with CI for fitted Y of ('cifynewlo','cifynewhi')
and PI of ('pinewlo',' pinewhi')';$
$endmac $
$return $
```

Chapter 4

Logistic Regression

Chapter 3 demonstrated that variables which are recorded on a continuous scale can be modelled using OLS regression. Many variables that one may wish to model are, however, discontinuous and need to be analysed using an alternative technique. The technique we consider in this chapter allows data which are constrained between two values to be modelled. Such data are relatively common and may consist of dichotomous classifications such as 'survived–died', 'waged–unwaged', 'employed–unemployed', 'succeed–fail', or measures of proportion constrained between 0 and 1 (proportion killed, proportion who succeed, the proportion of questions correctly answered etc.). Data that are constrained in this way may be analysed using logistic regression, a generalized linear modelling technique which allows predictions to be made of the response variable as well as an assessment to be made of the importance of individual and groups of explanatory variables (fulfilling the regression goals of prediction and explanation).

The three components of generalized linear models are a random component for the response variable, a systematic component representing the fixed values of the explanatory variables in terms of a linear function, and finally, a link function which maps the systematic component onto the random component. Whereas OLS regression assumes the errors of the random component to be Normally distributed, logistic regression assumes that the errors are distributed binomially. The systematic component in logistic regression is the same as that in OLS regression with explanatory variables assumed to be continuous and measured on at least an interval scale. Similar to OLS regression, discontinuous explanatory variables can be entered into the model using dummy variable coding techniques. Unlike OLS regression, the random and systematic components of the model do not map directly onto one another and a non-linear link function, known as the *logit*, is used. Logistic and OLS regression techniques have much in common and a number of the procedures and statistics discussed in this chapter, such as goodness-of-fit measures, confidence intervals, dummy variable coding, techniques of model building and the way in which regression coefficients are interpreted, are very similar to those already discussed in relation to OLS regression. It is therefore suggested that readers familiarize themselves with the descriptions of these procedures provided in Chapter 3.

4.1   Simple Logistic Regression

We will begin our description of logistic regression by focusing on a simple case which involves just two variables, a binary variable which we wish to model (the response variable) and a single explanatory variable. To demonstrate the modelling procedure we use a hypothetical data set showing the success of a treatment for a particular disease given the severity of the infection when the treatment was started. The response variable is binary and indicates two different treatment outcomes (those patients who survived and those who died) whilst the explanatory variable is continuous and is measured on a continuous scale which directly measures the severity of the infection (in this case, by measuring the concentration of bacteria in their blood).

Table 4.1: Treatment Outcome as a Function of Infection Severity (raw data)

Infection Severity	Treatment Outcome	Infection Severity	Treatment Outcome	Infection Severity	Treatment Outcome
9.3	survived	62.2	survived	90.9	died
18.2	survived	64.1	died	91.5	survived
22.7	survived	68.9	survived	96.6	survived
32.9	survived	71.2	survived	97.2	died
38.0	survived	72.3	died	101.6	survived
39.9	survived	73.0	died	104.8	died
44.0	survived	73.2	died	108.6	died
44.9	survived	74.6	survived	109.9	died
46.8	survived	75.3	died	111.3	died
47.7	survived	76.3	survived	113.2	died
49.1	died	77.7	died	118.8	died
49.7	survived	79.1	survived	127.0	died
50.9	survived	80.6	died	142.0	died
50.9	survived	85.0	survived	157.4	died
53.7	survived	86.0	died	169.2	died
60.1	died	89.4	died		
61.7	survived	90.0	survived		

Table 4.1 shows the treatment outcome and the severity of the infection when the treatment was started for 49 patients and provides some indication of the relationship between the two variables; namely, that as the severity of infection increases, fewer patients survive. Whilst this relationship can be

observed in the raw data, it is perhaps easier to see using the proportion of patients who die at different infection severities. Table 4.2 shows the information in Table 4.1 categorized into 17 equally-spaced groups of infection severity and the proportion of patients in each group who die. The use of proportions provides a clearer picture of the relationship between the variables. It should be noted that the data in Table 4.2 is only provided here to more clearly illustrate the relationship between the variables and to provide a convenient way of visually assessing the adequacy of the logistic regression model — it is not necessary to categorize the data in order to compute the regression model.

Table 4.2: Treatment Outcome as a Function of Infection Severity (categorized data)

Infection Severity	Total Number of Patients	Number Died	Proportion Died
0–10	1	0	0.00
10–20	1	0	0.00
20–30	1	0	0.00
30–40	3	0	0.00
40–50	6	1	0.17
50–60	3	0	0.00
60–70	5	2	0.40
70–80	9	5	0.56
80–90	5	3	0.60
90–100	4	2	0.50
100–110	4	3	0.75
110–120	3	3	1.00
120–130	1	1	1.00
130–140	0	0	—
140–150	1	1	1.00
150–160	1	1	1.00
160–170	1	1	1.00

Figure 4.1 provides a graphical representation of the relationship between the severity of infection and treatment outcome and shows that this relationship is not linear since it 'flattens out' at each extreme of infection severity producing an S-shaped curve which is constrained to lie between 0 and 1. In general, when the response variable is constrained between two extremes, the appropriate model will be S-shaped, or, more formally a sigmoid[1].

Although the non-linear nature of the relationship depicted in Figure 4.1 makes it inappropriate to model directly using a 'straight-line' technique such as OLS regression, it is possible to fit such a model as Figure 4.2 shows. We can

---

[1] Further examples of S-shaped distributions can be found in Agresti, 1996, and Collett, 1991.

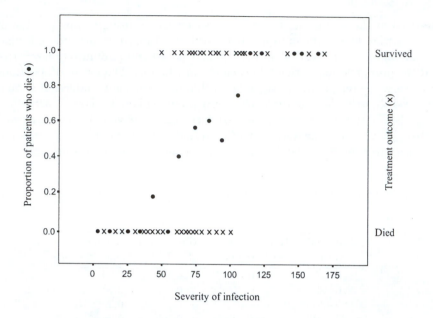

Figure 4.1: The relationship between infection severity and treatment outcome

see from the graph that even though a straight-line model appears to provide quite a good approximation of treatment outcome for mid-range values of infection severity, the predictions of treatment outcome become quite inaccurate at extreme values of infection severity. For example, the predicted probability of death when infection severity is equal to 160 is about 1.2, which indicates that out of a sample of 100, 120 patients are predicted to die. Similarly, at an infection severity equal to 10, the proportion of patients expected to die is about −0.1. In other words, out of 100 patients infected at this level it is predicted that 110 will survive. Clearly the OLS regression technique is not appropriate when *data* are constrained to lie between 0 and 1, as *predictions* from the model are not similarly constrained.

Although the relationship between treatment outcome and infection severity is non-linear, a generalized linear modelling technique can be successfully applied to these data. The technique used here is logistic regression which estimates the parameters of a linear model derived from the data and then transforms this into a non-linear S-shaped model. The process of logistic regression can therefore be seen as a transformation which converts a linear model (of the linear predictor) into a non-linear model (of the fitted values) which is more suited to the description of a binary response variable. The transformation in this case is the link function, which is commonly known as the logit (the log odds).

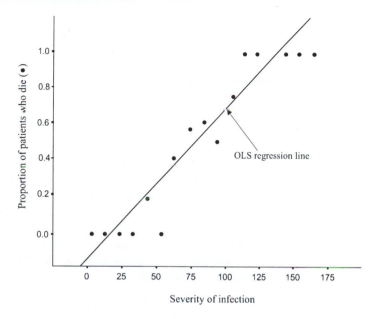

Figure 4.2: An OLS regression model of the relationship between infection severity and treatment outcome

4.1.1   The Regression Equation

There are a number of equations used in this chapter to describe the relationship between the linear predictor and the response variable. Although this requires some degree of mathematical knowledge, it is important that readers familiarize themselves with the following section since it introduces a number of important concepts and is crucial in understanding the way in which a measure representing the probability of a particular outcome (the S-shaped relationship) can be transformed into a linear function. We will begin our discussion with a non-linear equation showing how probability can be modelled and demonstrate how this can be transformed into a linear equation whose parameters can be estimated from the data.

The probability that a particular event will occur (for our example, this is the probability that a patient will die) can be modelled using Equation 4.1 overleaf. Figure 4.3 shows the graph which is produced using Equation 4.1 using parameters which have been calculated from the data in Table 4.1. The graph[2] is constrained to lie between 0 and 1 and appears to model the S-shaped relationship between severity of infection and treatment outcome much better than the OLS regression model depicted in Figure 4.2. Treatment outcome (p) is modelled using a linear predictor of the response variable (the systematic

---

[2]The procedure for producing this graph using software is provided in Section 4.6.

$$\text{probability of an event happening} = \frac{e^{(\alpha+\beta x)}}{1 + e^{(\alpha+\beta x)}} \qquad (4.1)$$

where e is the natural logarithm base,
α and β are parameters of the linear component of the model,
and x is the value of the explanatory variable.

component, $\alpha + \beta x$) together with a function to transform this straight line into an S-shaped curve (the logit link). Although the transformation of a linear function to an S-shaped function can appear confusing, it is relatively straightforward to demonstrate how it can be achieved. Firstly, one needs to transform the measure of probability into a measure of odds, which is defined as the ratio of the probability of an event occurring to the probability of an event not occurring. The odds of an event happening can be represented algebraically as shown in Equation 4.2 overleaf.

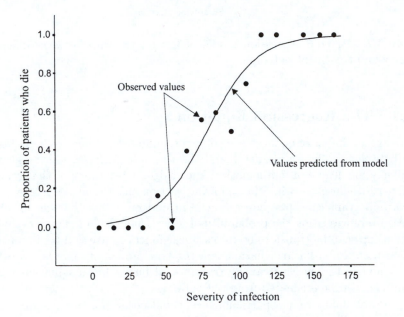

Figure 4.3: A logistic regression model of the relationship between infection severity and treatment outcome

The measures of odds and probability provide similar information, but must not be confused as they are distinct. For example, if there is a 50–50 chance of a patient dying due to an infection, the *probability* of death is 0.5 whereas the *odds* of death are 1.0 (0.5/0.5), which means that for each patient who

$$\text{odds of an event happening} = \frac{p}{1-p} \tag{4.2}$$

where p is the probability of an event happening,
and $(1-p)$ is the probability of an event not happening.

dies, one is expected to survive. If there is a relatively mild infection where
the probability of death is only 0.25, the odds of dying are 0.33 (0.25/0.75)
and for every 0.33 patient who dies, one will survive. This is equivalent to
saying that for every one patient who dies three will survive. If the infection
is relatively severe with a probability of death of 0.9, the odds of dying are 9
(0.9/0.1), which can be interpreted as odds of 9 to 1 in favour of dying. The
odds of an event happening can be derived using Equation 4.3.

$$\text{odds of an event happening} = e^{(\alpha+\beta x)} \tag{4.3}$$

Figure 4.4 is a graphical representation of Equation 4.3 and shows that the
predicted odds of dying increase as the severity of the infection increases. The
odds are constrained to assume any value above 0. This relationship is also

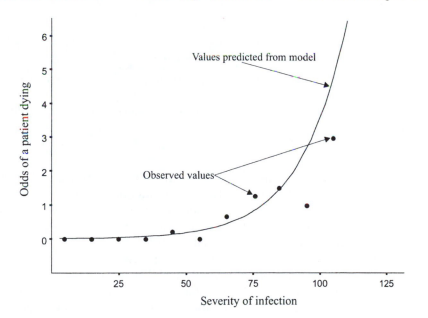

Figure 4.4: The relationship between infection severity and the odds of dying

non-linear. It is, however, a simple matter to represent it linearly by taking the natural log of the odds, which is commonly known as the *logit*. Logit(p) has a linear relationship with the explanatory variable (see Figure 4.5) and is represented algebraically in Equation 4.4[3].

$$\log[\text{odds of an event happening}] = \text{logit}(p) = \alpha + \beta x \qquad (4.4)$$

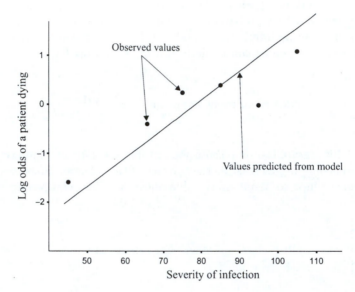

Figure 4.5: The relationship between infection severity and the log odds of dying

Equations 4.1 to 4.4 demonstrate how a non-linear relationship between a binary response variable and a continuous explanatory variable can be represented linearly when the response variable is described in terms of the log odds of the probability of a particular outcome. Using logit(p) instead of p enables linear parameters to be estimated from the data and the relationship between the variables to be modelled using a regression analysis. For ease of comparison, the transformation of the S-shaped distribution into a linear one is shown in Figure 4.6 along with the equations which have generated each of these graphs. It is important to point out that the three graphs and equations

---

[3]Logit(p) is also commonly known as logit[$\pi(x)$], where π = the probability of x and not 3.1416 ... , see Agresti, 1996; Hosmer and Lemeshow, 1989.

provide the same information about the relationship between the variables; it is just that this information is presented in different ways.

Calculating and Interpreting Model Parameters

The method of calculating regression parameters in logistic regression is different to that which is used in OLS regression (which uses the least-squares method; see Section 3.1.1). In logistic regression, a form of maximum likelihood estimation is used which selects parameters that make the observed results most likely for a response variable with binomial errors[4]. Although maximum likelihood estimation techniques are important, a detailed description is beyond the scope of this text, but may be found in a number of other publications (see, for example, Agresti, 1990; 1996; Collett, 1991; Elliason, 1993, and Hays, 1994).

The logistic regression procedure estimates the parameters of a linear model (parameters relating to $\text{logit}(p)$). Figure 4.5 and Equation 4.4 show clearly that the relationship between the explanatory variable and $\text{logit}(p)$ is a straight line ($\text{logit}(p) = \alpha + \beta x$). The parameters of the model are therefore interpreted in much the same way as they are in OLS regression with the gradient, or slope of the line, indicating the parameter β which is interpreted as the change in $\text{logit}(p)$ resulting from a unit change in x. Put another way, β represents the change in the log odds of an event happening for a unit change in x. The parameter α indicates the value of $\text{logit}(p)$ when $x = 0$, or the log odds of an event happening when $x = 0$. Table 4.3 shows a number of statistics which are typically provided by software as part of a logistic regression analysis. The regression parameters β (the regression coefficient for the explanatory variable) and α (the regression coefficient for the constant) are provided in the column labeled 'coefficient' along with the standard errors for these terms in the column labeled ASE (the asymptotic standard error[5]).

Table 4.3: Logistic Regression Model Parameters

	Coefficient	ASE	e^{β} (the odds ratio)
Variable x	0.142	0.028	1.15
(constant)	−2.641	1.389	

$\text{logit}(p) = -2.641 + 0.142x$

From Table 4.3 it can be seen that $\beta = 0.142$ and $\alpha = -2.641$. As the explanatory variable increases by 1, $\text{logit}(p)$ increases by 0.142. When the

---

[4]The least squares method of estimation used in OLS regression is, in fact, also a maximum likelihood estimation where the response variable has Normally distributed errors.

[5]Asymptotic standard errors are estimated when the maximum likelihood procedure is used to estimate the regression parameters.

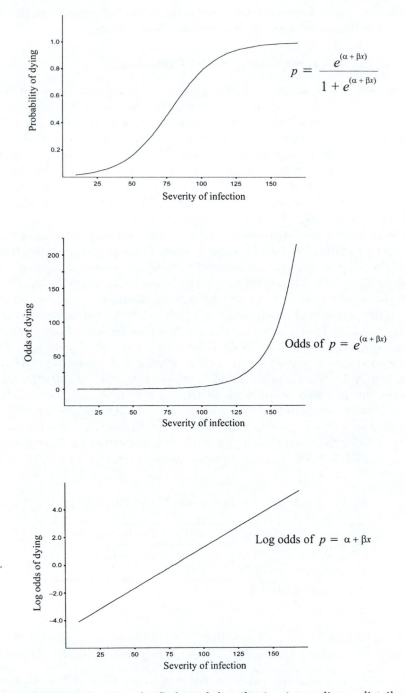

Figure 4.6: Transforming the S-shaped distribution into a linear distribution

explanatory variable is equal to 0, the value of logit(p) equals -2.641. It is, however, difficult to understand what the regression coefficient β means in practice as we do not tend to think in terms of logits. An easier interpretation of the regression coefficient can be obtained from the odds, which are obtained by taking the inverse of the natural log of logit(p), e^{β}. The e^{β} term represents the change in the odds of p which is associated with a unit change in x and is commonly termed the *odds ratio*. For the example above, $\beta = 0.142$, and $e^{0.142} = 1.15$ which indicates that for each unit increase in x the odds of p change to 115% of its previous value, an increase of 15%.

The odds ratio provides the ratio of the odds of p when the explanatory variable equals x to when it equals $x + 1$. It is particularly useful as it is a constant and allows a simple interpretation to be given to the relationship between the response and explanatory variables. For example, an odds ratio of 1 indicates that changes in the explanatory variable do not lead to changes in the odds of p (for each unit change in x there is no change in Y), a ratio of less than 1 indicates that the odds of p decrease as x increases, and a ratio greater than 1 indicates that the odds of p increase as x increases. Figure 4.4 shows that for our example data, the odds ratio has a positive value as the odds of p increase as the severity of the infection increases. It should be noted that, even though the change in p for each unit increase in the severity of the infection varies according to the level of severity (thus producing a non-linear graph), the odds ratio remains constant.

4.1.2   Confidence Intervals for β

Confidence intervals for β are provided by most statistical software packages or can be calculated by hand using Equation 4.5,

$$\text{confidence intervals for } \beta = \hat{\beta} \pm z_{\alpha/2}(\text{ASE}) \tag{4.5}$$

where $z_{\alpha/2}$ is the critical value of z with $N-2$ degrees-of-freedom at the desired level of α,

N is the number of cases,

and ASE is the asymptotic standard error of $\hat{\beta}$.

which, for relatively large samples (greater than about 30), can be simplified to Equation 4.6.

$$\text{confidence intervals for } \beta = \hat{\beta} \pm 1.96(\text{ASE}) \tag{4.6}$$

where 1.96 is the large sample approximation of t for a two-tailed, 95% confidence interval.

For logistic regression, β refers to the change in $\text{logit}(p)$ which results from a unit change in x. Similarly, the confidence intervals for β show the upper and lower limits of the expected change in $\text{logit}(p)$ for a unit change in x, assuming that the data are not under or overdispersed (see Section 4.1.4). Table 4.4 shows the 95% two-tailed confidence intervals which have been calculated using Equation 4.5 for the regression parameters provided in Table 4.3. From the table we can see that in 95% of cases a unit change in x will result in a change

Table 4.4: Example Logistic Regression Model Parameters

	Coefficient	ASE	95% CIs for β		95% CIs for e^{β}	
			Lower	Upper	Lower	Upper
Variable x	0.142	0.028	0.087	0.197	1.09	1.22
(constant)	−2.641	1.389				

$\text{logit}(p) = -2.641 + 0.142x$

in $\text{logit}(p)$ of between 0.086 and 0.197 with the odds expected to change from 1.09 (i.e., $e^{0.087}$) to 1.22 (i.e., $e^{0.197}$). For each unit increase in x, the odds of p can be expected to increase by at least 9% (109% of previous value) and at most 22% (122% of previous value). As both of these confidence intervals predict an increase in the odds ratio we can conclude that at the 95% two-tailed level of significance, variable x does have an affect on the response variable.

4.1.3   Confidence Intervals for Fitted y

In addition to determining confidence intervals for the explanatory variable, confidence intervals for fitted values of y can also be obtained. These intervals are calculated for the linear predictor, $\text{logit}(p)$, and are then transformed to show confidence intervals for p. The large sample approximation of the 95% two-tailed confidence intervals for the predicted mean value of $\text{logit}(p)$ can be calculated using Equation 4.7 (assuming that the data are not under or overdispersed — see Section 4.1.4).

$$\text{confidence intervals for } \text{logit}(p) = \text{logit}(\hat{p}) \pm 1.96(\text{ASE}) \qquad (4.7)$$

where ASE is the asymptotic standard error of $\text{logit}(\hat{p})$,
and 1.96 is the large sample approximation of t for a two-tailed 95% confidence interval.

Similar to OLS regression, confidence intervals are calculated for the linear relationship $\text{logit}(p) = \alpha + \beta x$. Using Equation 4.7 to compute the confidence intervals, it can be seen that these are curved in much the same way as they are with OLS regression (see Figure 4.7). The mean value of logit(p) can be more precisely estimated for non-extreme values of x.

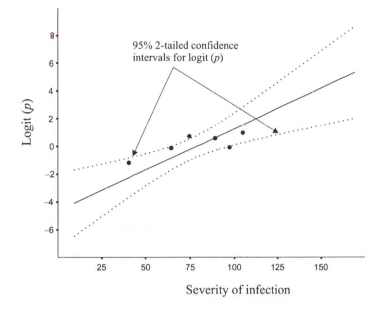

Figure 4.7: Confidence intervals for logit(p)

The confidence intervals for the probability of an event happening (p) can easily be obtained once the intervals for logit(p) have been derived. One simply transforms the graph so that the y axis represents p and not logit(p) (see Figure 4.8). It is interesting to note that the predicted values of y are not always in the middle of the confidence intervals as all values are constrained to lie between 0 and 1.

Relatively few statistical packages provide confidence intervals for logit(p) directly and these, therefore, often have to be calculated by hand[6]. The difficulty with calculating these intervals is in determining the asymptotic standard error (ASE) associated with the prediction. We provide two techniques for calculating the ASE for logit(p), the first of which relies on the generation of a variance-covariance matrix whilst the second is based on transforming the explanatory variable and recalculating the model. Both techniques are provided here since not all software programmes provide the necessary statistics to calculate the ASE based on the variance-covariance matrix and in cases where these statistics are provided, the calculation can be complex (particularly for problems with multiple variables, see Section 4.3.3). Due to the complexity of

---

[6]An exception to this is GLIM, which provides confidence intervals for logit(p) directly using the 'predict' command - see Section 4.6.2.

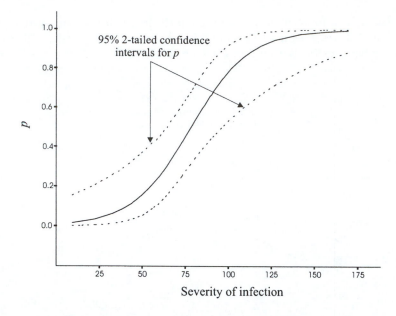

Figure 4.8: Confidence intervals for p.

calculating the ASE values for logit(p), the following section may be skipped upon first reading.

Computing the ASE for Logit(p): Method 1

When the variance-covariance matrix is available, the ASE for logit(p) for a logistic regression with a single explanatory variable can be calculated using Equation 4.8 (see Agresti, 1996).

$$\text{large sample ASE for logit}(p) = \sqrt{\text{Var}(\hat{\alpha}) + x^2\text{Var}(\hat{\beta}) + 2x\text{Cov}(\hat{\alpha}, \hat{\beta})} \quad (4.8)$$

where $\text{Var}(\hat{\alpha})$, $\text{Var}(\hat{\beta})$ and $\text{Cov}(\hat{\alpha}, \hat{\beta})$ are parameters obtained from the variance-covariance matrix,
and x is the value of the explanatory variable.

Values from the variance-covariance matrix and the value of the explanatory variable can be entered into Equation 4.8 and the ASE for the model calculated. Once this has been achieved, the confidence intervals for logit(p) can be determined using Equation 4.7. An example of the use of this method is provided in Section 4.2.

Computing the ASE for Logit(p): Method 2

If the variance-covariance matrix for the model is not available, the ASE for logit(p) can be calculated using a procedure which transforms the explanatory variable and recalculates the model (Crawley, 1993). Using this method one can obtain an estimate of the ASE for any particular value of x. For example, the procedure for accomplishing this when $x = 50$ is:

1. Subtract the value of the explanatory variable (x) you wish to use from each case of the original variable. Each value of the explanatory variable should now equal $x - 50$.

2. Calculate a logistic regression model using the new values of the explanatory variable.

3. In the output statistics, the ASE associated with the constant provides an estimate of the ASE for logit(p).

4. The confidence intervals for logit(p) when $x = 50$ can now be calculated using Equation 4.7.

As we can see from the procedures above, the ASE associated with logit(p) changes as a function x and has to be calculated for each value of x we are interested in. The 95% two-tailed confidence intervals for logit(p) indicate the mean value of logit(p) which can be expected in 95% of cases given a particular value of x. If, for example, at a given value of x, the 95% confidence intervals for logit(p) are 1.431 and 2.243, we can conclude that in 95% of cases logit(p) can be expected to vary from 1.431 to 2.243. Converting these figures to probabilities using Equation 4.1 we can see that in 95% of cases, the probability of an event happening is between 0.81 (calculated from $e^{1.431}/(1+e^{1.431})$) and 0.90 (calculated from $e^{2.243}/(1+e^{2.243})$). A worked example of a logistic regression with a single explanatory variable showing the calculation of the ASE and the confidence intervals for fitted Y is provided in Section 4.2.

4.1.4 Under and Overdispersion

As discussed in Chapter 2 on Data Screening, the logit link is an example of a GLM where the variance of the probability distribution for the response variable is a fixed function of the mean (see Section 2.10.1). It is recommended that any good-fitting models are checked for under and overdispersion, which occurs when the sample variability departs from that expected by the theoretical distribution. Cases of moderate departure from the expected variance can be compensated for by an adjustment to the standard errors using Equation 2.6. Correcting the standard error will have the effect of altering the range of the confidence intervals for the estimated parameters.

4.1.5   Goodness-of-fit Measures

There are a number of ways in which the goodness-of-fit of a logistic regression model can be assessed. Perhaps the most widely used and most powerful, is the log-likelihood statistic and this is explained in some detail below. The Wald statistic and analyses based on classification tables are also commonly used to evaluate model fit and are therefore also discussed as goodness-of-fit measures.

The Log-Likelihood Statistic

The log-likelihood statistic provides a measure of deviance for a logistic regression model (that is, a measure of the difference between the observed values and those predicted from the model) and can be used as a goodness-of-fit statistic. The derivation of $-2LL$ is beyond the scope of this chapter, but interested readers may consult Collett, 1991, and Lyndsey, 1995, for a full discussion of the likelihood function. For the purposes of this book, it is sufficient to obtain $-2LL$ from software. The goodness-of-fit statistic is usually quoted as -2 times the log-likelihood $(-2LL)$ as this has approximately a χ^2 distribution, thus enabling significance to be evaluated. The interpretation of $-2LL$ is quite straightforward – the smaller its value, the better the model fit (a $-2LL$ score equal to 0 indicates a perfect model where there is no deviance).

An indication of the goodness-of-fit of a model can be obtained by comparing its $-2LL$ value with $-2LL$ for the null model. This statistic, which we will call $-2LL_{\text{diff}}$, is shown in Equation 4.9.

$$-2LL_{\text{diff}} = (-2LL_0) - (-2LL_1) \qquad (4.9)$$

where $-2LL_0$ is the measure of deviance in the null model $\text{logit}(p) = \alpha$, and $-2LL_1$ is the measure of deviance in the model $\text{logit}(p) = \alpha + \beta x$.

The change in the value of $-2LL$ represents the effect that the explanatory variables have on the deviance in the model, an effect which can be evaluated for significance using the χ^2 distribution with the number of degrees-of-freedom equal to the difference in the number of terms between the two models. For the example above, the effect that variable x has on the model can be assessed using the $-2LL_{\text{diff}}$ statistic with 1 degree-of-freedom.

Statistics based on $-2LL$ have a close relationship with the goodness-of-fit statistics used in OLS regression (refer to Sections 3.1.5 and 3.3.5). In fact, the residual sum of squares, which is a measure of deviance in OLS regression, can be viewed as being analogous to $-2LL$ which is a measure of deviance for the logit link. Similarly, the F-statistic used in OLS regression can be seen as being analogous to the χ^2 statistic used in logistic regression (see Table 4.5).

Table 4.5: OLS and Logistic Regression Goodness-of-fit Statistics

	Measure of Deviance	Reference Distribution
OLS regression	Residual Sum of Squares (RSS)	F
Logistic regression	log-likelihood $(-2LL)$	χ^2

The Wald Statistic

The Wald statistic is implemented by a number of statistical packages and is broadly comparable with $-2LL$. It tests the hypothesis that the regression coefficient for the explanatory variable is zero (that is, the explanatory variable has no effect on the response variable). The Wald statistic is calculated using Equation 4.10.

$$\text{Wald statistic} = \frac{\beta^2}{\text{ASE}_\beta} \qquad (4.10)$$

where β is the regression coefficient,

and ASE_β is the asymptotic standard error of β.

The Wald statistic has an approximate standard Normal distribution and is tested for significance using the standard Normal table to obtain one or two-sided P-values (see Agresti, 1996, for a discussion of this). A significant Wald statistic suggests that the explanatory variable has an effect on the response variable. The Wald statistic is easy to calculate and interpret, yet it should be used with caution as it tends to exaggerate the significance of variables which have high coefficient values, and can also prove to be unreliable for small samples. Given these restrictions to its use we recommend that the goodness-of-fit of a logistic regression model is assessed using statistics based on $-2LL$.

Analysis of Classification Table Data

The predictive efficiency of a particular model can be calculated using a classification table which compares frequencies observed in the sample to those which are predicted from the model. When dealing with a binary response variable, this information is presented in a 2 by 2 contingency table. Table 4.6 shows a classification table where $(x_1 + x_4)$ cases are correctly classified (see section 4.2 for a worked example of a classification table analysis).

There are a number of statistical tests which can be used to assess the significance of the relationship between the predicted and observed values

Table 4.6: Predictive Efficiency Using a Classification Table

		Predicted	
		0	1
Observed	0	x_1	x_2
	1	x_3	x_4

shown in the classification table (for example, Goodman and Kruskal's λ and τ, Kendall's τ and ϕ, Pearson's r and the odds ratio; see Menard, 1995). These tests will not be discussed here as they are usually considered to be inferior to the significance tests based on the $-2LL$ statistic and are not routinely provided by software.

4.2   A Worked Example of Simple Logistic Regression

The example we are to use here is the severity of infection and treatment outcome data already described in this chapter and presented in Table 4.1. The aim of this analysis is to model treatment outcome (the response variable) using the severity of infection when the treatment was started as the explanatory variable. For this demonstration we can assume that there are no significant outliers, the data are not over or underdispersed, and that neither of the variables require transforming.

Having entered the data into a statistical programme in an appropriate format (representing the binary response variable as 0 and 1; in this case 0 represents a patient who survives and 1 represents a patient who succumbs to the infection), a logistic regression model can be computed. The calculated regression parameters for the model predicting treatment outcome from severity of infection are given in Table 4.7 with the regression equation shown in Equation 4.11.

$$\text{logit}(p) = \alpha + \beta x = -4.640 + 0.059x \qquad (4.11)$$

A unit increase in the severity of the infection (x) results in an increase of 0.059 in the log odds of the probability, $\text{logit}(p)$, of the patient succumbing to the infection. Using the odds ratio, e^β, one can also state that for each unit increase in the severity of infection, the odds of succumbing to the disease increase by 6%. The large sample 95% two-tailed confidence intervals associated with β are 0.025 to 0.094 which means that in 95% of samples we

Table 4.7: Model Parameters

	Coefficient	ASE	95% CIs for β Lower	95% CIs for β Upper	e^{β}
Severity	0.059	0.018	0.025	0.094	1.06
(constant)	−4.640	1.383			

would expect $\text{logit}(p)$ to increase by somewhere between 0.025 and 0.094 for each unit increase in x (these intervals can be obtained from software or can be calculated from the parameters given in Table 4.7 using Equation 4.5). For each unit increase in infection severity, the odds of a patient succumbing to the infection are likely to increase somewhere between 3% and 10% ($e^{0.025}$ and $e^{0.094}$ respectively).

The confidence intervals for fitted y can also be calculated for this model. Section 4.6.2 demonstrates how these intervals can be derived directly using the 'predict' command in GLIM, whilst two alternative methods are provided below. The first task in obtaining confidence intervals for fitted y is to determine the ASE for $\text{logit}(p)$. If these are not provided by software, they can be obtained using one of the methods demonstrated below (see Section 4.3.3 for a description of these techniques). The first method utilizes the information in the variance-covariance matrix which is provided by some software, whilst the second relies on transforming explanatory variables and recalculating the regression model.

Table 4.8: Variance-Covariance Matrix

	Constant	Severity
Constant	1.89769	
Severity	−0.02326	0.00031

Using the parameters $\text{Var}(\hat{\alpha}) = 1.89769$, $\text{Var}(\hat{\beta}) = 0.00031$, and $\text{Cov}(\hat{\alpha}, \hat{\beta}) = -0.02326$ derived from the variance-covariance matrix in Table 4.8, the large sample ASE can be computed for any value of x by substituting these values into Equation 4.8. For example, the large sample ASE for $\text{logit}(p)$ when $x = 50$ is:

$$\text{ASE for logit}(p) = \sqrt{\text{Var}(\hat{\alpha}) + x^2\text{Var}(\hat{\beta}) + 2x\text{Cov}(\hat{\alpha}, \hat{\beta})}$$

$$= \sqrt{1.89769 + 50^2(0.00031) + 2(50)(-0.02326)}$$

$$= 0.589.$$

If the variance-covariance matrix is not available, the ASE for logit(p) can be calculated by transforming the explanatory variable and recalculating the model. For example, at an infection severity of 50, the ASE of logit(p) can be estimated by calculating the regression model using values of $x - 50$ instead of the original explanatory variable (x). The recalculated model is shown in Table 4.9.

Table 4.9: Logistic Regression Model Parameters

	Coefficient	ASE	e^β (the odds ratio)
$x - 50$	0.059	0.018	1.06
(constant)	−1.680	0.583	

From Table 4.9 the estimate of the ASE for logit(p) is the ASE associated with the constant, which in this case is 0.583. This is close to the value calculated using the variance-covariance matrix which provided a value of the ASE for logit(p) when $x = 50$ of 0.589.

Having calculated the ASE for logit(p) it is relatively simple to calculate the confidence intervals for fitted y at any level of x. For example, when $x = 50$, logit(p) can be calculated using the equation of the regression model, $\alpha + \beta x$. For this example, logit(p) is equivalent to $-4.64 + (0.059 \times 50)$, which equals -1.69. The large sample 95% two-tailed confidence intervals associated with this value of logit(p) can be determined using Equation 4.7. For this example, we will use the ASE estimate derived from the variance-covariance matrix. The large sample 95% two-tailed confidence intervals are derived using the following calculation:

$$\text{confidence intervals for logit}(p) = \text{logit}(\hat{p}) \pm 1.96(\text{ASE})$$

$$= -1.69 \pm (1.96 \times 0.589)$$

$$= -2.84, -0.54.$$

In order to understand more fully the predictions made from the model, all values can be transformed into direct measures of probability (instead of the log odds) by using Equation 4.1. Applying this transformation, one can see that the probability of dying due to an infection of severity 50 is predicted to be 0.16 (see Equation 4.12, overleaf). It is an easy matter to recalculate the ASE for different values of x and obtain predictions and confidence intervals for fitted y for a whole range of values of the explanatory variable. Table 4.10 shows the ASEs, the logits and the probabilities associated with the predicted values of the response variable and the 95% two-tailed confidence intervals

$$\text{probability of death} = \frac{e^{(\alpha+\beta x)}}{1 + e^{(\alpha+\beta x)}} \qquad (4.12)$$

$$= \frac{e^{(-4.640+(0.059\times 50))}}{1 + e^{(-4.640+(0.059\times 50))}}$$

$$= 0.16$$

for a number of different infection severities using ASE values calculated from both methods demonstrated above. It is interesting to note that the results are very similar (in fact, the predicted probability of dying is identical to two decimal places).

Table 4.10: Predictions Derived from the Regression Model

Infection Severity	ASE for logit(p)	Logit(p) Predicted	Logit(p) 95% CIs		Probability (of dying) Predicted	Probability (of dying) 95% CIs	
ASE calculated using variance-covariance matrix							
0	1.377	−4.64	−7.34	−1.94	0.01	0.00	0.13
50	0.589	−1.69	−2.84	−0.54	0.16	0.06	0.37
100	0.588	1.26	0.11	2.41	0.78	0.53	0.92
150	1.376	4.21	1.51	6.91	0.99	0.82	1.00
200	2.235	7.16	2.78	11.54	1.00	0.94	1.00
ASE calculated using model recalculation							
0	1.383	−4.64	−7.35	−1.93	0.01	0.00	0.13
50	0.583	−1.69	−2.83	−0.55	0.16	0.06	0.37
100	0.558	1.26	0.17	2.35	0.78	0.53	0.92
150	1.352	4.21	1.56	6.86	0.99	0.83	1.00
200	2.211	7.16	2.83	11.45	1.00	0.94	1.00

The goodness-of-fit of the model can be calculated using the $-2LL$ statistic. From software we find that the initial log likelihood function (the value of $-2LL$ when no explanatory variables are included in the model) equals 67.745. When the explanatory variable is included, $-2LL$ drops to 45.981, a reduction of 21.764. This reduction in $-2LL$ indicates that the model which includes the explanatory variable is a better fit than the model which does not (there is less deviance). This change in $-2LL$ is significant as determined by the chi-square test ($\chi^2 = 21.764$, with 1 degree-of-freedom; $P < 0.00005$).

Some indication of goodness-of-fit is also provided by the classification table, which gives the predictive efficiency of the model. Table 4.11 shows the classification table for the above example where it can be seen that 71.43% of cases are correctly predicted by the model (that is, given the severity of the infection, one is able to correctly predict treatment outcome in 71% of cases).

Table 4.11: Predictive Efficiency

		Predicted		
		Survived	Died	% correct
	Survived	20	6	76.92
Observed				
	Died	8	15	65.22
			Overall	71.43

This analysis has demonstrated the use of simple logistic regression in modelling a binary response variable. The analysis not only showed that the severity of infection was significantly related to the outcome of the treatment, but through the calculation of confidence intervals also gave an indication of the expected range of this effect. Predictions were also made regarding the likely outcome given a number of different infection severities with full information provided on the confidence intervals surrounding these predictions. In practice, one would also analyse the residuals, check for overdispersion and correct any anomalies using one of the techniques discussed in Chapter 2 before deciding on the final model.

4.3 Multiple Logistic Regression

Logistic regression models can be built for a binary response variable using any number of explanatory variables. As with OLS regression, these explanatory variables may be continuous or discrete. The systematic component of the model (that is, the fixed structure of the explanatory variables) is similar to OLS regression and therefore many of the same considerations regarding dummy variable coding, multicollinearity and model building apply.

4.3.1 The Regression Equation

The logistic regression equation for multiple explanatory variables is similar to the case where there is just one explanatory variable except that it allows more than one variable to be entered into the model (the systematic component of the model may be determined by more than one variable). When there is more than one explanatory variable, the logistic regression model can be written as shown in Equation 4.13.

$$\text{probability of an event happening} = \frac{e^z}{1 + e^z} \qquad (4.13)$$

where e is the natural logarithm base,

and z is the linear (systematic) component of the model and equals $\alpha + \beta_1 x_1 + \beta_2 x_2 + \beta_3 x_3, \ldots, +\beta_k x_k$.

The relationship between the probability of an event happening (p) and the linear predictor (z) in Equation 4.13 is non-linear. However, if p is transformed to logit(p) (i.e., the log odds of p), this relationship can be made linear as Equation 4.14 shows.

$$\text{logit}(p) = \alpha + \beta_1 x_1 + \beta_2 x_2 + \beta_3 x_3, \ldots, +\beta_k x_k. \qquad (4.14)$$

where logit(p) is the log odds of an event happening.

The parameters calculated on the linear component of the model refer to logit(p), which, is difficult to interpret. A simpler interpretation of the model parameters is obtained using the odds, which can be derived from Equation 4.15.

$$\frac{p}{1 - p} = e^{\alpha + \beta_1 x_1 + \beta_2 x_2 + \beta_3 x_3, \ldots, +\beta_k X_k} \qquad (4.15)$$

where p is the probability of an event happening,

and $1 - p$ is the probability of an event not happening.

Interactions and Curvilinearity

As with OLS regression it is possible to include interaction and curvilinear terms into a logistic regression model. Interactions can be accounted for by including additional terms in the systematic component of the model which show the product of the explanatory variables interacting. For example, if there is an interaction between x_1 and x_2, the linear component of the model can be represented as $\alpha + \beta_1 x_1 + \beta_2 x_2 + \beta_3 x_1 x_2$. The main effect of each explanatory variable (that is, the effect that variables x_1 and x_2 by themselves have on the response variable) are included in the model along with the effect of the interaction, $x_1 x_2$ (that is, the effect that the interaction between x_1 and x_2 has on the response variable).

In addition to interactions, curvilinear relationships can also be accounted for by including additional polynomial terms in the systematic component of the model. For example, if the variable x_2 showed a curvilinear relationship with the response variable, a quadratic term such as x^2 could be entered into the equation to take account of this (see Chapter 2 for more detailed information about entering polynomial terms). A model containing two explanatory variables, one which shows a curvilinear relationship with the linear predictor (in this case, a squared relationship) could be represented as $\text{logit}(p) = \alpha + \beta_1 x_1 + \beta_2 x_2 + \beta_3 x_2^2$. The main effects of x_1 and x_2 are included in the model together with an additional term which takes account of the curvilinear relationship between x_2 and $\text{logit}(p)$ $(\beta_3 x_2^2)$.

Although the regression equation can deal with interactions and curvilinear relationships, for the purpose of exposition, the present treatment of logistic regression will only include the main effects since these models contain fewer terms and are often easier to understand. Further information about identifying interaction and curvilinear effects and including these in logistic regression models can be found in Afifi and Clark, 1996; Agresti, 1996; and Menard, 1995.

Calculating and Interpreting Model Parameters

Model parameters are calculated using the maximum likelihood method and are interpreted in much the same way as discussed in Section 4.1.1. The parameter values β (the coefficients for the explanatory variables) show the change in $\text{logit}(p)$ that is associated with a unit change in the explanatory variable when all other variables in the model are held constant. Table 4.12 show a number of statistics output from a logistic regression analysis.

Table 4.12: Example Logistic Regression Model Parameters

	Coefficient	ASE	e^β (the odds ratio)
x_1	0.148	0.023	1.16
x_2	1.342	0.929	3.83
x_3	−1.980	1.947	0.14
(constant)	−2.650	1.380	

For a unit increase in variable x_1, when all other variables are held constant, $\text{logit}(p)$ increases by 0.148. Similarly, for a unit increase in variables x_2 and x_3, when all other variables are held constant, $\text{logit}(p)$ increases by 1.342 and −1.980 respectively. The coefficient for the constant (α) shows the value of $\text{logit}(p)$ when all explanatory variables have a value of zero. These regression coefficients can be more easily understood if quoted as odds ratios, which show the change in the odds of p associated with a unit change in x whilst all other variables are held constant. For the data in Table 4.12, for each unit change in variable x_1, whilst all other variables are held constant, the odds of p increase to 116% of its previous value (an increase of 16%, or an increase by a factor of

1.16). Similarly, a unit increase in variable x_2 results in an increase in the odds of p of 383% of its previous value (an increase of 283%), and a unit increase in variable x_3 results in a decrease in the odds of p by a factor of 0.14 (14% of previous value, a decrease of 82%).

4.3.2   Confidence Intervals for β

Confidence intervals for logistic regression models containing multiple explanatory variables can be calculated for the regression coefficient β in much the same way as they were in the case where there was only one explanatory variable. Confidence intervals for β are provided by most standard software packages or can be computed using Equation 4.16, which assumes that the data are not under or overdispersed (see Section 4.1.4):

$$\text{confidence intervals for } \beta = \hat{\beta} \pm 1.96(\text{ASE}) \tag{4.16}$$

where 1.96 is the large sample approximation of t for two-tailed, 95% confidence intervals,

and ASE is the asymptotic standard error of $\hat{\beta}$.

Table 4.13 shows confidence intervals which have been calculated for the regression parameters presented in Table 4.12.

Table 4.13: Example Logistic Regression Model Parameters

	Coefficient	ASE	95% CIs for β		95% CIs for e^{β}	
			Lower	Upper	Lower	Upper
x_1	0.148	0.023	0.10	0.19	1.11	1.21
x_2	1.342	0.929	−0.48	3.16	0.62	23.57
x_3	−1.980	1.947	−5.80	1.84	0.00	6.30
(constant)	−2.650	1.380				

The confidence intervals for variable x_1 indicate the effect that a unit change in this variable has on the response variable when all other variables in the model are held constant. In this case, logit(p) can be expected to increase between 0.10 and 0.19 for each unit increase in variable x_1. Interpreting these values in terms of odds, we find that in 95% of cases a unit increase in x_1 can be expected to result in at least an 11%, and at most, a 21% increase in the odds of p. Similarly, for a unit increase in variable x_2, in 95% of cases we can expect the odds of p to lie between a decrease of 38% and an increase of 2,257% (as the confidence intervals predict both an increase and a decrease, this result is non-significant). In 95% of cases, each unit increase in variable

x_3 results in a decrease in the odds of p of at least 99.5% (a maximum of 0.005 of previous value) to an increase of 530% (630% of previous value), as these confidence intervals include the value 1, this result is also non-significant.

4.3.3   Confidence Intervals for Fitted y

Confidence intervals for models containing multiple explanatory variables can be calculated for fitted y in much the same way as they were in the case where there was only one explanatory variable. These intervals are first calculated for logit(p) and are then transformed to represent the intervals for p. Confidence intervals for logit(p) (assuming no under or overdispersion) can be computed using Equation 4.17.

$$\text{confidence intervals for logit}(p) = \text{logit}(\hat{p}) \pm 1.96(\text{ASE}) \qquad (4.17)$$

where 1.96 is the large sample approximation of t for two-tailed, 95% confidence intervals,
and ASE is the asymptotic standard error of logit($\hat{p}$).

As in the case for a single explanatory variable, confidence intervals for logit(p) often have to be calculated by hand since many statistical software packages do not allow these to be computed directly. The difficulty with calculating these intervals is in determining the ASE associated with the prediction. When confidence intervals cannot be obtained directly through software, one of the following two techniques may be used to calculate the ASE for logit(p). This enables one to calculate confidence intervals for fitted y using any standard statistical software. The first technique relies on the generation of a variance-covariance matrix whilst the second is based on transforming the explanatory variable and recalculating the model.

Computing the ASE for Logit(p): Method 1

If the variance-covariance matrix is available, the large sample ASE of logit(p) may be calculated using Equation 4.18 (see Collett, 1991).

$$\text{ASE of logit}(p) = \sqrt{\sum_{j=1}^{k} x_{j0}^2 \, \text{Var}(\hat{\beta}_j) + 2 \sum_{j=1}^{k} \sum_{h=1}^{j} x_{h0} x_{j0} \, \text{Cov}(\hat{\beta}_h, \hat{\beta}_j)} \qquad (4.18)$$

where $\text{Var}(\hat{\beta}_j)$ and $\text{Cov}(\hat{\beta}_h, \hat{\beta}_j)$ are parameters obtained from the variance-covariance matrix,
and x is the value of the explanatory variable.

As can be seen from Equation 4.18, the calculation of the ASE associated with logit(p) is complex and needs to be calculated for each combination of explanatory variables we are interested in. Once the ASE for logit(p) has been determined for a particular combination of x values, it can be entered into Equation 4.17 and the confidence intervals for logit(p) determined.

Computing the ASE for Logit(p): Method 2

If the variance-covariance matrix is not available, the ASE for logit(p) can be calculated using a procedure which transforms each explanatory variable and recalculates the model. Using this method we can obtain an estimate of the ASE for any particular combination of x values. For a multiple logistic regression, the procedure for accomplishing this is as follows:

1. Create new explanatory variables by subtracting the chosen value of the explanatory variable from each case of the original variable.

2. Recalculate the model using the new explanatory variables.

3. The ASE associated with the constant provides an estimate of the ASE for logit(p).

4. The confidence intervals for logit(p) can be calculated using Equation 4.17.

The 95% confidence intervals for logit(p) are interpreted as the range of values of logit(p) which one can expect to obtain in 95% of cases. Once the ASE of logit(p) has been derived, it is a relatively simple matter to calculate the confidence intervals for fitted y by transforming the intervals obtained for logit(p) using Equation 4.13. An example of calculating the confidence intervals for logit(p) and how these are transformed to represent intervals for fitted y is provided in Section 4.4.

4.3.4   Goodness-of-fit Measures

The goodness-of-fit of a multiple logistic regression model can be derived using the same statistics as are used in simple logistic regression. Using these statistics it is also possible to evaluate the effect that individual or groups of variables have on the model fit. Although the log-likelihood, the Wald statistic and the analysis of classification tables can all be used to represent model fit, only the statistics based on the log-likelihood will be discussed here as they are generally considered to provide the best indication.

The Log-Likelihood Statistic

Statistics based on the log-likelihood are the most popular method of determining the goodness-of-fit of a logistic regression model. The log-likelihood is usually quoted as $-$two times the log-likelihood (i.e., $-2LL$) because this approximates to the chi-square distribution and enables significance levels to be determined. Using $-2LL$, the contribution made by all as well as individual and groups of explanatory variables can be determined.

The Overall Model

A measure of the effect that *all* explanatory variables in the model have on the response variable can be obtained by comparing $-2LL$ for a model with no explanatory variables (the null model) with $-2LL$ for a model which includes all explanatory variables. $-2LL$ for the null model is commonly called the initial log-likelihood function. The difference in $-2LL$ between these two models represents the effect that the explanatory variables have (that is, the improvement in the model fit which can be attributed to the explanatory variables). As $-2LL$ approximates to a χ^2 distribution, the significance of the change in $-2LL$ can be determined using degrees-of-freedom equal to the number of parameters in the model excluding the constant. For example, if the initial log-likelihood function equals 50, and the log-likelihood function for a model with five terms equals 35, the significance of the change in $-2LL$ (15) can be calculated using the χ^2 distribution with 5 degrees of freedom ($\chi^2 = 15; df = 5; P = 0.010$). In this case we would conclude that the model with five terms provides a better fit to the data than the null model. This statistic is sometimes referred to as the *model* chi-square[7]. The model chi-square can be seen as analogous to the F statistic in OLS regression in that it provides the goodness-of-fit of a model compared to the null model. The model chi-square can be derived using Equation 4.19[8].

$$\text{model chi-square} = (-2LL_0) - (-2LL_1) \qquad (4.19)$$

where $-2LL_0$ is a measure of deviance for the null model $\text{logit}(p) = \alpha$, and $-2LL_1$ is a measure of deviance for the model $\text{logit}(p) = \alpha + \beta_1 x_1 + \beta_2 x_2 + \beta_3 x_3, \dots, +\beta_k X_k$.

Individual Variables

The effect that individual or groups of variables have on the model fit can be determined by comparing the fit of nested models. The amount by which $-2LL$ decreases when additional variables are added to the model indicates the size of the effect that these variables have. The significance of the change

---

[7]The term model chi-square is in common use in many statistical packages though it should be noted that chi-square is actually the reference distribution for evaluating the difference in deviance.

[8]You will note that the model chi-square equation is a special case of $-2LL_{\text{diff}}$ (see Equation 4.20), where a comparison is made with the null model.

in $-2LL$ is determined by the χ^2 test with degrees-of-freedom equal to the difference in the number of terms between the two models. For example, if $-2LL$ for a model containing three variables is equal to 35 and this changes to 32.5 when an additional variable is added, the significance of the change in $-2LL$ (2.5) can be determined by using the χ^2 distribution with 1 degree-of-freedom ($\chi^2 = 2.5; df = 1; P = 0.114$). In this case we would conclude that the addition of the fourth term does not result in a significant improvement. We shall refer to this statistic as $-2LL_{\text{diff}}$ because it explicitly tests the difference in $-2LL$ between nested models[9]. $-2LL_{\text{diff}}$ can be seen as analogous to the partial-F statistic in OLS regression in that it provides the goodness-of-fit of one particular model compared to a nested model. $-2LL_{\text{diff}}$ can be derived using Equation 4.20.

$$-2LL_{\text{diff}} = (-2LL_p) - (-2LL_{p+q}) \qquad (4.20)$$

where p is the smaller, nested model,
and $p + q$ is the larger model.

$-2LL_{\text{diff}}$ evaluates the effect of individual and groups of variables on the model fit and is used extensively in model selection. Section 4.3.7 demonstrates how $-2LL_{\text{diff}}$ may be used to select a regression model.

4.3.5 Multicollinearity

Multicollinearity affects logistic regression in much the same way as it does OLS regression. Variables which show high levels of multicollinearity provide little unique information which leads to high standard errors and regression coefficients that are unlikely to accurately reflect the impact that x_i has on y in the population. It is, therefore, important that instances of high multi-collinearity are identified and dealt with before the regression model is built using the methods outlined in Chapter 3.

4.3.6 Dummy Variable Coding Discontinuous Data

Whenever a model is built that includes a categorical variable, a frame of reference must be established for it. For example, if there are four distinct geographical locations coded as a single variable, one can't make an absolute statement about the effect of region A — and can only compare region A to other regions. Any comment about region A depends on a frame of reference which is determined by dummy coding, or as it is also known, aliasing. As in OLS regression, categorical variables can be included in a model, provided that they are appropriately coded as dummy variables (see Section 3.3.7). Ordinal

---

[9]$-2LL_{\text{diff}}$ is also sometimes referred to as the *improvement* chi-square.

variables are a little more complex to deal with and as such have traditionally been assumed to be continuous (assuming information not always present in the data), or assumed to be categorical and dummy coded (thereby losing the information about order in the data). Although not explicitly discussed in this chapter, there are techniques for preserving information about ordinality and Chapter 5 presents a discussion of these. It is, however, important to know that the quality of ordinal data can be preserved without the need to assume that it is continuous or to code it as categorical.

Table 4.14: Recovery as a Function of Illness Severity and Hospital Attended

Severity	Outcome	Hospital	Severity	Outcome	Hospital
9.3	survived	C	75.3	died	B
18.2	survived	B	76.3	survived	A
22.7	survived	A	77.7	died	C
32.9	survived	C	79.1	survived	A
38.0	survived	A	80.6	died	C
39.9	survived	B	85.0	survived	C
44.0	survived	A	86.0	died	A
44.9	survived	B	89.4	died	C
46.8	survived	A	90.0	survived	B
47.7	survived	B	90.9	died	C
49.1	died	C	91.5	survived	B
49.7	survived	B	96.6	survived	A
50.9	survived	A	97.2	died	C
50.9	survived	B	101.6	survived	A
53.7	survived	A	104.8	died	C
60.1	died	C	108.6	died	A
61.7	survived	A	109.9	died	C
62.2	survived	B	111.3	died	B
64.1	died	A	113.2	died	C
68.9	survived	B	118.8	died	C
71.2	survived	A	127.0	died	B
72.3	died	B	142.0	died	C
73.0	died	C	157.4	died	A
73.2	died	B	169.2	died	C
74.6	survived	A			

To demonstrate the use and interpretation of dummy variables in a logistic regression model, an additional variable has been added to the example data set used earlier (see Table 4.1). The new variable indicates one of three hospitals at which patients were treated (see Table 4.14). Hospitals A and B have similar records in treatment outcome whilst Hospital C appears to provide relatively poor patient care as it shows a higher mortality rate. However, since Hospital C tends to deal with cases which are more severe, we would expect there to be a higher mortality rate. Basic statistics for the three hospitals are shown in Table 4.15.

Table 4.15: Comparison of Hospitals

Hospital	Number Treated	Number Died	Proportion Died	Mean Severity of Infection
A	17	4	0.24	72.5
B	15	5	0.33	68.2
C	17	14	0.82	88.4

As with OLS regression, a number of dummy variable coding schemes can be used. Here we will discuss two of the more commonly used techniques, the indicator method, which allows a direct comparison with a reference category, and the deviation coding method, which allows comparison with an overall mean for the group.

Indicator Coding

The technique of indicator dummy coding used in logistic regression is identical to that used in OLS regression and will not, therefore, be discussed in detail here. What will be discussed is the interpretation of the regression parameters. If one was to model treatment outcome from the data in Table 4.14 using the categorical variable Hospital which has been dummy coded with Hospital A identified as the reference category, we would obtain the regression parameters in Table 4.16.

Table 4.16: Logistic Regression Model Parameters: Hospital A = Reference

	Coefficient	ASE	95% CI for β Upper	95% CI for β Lower	e^{β}
Severity	0.062	0.020	0.02	0.10	1.06
Hospital dummy variables					
Hospital B	0.983	1.013	−1.00	2.97	2.67
Hospital C	3.366	1.202	1.01	5.72	28.97
(constant)	−6.189	1.818			

$\text{logit}(p) = -6.189 + 0.062 \text{ Severity} + 0.983 \text{ Hospital B} + 3.366 \text{ Hospital C}$

Model chi-square $= 33.003$, $df = 3$, $P < 0.00005$

The parameter coded Hospital B in Table 4.16 refers to the comparison between Hospitals B and A whilst the parameter coded Hospital C refers to the comparison between Hospitals C and A. The value of the coefficient for

Hospital B refers to the difference in logit(p) which would be expected if the patient was treated in Hospital B compared to Hospital A. Computing the odds we can see that a patient in Hospital B is 2.67 times as likely to die as a patient in Hospital A. This result is not significant as the confidence intervals for e^β (the odds ratio) predict that it is likely to range from 0.37 ($e^{-1.00}$, a decrease of 63%) to 19.49 ($e^{2.97}$, an increase of 1,849%). The coefficient for Hospital C indicates that logit(p) increases by 3.366 for Hospital C compared to Hospital A, whilst a patient in Hospital C is 28.97 times as likely to die as a patient treated in Hospital A. This result is significant at the 95% level with the odds expected to change from 2.75 (i.e., $e^{1.01}$) to over 300 (i.e., $e^{5.72}$).

As with OLS regression, the choice of reference category is essentially arbitrary. The same amount of variance is accounted for each time — only the comparisons change. If we had chosen Hospital C as the reference category (as is the case in Table 4.18) we would have obtained different comparisons, but the same parameters would have been obtained for Severity and the models would have identical model chi-square values.

Deviation Coding

Deviation dummy coding enables comparisons to be made between each category and the mean of all categories. Using Deviation coding, the logistic regression coefficients indicate how much better or worse each category is when compared to the *average effect of all categories* (refer to Section 3.3.7 for a description of deviation coding). The advantage of this method is that it sometimes makes more sense to compare each category against an average value as there is not always an obvious choice of reference category, and a regression coefficient can be obtained for all categories. Table 4.17 shows the results of a logistic regression when the variable Hospital has been coded using the deviation method. For this example, the regression coefficients for each of the dummy codes (Hospitals A to C) indicate the difference between each hospital compared to the average of all hospitals. Although Table 4.17 shows parameters for all of the hospitals (j dummy variables), many statistical packages require a 'reference' category[10] to be identified to avoid the situation where perfect multicollinearity exists (see Section 3.3.6). To obtain all of the regression parameters shown in the table it might be necessary to calculate more than one model (using a different reference category in each case). Unlike indicator coding, the choice of reference category makes no difference to the parameters for each dummy variable (Hospital A has the same parameters associated with it no matter which of the other hospitals are chosen as the 'reference' category) because these represent a comparison between the mean of all groups — the mean is not dependent upon the choice of reference category.

---

[10]The use of the term 'reference' can be confusing since the reference category in deviation coding is not the comparison group — a reference is selected for purely practical reasons (it eliminates multicollinearity).

Table 4.17: Logistic Regression Model Parameters: Deviation Coding

	Coefficient	ASE	95% CI for β Upper	Lower	e^{β}
Severity	0.062	0.020	0.02	0.10	1.06
Hospital dummy variables					
Hospital A	−1.450	0.640	−2.70	−0.20	0.23
Hospital B	−0.467	0.589	−1.62	0.69	0.63
Hospital C	1.917	0.698	0.55	3.28	6.80
(constant)	−4.739	1.522			

logit(p) = −4.739 + 0.062 Severity − 1.450 Hospital A − 0.467 Hospital B
+1.917 Hospital C

Model chi-square = 33.003, df = 3, $P < 0.00005$

From Table 4.17 we can see that Hospitals A and B are below average mortality (both have negative coefficients) whilst Hospital C is above average. From the coefficient we can see that logit(p) decreases by 1.450 for a patient in Hospital A compared to the average of all three hospitals. Interpreting the odds, one can conclude that patients in Hospital A are 0.23 times as likely to die of the infection compared to the average (alternatively, they are about 4.35 times as likely to survive, 1/0.23). The confidence intervals for the odds ratio (e^{β}) indicate that the odds of dying at Hospital A compared to the average are expected to be between 0.07 and 0.82 ($e^{-2.70}$ and $e^{-0.20}$). Similarly, the regression coefficient shows that, compared to the average, logit(p) is 1.917 times higher for patients in Hospital C. The odds ratio for Hospital C equals 6.80, which indicates that patients in Hospital C are 6.8 times as likely to die of the infection. The confidence intervals for the odds associated with this result are 1.73 and 26.58 ($e^{0.55}$ and $e^{3.28}$ respectively), which indicate that patients in Hospital C are at least 1.73 and at most 26.58 times as likely to die of the infection compared to the average of all three hospitals.

4.3.7   Model Selection

As with OLS regression, the amount of deviance in the model (as measured by $-2LL$) can be minimized by including as many explanatory variables as possible. Maximizing the explanatory power of the model in this way is not always beneficial as the inclusion of irrelevant variables may add a little to the explanatory power, but may increase the standard errors associated with the prediction and thereby have an adverse effect on the model fit. A model which includes all variables regardless of their importance will also lack parsimony. For these reasons it is useful to reduce the number of variables in the model by eliminating those which do not exert a significant influence.

Criteria for Including and Removing Variables

Decisions about which variables may be entered or removed from a logistic regression model can be made on the basis of $-2LL_{\text{diff}}$. Using Equation 4.20, nested regression models can be compared to assess the effect that individual or groups of explanatory variables have on the response variable. For example, to assess the contribution made by the categorical variable Hospital one would compare $-2LL$ for the model containing the variable Hospital with $-2LL$ for a nested model excluding Hospital (see Equation 4.21).

$$-2LL_{\text{diff}} = (-2LL_p) - (-2LL_{p+q}) \qquad (4.21)$$

$$= 45.994 - 34.742$$

$$= 11.252$$

where p is the nested model with the linear component $\alpha + \beta_1$ Severity,

and $p + q$ is the model with the linear component $\alpha + \beta_1$ Severity+
β_2 Hospital A + β_3 Hospital B.

$-2LL_{\text{diff}}$ indicates the effect that the variable Hospital has, and can be tested for significance using the chi-square distribution with 2 degrees-of-freedom (the difference in the number of parameters between the two models). In this example, Hospital has a significant effect on the model ($\chi^2 = 11.252$ with 2 df, $P=0.0036$). Table 4.18 shows the $-2LL_{\text{diff}}$ statistics for the variables Severity and Hospital. These statistics show the fall in $-2LL$ which would result if either of these variables were to be removed from the model. Since the variable Hospital is categorical it is represented here as two dummy categories ($j - 1$) and therefore has 2 degrees-of-freedom associated with it. The model which is being tested in Table 4.18 is logit$(p) = \alpha + \beta_1$ Severity + β_2 Hospital A + β_3 Hospital B. On the evidence presented in the table, removing Severity or Hospital would lead to a significant decrease in the model fit and so both variables should be left in.

Table 4.18 shows $-2LL_{\text{diff}}$ statistics for the variable Hospital and also for each individual dummy variable. When coded using the indicator coding method detailed above, each of the individual hospitals may be converted into individual variables coded 0 and 1. The effect of each of the dummy variables can be assessed using $-2LL_{\text{diff}}$ with 1 degree-of-freedom.

Automated Model Selection

As with OLS regression, there are a number of automated procedures that can be used to derive a final model. These procedures are almost identical to those discussed in Section 3.3.9 and will not therefore be discussed in any

Table 4.18: Logistic Regression Model Selection

	Coefficient	ASE	$-2LL_{\text{diff}}$	df	P
Severity	0.062	0.020	18.75	1	0.000
Hospital dummy variables			11.25	2	0.004
Hospital A	−3.366	1.202	10.85	1	0.001
Hospital B	−2.383	1.121	5.35	1	0.021
(constant)	−2.822	1.497			

logit(p) = −2.822 + 0.062 Severity − 3.366 Hospital A − 2.383 Hospital B

Model chi-square = 33.003, $df = 3$, $P < 0.00005$

detail here. The only important difference between the techniques is in the statistics used to assess model fit (OLS techniques rely on changes in the sum of squares whilst logistic regression relies on changes in $-2LL$). The specific details relating to the selection and removal of variables are covered in Chapter 3 and readers are advised to consult this for more detailed information about automated model selection procedures.

4.4 A Worked Example of Multiple Logistic Regression

The following example shows an analysis of a data set using logistic regression. The primary purpose of this exercise is to demonstrate the logistic regression procedure rather than provide a 'best' model. The data to be used has been taken from a study into child eyewitness testimony (Hutcheson, Baxter, Telfer and Warden, 1995) and adapted so that certain procedures can be demonstrated (see Table 3.11 for the data to be used in this analysis). The overall aim is to model the probability that a case will be heard in court (the variable 'Prosecute') given a number of pieces of information about the child and details about the child's testimony. The explanatory variables which are to be considered for inclusion in the model are the child's age (children from two different age groups took part in the study, 5–6-year-old children attending Primary 1 and 8–9-year-old children attending Primary 4), the child's gender, how coherent the information was that the child presented to the interviewer, the overall quality of the testimony (based on its completeness and accuracy), the location where the child provided the testimony (the child's home, school, in a 'standard' police interview room, or a specially constructed children's interview room), and the time between the incident and the child providing the testimony.

Some of these data have already been analysed in Section 3.4 where the quality of the testimony was modelled using OLS regression. This analysis found a high degree of multicollinearity between two variables in the data set (the variables Coherence and Maturity) and it was decided that Maturity should be removed from the analysis. An investigation into the relationship between the explanatory variables to be considered for inclusion in this model revealed that all tolerance and VIF values were within acceptable limits (see Section 3.3.6). For simplicity, we will assume that none of the variables we are to use require transforming, that there are no significant outliers and that there is no under or overdispersion. We will also assume that there are no significant interactions or curvilinear relationships and will therefore only include the 'main effects' in the model. The logistic regression model which includes all variables of interest is shown in Table 4.19. The variable Location has been coded using the indicator coding method with the 'standard police interview room' as the reference category (this makes theoretical sense since the 'standard police interview room' is the location which is normally used). The variables Gender and Age have also been dummy coded using the indicator method so that the coefficients generated by software refer to comparisons between age groups (8–9-year-olds are the reference category) and between genders (females are the reference category).

Table 4.19: Predicting Prosecution Using All Explanatory Variables

	Coefficient	ASE	$-2LL_{\text{diff}}$	df	P
Age	−0.895	0.673	1.79	1	0.18
Coherence	−0.270	0.385	0.50	1	0.48
Delay	−0.004	0.012	0.09	1	0.76
Gender	−0.061	0.585	0.01	1	0.92
Location dummy variables			2.26	3	0.52
Home	−0.602	0.796	0.58	1	0.45
School	−0.038	0.775	0.00	1	0.96
Special	0.598	0.873	0.47	1	0.49
Quality	0.039	0.036	1.27	1	0.26
(constant)	−1.128	3.001			

From software, the model chi-square of the model in Table 4.19 is equal to 16.364 with 8 df; $P = 0.0375$. We can conclude from this result that the model containing the eight parameters is significantly better than the null model. However, this model has limitations when it is used to describe the effect that individual explanatory variables have since it appears that no single variable is significantly related to the response variable, as determined by the $-2LL_{\text{diff}}$ statistics (this statistic shows the change in $-2LL$ which would result if a term was omitted from the model). In order to obtain a more useful model for explanatory purposes we need to remove those variables from the model which do not play a significant role in predicting prosecution.

Table 4.20 shows the models analysed using a backward elimination model selection procedure (that is, removing variables one at a time on the basis of the $-2LL_{diff}$ statistic) and shows how the model fit changes as variables are omitted. The model chi-square shows the goodness-of-fit statistic for the full model compared to the null model, and the $-2LL_{diff}$ shows the change in $-2LL$ from the previous (larger) model. The final model selected using the automated selection procedure contains just the variable Quality and shows a significant model chi-square ($\chi^2 = 11.45; df = 1; P = 0.001$).

Table 4.20: Backward Elimination Model Selection

Variables Included in the Model	Model Chi-Square			$-2LL_{diff}$		
	Deviance Change	df	P	Deviance Change	df	P
Age, Coherence, Delay, Gender, Location, Quality	16.36	8	0.038	—	—	—
Age, Coherence, Delay, Location, Quality	16.35	7	0.022	0.011	1	0.916
Age, Coherence, Location, Quality	16.25	6	0.013	0.101	1	0.751
Age, Coherence, Quality	13.76	3	0.003	2.496	3	0.476
Age, Quality	13.23	2	0.001	0.531	1	0.466
Quality	11.45	1	0.001	1.775	1	0.183

A model containing just the variable Quality might be acceptable as a predictive model, but as location and age are important theoretically (the study was originally designed to explicitly investigate the effect of these variables) they are also to be included in the model. The inclusion of the variables Age and Location also enables us to demonstrate how predictions can be made from models containing more than one explanatory variable. The chosen model can be seen in Table 4.21.

The regression parameters in Table 4.21 illustrate the effects that each of the variables has in determining whether a case is prosecuted. For example, compared to 8–9-year-old children, testimonies from 5–6-year-olds are only 0.404 as likely (the odds ratio e^β) to lead to prosecution. This result is non-significant as the 95% confidence intervals for e^β show that the odds ratio can be expected to be between 0.116 and 1.409.

It is also possible to predict the value of fitted y and to provide confidence intervals for this prediction. For 5–6-year-old children, who are interviewed at home and provide a testimony with a quality of 50, logit(p) is predicted as:

$$\begin{aligned} \text{logit}(p) \quad &= \quad \alpha + \beta_1 \text{Quality} + \beta_2 \text{Age} + \beta_3 \text{Home} \\ &= \quad -2.82 + (0.05 \times 50) - 0.907 - 0.452 \\ &= \quad -1.679. \end{aligned}$$

Table 4.21: Predicting Prosecution: Final Model

	Coefficient	ASE	e^β	95% CIs for e^β Lower	Upper
Quality	0.050	0.033	1.051	0.984	1.122
Age	−0.907	0.637	0.404	0.116	1.409
Location					
Home	−0.452	0.752	0.636	0.150	2.775
School	0.070	0.758	1.072	0.243	4.739
Special	0.773	0.810	2.166	0.442	10.601
(constant)	−2.820	2.168			

logit$(p) = -2.820 + 0.05$ Quality $- 0.907$ Age $- 0.452$ Home
$+0.07$ School $+ 0.773$ Special

Model chi-square $= 15.729$, $df = 5$, $P = 0.0077$

Logit(p) for the example above is equivalent to -1.679, which equates to a probability of 0.157 (i.e., $e^{-1.679}/(1 + e^{-1.679})$). By substituting different values into the model we can obtain predictions for logit(p) for any combination of explanatory variable values. The estimated values of logit(p) are, however, considerably more meaningful when quoted in conjunction with their confidence intervals. As the confidence intervals for logit(p) are not provided by all statistical packages, two methods for estimating them are demonstrated here. The first method uses the variance-covariance matrix for the model, whilst the second involves transforming variables and recalculating the model (Section 4.6 shows how the ASE can be derived using these methods and directly using GLIM).

The variance-covariance matrix for the model in Table 4.21 is shown in Table 4.22. From the data in this table the large sample ASE for logit(p) can be calculated using Equation 4.18 and our designated values for Age (1), Location (Home = 1, all others = 0) and Quality (50):

$$\begin{aligned} \text{ASE} \quad &= \quad \sqrt{[4.668 + 0.405 + 0.562 + (50^2 \times 0.001) + 2(-0.818 - 0.135 +} \\ & \qquad (50 \times -0.069) + 0.004 + (50 \times 0.011) + (50 \times -0.002))] \\ &= \quad 0.647. \end{aligned}$$

Table 4.22: Variance-Covariance Matrix

	Constant	Age	School	Home	Special	Quality
Constant	4.667920					
Age	−.817716	.404895				
School	−.178822	.021321	.572003			
Home	−.135454	.003707	.283277	.561751		
Special	.231957	−.065487	.291245	.295162	.653605	
Quality	−.068954	.010732	−.001846	−.002448	−.008209	.001100

Using the original values from the table (for the purpose of reducing rounding error), the ASE for the model equals 0.647. Inputting this value into Equation 4.17 we can easily calculate the confidence intervals for logit(p) as $-1.679 \pm (1.96 \times 0.647)$, giving $-2.947, -0.411$ and convert these into estimates for p (using the equations $e^{-2.947}/(1 + e^{-2.947})$ and $e^{-.411}/(1 + e^{-.411})$ to calculate the intervals 0.050, 0.399).

Confidence intervals for logit(p) can also be determined by recalculating the model using transformed variables. The method used to achieve this is identical to that demonstrated for a model with a single explanatory variable (see Section 4.2). Essentially, new variables are computed where a value is deleted from each case which corresponds to the variable value we wish to predict (predicting the probability of a case being heard in court for a 5–6-year-old child, interviewed at home and who obtains a score of 50 for quality, we would delete 1 from Age (assuming that 5–6-year-old children are coded as 1, if they are coded as 0, then the variable should be left as it is), 1 from Home (the dummy variable home is coded 0 and 1) and 50 from Quality. These new variables are then entered into the model in place of the original variables (remember to include $j − 1$ dummy location variables). The model is recalculated and the ASE for the constant term provides the estimate of the ASE for logit(p). For this example, the ASE is predicted as 0.6499. The 95% confidence intervals for logit(p) are therefore $-1.679 \pm (1.96 \times 0.6499)$, giving intervals of -2.953 and -0.405 for logit(p), with the corresponding confidence intervals for p being equivalent to 0.050, 0.400 (these values are very similar to those calculated using the variance-covariance matrix (see above), and those calculated directly using GLIM (see Section 4.6.2)).

If our primary interest in modelling the data is to predict likelihood of prosecution, it is important to keep the width of the confidence intervals as narrow as possible. For the above example, we have included explanatory variables in the model which are not necessarily important for prediction. Removing relatively unimportant variables from the model can improve the overall model fit and reduce the width of the confidence intervals. Consider the model obtained using a backward elimination procedure where Quality is the only variable included. The model we obtain in this case has a model chi-square value of 11.451, with $df = 1$, $P = 0.0007$, and the equation:

$$\text{logit}(p) = -5.1971 + (0.0833 \times \text{Quality}).$$

When Quality is equal to 50, the predicted value of $\text{logit}(p)$ is -1.032. The confidence intervals associated with $\text{logit}(p)$ are -1.847 and -0.217 (these intervals can be calculated using one of the methods above, however, we have calculated them using GLIM). The predicted value for p is 0.263 with associated 95% confidence intervals equal to 0.136 and 0.446. These are narrower than the intervals calculated for the larger model above even though more information was used in that model. When the purpose of the regression model is to predict the response variable, it is important to only include those explanatory variables in the model which are important for prediction. For this example, the model which contains just one explanatory variable provides the better prediction.

4.5   Summary

Logistic regression provides a model-building approach to the analysis of binary (or proportional) data. It is a generalized linear model that maps the random component (the response variable) onto the systematic component (the explanatory variables expressed as a linear function) using a logit link (the log odds). It is a versatile analytic technique since it allows dichotomous data to be modelled using both continuous and discontinuous explanatory variables. This chapter has demonstrated how logistic regression can be used to model quite complex data sets and has also shown the similarities between this technique and the other generalized linear modelling techniques discussed in this book.

4.6   Statistical Software Commands

Detailed discussions of the SPSS procedures outlined in this section can be found in the appropriate SPSS manuals (see, for example, SPSS Inc., 1996b).

4.6.1   SPSS

Calculating and Displaying the Logistic Regression Curve

The first task in graphing the logistic regression model shown in Figures 4.3 and 4.6 is to generate a regression model using the data presented in Table 4.1. Input the data from this Table into a spreadsheet in two columns labelled Outcome and Severity.

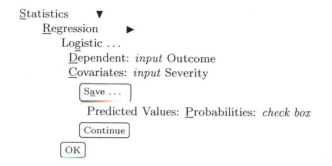

The above commands will compute the regression model and save predicted values for p under the variable name pre_1. The regression equation calculated above is:

$$\text{logit}(p) = -4.6401 + 0.0592 \text{ Severity}.$$

Whilst this equation could be used to determine predicted values, these have already been saved under the variable name pre_1. It is now possible to graph the logistic regression curve and the original data values using the commands:

Graphs   ▼
    Scatter ...
      Define: *indicate an overlay plot*
      [Define]
      input variables to be plotted ...
        Outcome - Severity
        pre_1 - Severity
    [OK]

You will note that the data points fall on two lines, similar to Figure 4.1. To get a better assessment of the model fit one could plot the proportion of patients who died from data which has been categorized as presented in Table 4.2. This will provide the graph shown in Figure 4.3.

Calculating Confidence Intervals for Fitted y

To calculate the confidence intervals for fitted y we first need to determine the ASE associated with $\text{logit}(p)$. In SPSS, when Severity is equal to 50, this can be calculated using the model recalculation method:

First, compute a new variable equal to Severity $-$ 50 (Call it sev_50) using the commands:

Transform   ▼
    Compute ...
      Target Variable: *input* Sev_50

Numeric Expression: *input* Severity − 50

[OK]

Use the variable Sev_50 to derive the ASE by computing a logistic regression model using the following commands:

Statistics   ▼
   Regression   ►
     Logistic . . .
      Dependent: *input* Outcome
      Covariates: *input* Sev_50
       [Continue]
    [OK]

The ASE for logit(p) is given by the ASE for the constant, which in this case is 0.583. Using this value, one can calculate the confidence intervals for logit(p) using the equation logit(p) $\pm$ (1.96 × 0.583). When severity is equal to 50, the predicted value of logit(p) is −1.68 (calculated using the logistic regression equation logit(p) = −4.6401 + 0.0592 × Severity derived above). This gives confidence intervals for logit(p) of (−2.822, −0.537). These values can easily be converted into direct probabilities using the equation $e^z/(1 + e^z)$, which gives confidence intervals for treatment outcome when severity of infection is equal to 50 of (0.056 to 0.37).

If the above procedure is repeated for a number of values of severity, the graphs depicted in Figures 4.7 and 4.8 can be constructed using overlay scatterplots as described above.

Dummy Variable Coding

Categorical explanatory variables can be entered into a logistic regression model directly, without the need for prior coding. The categorical variable is dummy coded in exactly the same way as for OLS regression, but this coding can now be completed internally and new variables need not be constructed by the user. For the example shown above in Table 4.14 the variable Hospital can be dummy coded using the commands:

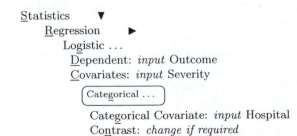

Statistics   ▼
   Regression   ►
     Logistic . . .
      Dependent: *input* Outcome
      Covariates: *input* Severity
      [Categorical . . .]
       Categorical Covariate: *input* Hospital
       Contrast: *change if required*

Reference Category: *change if required*

Continue

OK

Using the commands above, categorical variables can be dummy coded according to a variety of schemes and with a choice of reference categories.

Specific Code Relating to the Example in Section 4.4

Load the data from Table 3.11 using the following coding scheme:

Prosecute: no = 0, yes = 1.

Age: 5–6-year-old children = 0, 8–9-year-old children = 1.

Gender: male = 0, female = 1.

Location: Home = 1, School = 2, Special = 3, Standard = 4.

Run the full logistic regression model shown in Table 4.19:

<u>S</u>tatistics   ▼
   <u>R</u>egression   ►
      Lo<u>g</u>istic ...
         <u>D</u>ependent: *input* Prosecute
         <u>C</u>ovariates: *input* Age, Coherence, Delay
                      Gender, Location *and* Quality

         Cate<u>g</u>orical ...

         Categorical Covariate: *input* Age, Gender *and* Location

         Continue

      OK

To obtain the models shown in Table 4.20, a backward elimination procedure can be used utilizing statistics based on $-2LL$. The commands to run such a modelling process are basically the same as that provided above, except that the <u>M</u>ethod: used is Backward:LR instead of Enter.

To calculate the ASE when there are multiple variables, the model recalculation procedure can be used. Using the example in Section 4.4, the ASE for logit(p) can be calculated for a 5–6-year-old child, interviewed at home and producing an interview of quality 50 using the procedure:

Create dummy variables for Location (see Chapter 3 for explicit instructions on how this can be achieved). Create new variables for Age, Home, and Quality subtracting the designated value from the variable. Home becomes Home − 1, Quality becomes Quality − 50 and Age becomes Age − 0. Call the variables

Qual_new, Home_new, and Age_new. Input these variables into the logistic regression model:

<u>S</u>tatistics   ▼
    <u>R</u>egression   ▶
        <u>L</u>ogistic ...
            <u>D</u>ependent: *input* Prosecute
            <u>C</u>ovariates: *input* Age_new, Home_new, School,
                     Special *and* Qual_new

             ⌐OK¬

In the output, the ASE associated with the constant provides the estimate of the ASE for logit(p). In this case the estimate equals 0.6499.

4.6.2   GLIM

In order to run the GLIM examples presented below, type in the following command from within GLIM: `$INPUT 'FILENAME.EXT'$`, replacing `FILENAME.EXT` with that of each example file. To aid the reader, we have commented the commands extensively within each file. All macros which have been used are included at the end of this section.

Example from the Data Set in Table 4.14

```
$echo on $
!        First input any macros that we require.
$input 'logistic.mac' $
!        Read in the data set, declaring HOSPITAL to be a
!        factor with level 3 as the reference category.
$slen   49 $
$factor HOSPITAL 3 (3) $
$data SEVERITY HOSPITAL DIED $
$read
9.3      3         0
18.2     2         0
etc.
etc.
157.4    1         1
169.2    3         1
$
!        Declare the response variable.
$yvar DIED$
!        For binary data the binomial denominator is set to one
!        so we set up a variate containing all values of 1.
$calc total=1 $
!        Set the error term to binomial errors and declare which variable
!        is the binomial denominator.
$error b total $
!        Fit the model to be tested.
$fit SEVERITY $
```

```
!        Display parameter estimates and standard errors.
$dis e $
!        Call macro to calculate 95% CI's for parameters and odds ratios.
$use cior $
!        Call macro to set the deviance and df for fitted model.
$use devdf1 $
!        Remove the tested model term.
$fit -SEVERITY$
!        Call macro to set the deviance and df for reduced model.
$use devdf2$
!        Call macro to calculate -2 log likelihood test.
$use min2ll $
!        Refit model of interest.
$fit +SEVERITY $
!        Predict fitted values for the original values of the
!        explanatory variables.
$predict SEVERITY=SEVERITY $
!        Call macro to tabulate logit P, ASE and 95% confidence
!        intervals for logit P, as well as the fitted Y and 95%
!        confidence intervals for fitted Y, with the original
!        values of the explanatory variables.
$use cipiori $
!        Call the macro to display the classification table and
!        predictive efficiency for the fitted model.
$use predeff $
!        Predict fitted value for a new value of the explanatory
!        variable.
$predict SEVERITY=0 $
!        Call macro to display logit P, ASE and 95% confidence
!        intervals for logit P, as well as the fitted Y and 95%
!        confidence intervals for fitted Y, for a new value of
!        each explanatory variable.
$use cipinew $
$predict SEVERITY=50 $
$use cipinew $
$predict SEVERITY=100 $
$use cipinew $
$predict SEVERITY=150 $
$use cipinew $
$predict SEVERITY=200 $
$use cipinew $
!        Add the factor HOSPITAL to the model
$fit +HOSPITAL $
$dis e $
$use cior $
$return $
```

Example from the Data Set in Table 3.11 — a Further Analysis

```
$echo on $
!        First input any macros that we require.
$input 'logistic.mac' $
$slen  70 $
```

```
$factor age 2 (2) gender 2 location 4 (3) $
$data AGE GENDER LOCATION COHERENC DELAY MATURITY QUALITY PROSECUT $
$read
1 1 3 3.81 45 3.62 34.11  0
1 2 2 1.63 27 1.61 36.59  0
etc.
etc.
2 2 2 1.94 46 1.99 80.67  1
2 1 4 1.89 15 1.87 83.15  1
$
$yvar prosecut $
!       For binary data the binomial denominator is set to one
!       so we set up a variate containing all values of 1.
$calc total=1 $
!       Set the error term to binomial errors and declare which variable
!       is the binomial denominator.
$error b total $
!       Fit the full main-effects model.
$fit AGE+GENDER+LOCATION+COHERENC+DELAY+QUALITY $
$use predeff $
$dis e $
$use cior $
$use devdf1 $
!       Test against the null model to obtain a deviance statistic
!       that corresponds to the Model Chi-square statistic.
$fit $
$use predeff $
$use devdf2$
$use min2ll $
!       Refit the full main-effects model.
$fit AGE+GENDER+LOCATION+COHERENC+DELAY+QUALITY $
!       Remove and evaluate the tested model terms using
!       the sequence of backward elimination given in the chapter,
!       evaluating each model term by the change in the deviance.
$fit -GENDER$
$use predeff $
$use devdf2$
$use min2ll $
$use devdf1 $
$fit -DELAY$
$use predeff $
$use devdf2$
$use min2ll $
$use devdf1 $
$fit -LOCATION$
$use predeff $
$use devdf2$
$use min2ll $
$use devdf1 $
$fit -COHERENC$
$use predeff $
$use devdf2$
$use min2ll $
```

```
$use devdf1 $
$fit -AGE$
$use predeff $
$use devdf2$
$use min2ll $
!      Fit the final model
$fit AGE+LOCATION+QUALITY $
$use predeff $
$dis e $
$use cior $
$use devdf1 $
!      Compare to the model without LOCATION.
$fit -LOCATION$
$use predeff $
$use devdf2$
$use min2ll $
!      Refit Final Model.
$fit +LOCATION $
!      Predict fitted value for a new value of each explanatory
!      variable.
$predict AGE=1 LOCATION=1 QUALITY=50 $
$use cipinew $
!      Fit QUALITY alone.
$fit QUALITY $
$predict QUALITY=50 $
$use cipinew $
$return $
```

GLIM Macros for Logistic Regression

```
$mac cior
!      Produces a table of 95% CI's for the model parameters
!      and corresponding exponentiated values.
$num td95 $
$extract %pe %se $
$calc or=%exp(%pe)
$calc td95=%td(0.975,%df) $
$calc pelo=%pe-(td95*%se)
$calc pehi=%pe+(td95*%se)
$calc orlo=%exp(pelo) $
$calc orhi=%exp(pehi) $
$acc 4 3 $ $look %pe %se pelo pehi or orlo orhi $ $pr $ $acc $
$delete pelo pehi or orlo orhi $
$endmac $

$num dev1 dev2 df1 df2 df21 s2 dev21  p $

$mac devdf1 $assign dev1=%dv: df1=%df $ $endmac $

$mac devdf2 $assign dev2=%dv: df2=%df $ $endmac $

$mac min2ll
!      Calculates -2 log likelihood and its associated p-value.
```

```
$calc dev21=dev2-dev1: df21=df2-df1 $
$calc p= 1-%chp(dev21, df21) $
$pr '-2 log likelihood  ='dev21' with 'df21' df and P ='p ;$
$endmac $


$mac cipiori
!         Calculate and tabulate logit P, ASE and 95 % confidence
!         intervals for logit P, as well as the fitted Y and 95 %
!         confidence intervals for fitted Y, with the original
!         values of the explanatory variables.
$calc td95=%td(.975,%df): ase=%sqrt(%pvl) $
$calc pilplo=%plp-td95*ase:
         pilphi=%plp+td95*ase$
$calc pilo=1/(1+%exp(-(pilplo))):
         pihi=1/(1+%exp(-(pilphi)))$
$acc 4 3 $ $look %plp ase pilplo pilphi %pfv pilo pihi$ $pr $ $acc $
$endmac $


$mac cipinew
!         Calculate and display logit P, ASE and 95 % confidence
!         intervals for logit P, as well as the fitted Y and 95 %
!         confidence intervals for fitted Y, for a new value of
!         each explanatory variable.
$num cifynewlo cifynewhi pinewlo pinewhi  asenew $
$calc td95=%td(.975,%df): asenew=%sqrt(%pvl) $
$calc pilpnewlo=%plp-td95*asenew:
         pilpnewhi=%plp+td95*asenew$
$calc pinewlo=1/(1+%exp(-(pilpnewlo))):
         pinewhi=1/(1+%exp(-(pilpnewhi))) $
$pr 'Logit P='%plp' ASE='asenew' with 95% CI of ('pilpnewlo','
pilpnewhi')'$
$pr 'Fitted P='%pfv' with 95% CI of ('pinewlo','pinewhi')';$
$endmac $


$mac predeff
!         Displays the classification table and predictive efficiency
!         for the fitted model.
$num true0sum true1sum false0sum false1sum pc0true pc1true pcoverall$
$calc binpred=%ge(%fv,0.5) $
$calc true0=%if(%eq(%yv,0),%eq(%yv,binpred),0):
         true1=%if(%eq(%yv,1),%eq(%yv,binpred),0):
         false0=%if(%eq(%yv,0),%ne(%yv,binpred),0):
         false1=%if(%eq(%yv,1),%ne(%yv,binpred),0) $
$calc true0sum=%cu(true0): true1sum=%cu(true1):
          false0sum=%cu(false0): false1sum=%cu(false1)$
$calc pc0true=true0sum/(true0sum+false0sum)*100 $
$calc pc1true=true1sum/(true1sum+false1sum)*100 $
$calc pcoverall=(true0sum+true1sum)/
(true0sum+true1sum+false0sum+false1sum)*100 $
$acc 4 2 $          -
$pr ;'Predictive Efficiency:' $
$pr '                        Predicted' $
$pr '                 0       1       % correct'; $
```

```
$pr 'Observed   0         ' true0sum false0sum pc0true'%' $
$pr '           1         ' false1sum true1sum pc1true'%'; $
$pr 'Overall correct ='pcoverall'%'; $
$acc $
$endmac $
$return $
```

Chapter 5

Loglinear Analysis

Loglinear models are a class of generalized linear model which can be used to model categorical response variables, both with nominal and ordered categories. In this chapter, we shall emphasize the model-building approach, introduced earlier for data meeting the assumptions of OLS and logistic regression, as a method of investigating the relationships amongst categorical variables. Such data may be nominal, where the data consist of discrete categories, e.g., ethnic origin, or type of therapy, or they may be ordered categories, consisting of discrete data which can be ranked, e.g., statements of the degree of agreement to a question measured with a Likert scale, or a grouped continuous variable such as low, medium and high levels of smoking. Here, we shall present loglinear models which are designed for use with categorical data and which have extensions to take into account the additional information available in ordered categorical data. In addition, these methods may be of interest when discrete numerical scales are restricted to a small number of possible values, such as the number of cylinders in a motorcar engine, i.e., 2, 3, 4, 6, 8, or 12, or the number of bits in the main microprocessor of a computer, i.e., 8, 16, 32 or 64 bits.

Placing loglinear models within the context of generalized linear models, they consist of three components. The Random component is the probability distribution of the response variable, and for categorical data that consists of frequency counts which have a Poisson distribution. This is a convenient simplification, but allows a wide variety of data sets to be fitted. The Systematic component is the fixed structure of the explanatory variables which is specified by a linear function between them, i.e., $\alpha + \beta x_1 + \beta x_2 +, \ldots, + \beta x_j$ for a set of j explanatory variables. The Link function maps the systematic component onto the random component and for Poisson random components this is the log link, the natural logarithm of the linear predictor from the systematic component. The use of non-linear links to the systematic component allow the development of generalized linear models without the assumptions of Normality and constant variance in the response variable, required by ordinary least-squares regression technique, and other techniques assuming an identity link. The principle concern is to obtain additivity in the combination of the explanatory variables in model. This is the role of the link function in a generalized linear model.

In generalized linear models, the single response variable is predicted by a linear combination of the explanatory variables, through the link function. The family of models can therefore be considered univariate in nature, with multiple explanatory variables. However, in the case of a loglinear model, all the variables are entered into the systematic component and through the logarithmic link function predictions of the frequency count of each cell of the contingency table can be made. It is possible to examine standard univariate models with explanatory variables of known fixed values and a single response variable, as well as multivariate models with more than one response variable, in which case one can estimate the size of the associations between all of the variables. This provides us with a powerful modelling technique, at the expense of a somewhat cumbersome notation since all the variables, regardless of explanatory or response status are entered into the right-hand side of the equation. Since all the variables are categorical, either nominal or with ordered categories, we shall refer to them as *factors*, and draw a distinction between their status as response or explanatory when it is useful to do so.

The loglinear technique is also useful if one is interested in predicting the occurrence of the categories of a response factor from a series of explanatory factors. In such cases, a logit function forms the link to the random component. There is a close correspondence between the two types of model with certain logit models having loglinear representations. Chapter 4 developed the logit model in the context of logistic regression, here we will show the correspondence between logit and loglinear models for data in the form of contingency tables.

Loglinear modelling is a versatile technique which can be applied to the analysis of a wide variety of data. It should be noted, however, that there are limitations to the technique which have implications for the way in which these models can be applied. Perhaps the most notable of these are the problems associated with sparse cells and the need to reduce continuous variates to grouped factors with scores representing the values of the ordered categories[1].

5.1   Traditional Bivariate Methods

5.1.1   Hypothesis Testing with Significance Tests

Statistical methods for categorical data have tended to concentrate upon bivariate data, with additional special techniques for two-by-two contingency ta-

---

[1]It is possible to use a form of dummy coding to include continuous variables alongside factors, but since this is not easily implemented in most statistical packages, we restrict ourselves to loglinear models with nominal and ordered categories.

bles. When one is considering a single bivariate association, then the Pearson X^2 statistic has traditionally been used. Other methods include Fisher's Exact test for two-by-two tables with small expected frequencies, and non-parametric methods for ordered categorical data, such as the Mann–Whitney U test and the Kruskal–Wallis one-way Analysis of Variance (Siegel & Castellan, 1988). We shall briefly consider traditional categorical methods for nominal factors, before moving onto multivariate data and the model-building approach.

5.1.2   Goodness-of-fit Statistics

Consider the data presented in Table 5.1. These represent a hypothetical study to examine the association between the job of two professional groups, doctors and dentists, and a binary classification of whether they are satisfied with their job. The goodness-of-fit test compares the observed cell counts with the expected cell counts for the null hypothesis of independence amongst the two factors, H_0. A number of statistical methods exist for this purpose, we consider Pearson's X^2 because of its traditional usage, and G^2 which approximates the distribution of χ^2 with large samples and has advantages when developing loglinear models with multivariate data.

Table 5.1: Contingency Table of Job Satisfaction for Doctors versus Dentists

	Satisfaction	
Job	Yes	No
Doctors	293	98
Dentists	223	114

The Pearson X² Statistic

The Pearson statistic is shown in Equation 5.1.

$$X^2 = \sum_{ij} \frac{(o - e)^2}{e} \tag{5.1}$$

where o is the observed frequency for a particular cell ij,

and e is its expected frequency.

The values are generated by commonly available statistical software, and for our example data, a value of $X^2 = 6.735$ with $df = 1$ is obtained. This corresponds to a P-value of 0.010, a significant overall difference from the expected values of the null hypothesis of no association, H_0. It suggests that there is an association between profession and job satisfaction, for doctors compared to dentists.

The G^2 Statistic

An alternative statistic to Pearson X^2 is G^2, the *likelihood ratio* statistic, which has advantages when multivariate data are examined. The equation for two-way contingency tables is shown in Equation 5.2.

$$G^2 = 2 \sum_{ij} o(\log \frac{o}{e}) \qquad (5.2)$$

Using software to analyse the data in Table 5.1, we obtain $G^2 = 6.725$. Since G^2 has the same distribution as X^2, for large samples, it allows tables of χ^2 to be used to evaluate the statistical significance — with $df = 1$, we obtain a P-value of 0.010. Once more we obtain evidence of an association between profession and job satisfaction.

When associations are successively examined amongst a number of factors, then a problem occurs which is similar to that found with repeated pairwise correlations and regression analysis — the same variance is analysed over again, and the likelihood of a Type I error increases with the number of tests carried out. A Type I error refers to rejecting the null hypothesis, H_0, when it is, in fact, true. The end result is that X^2 tests for individual effects do not sum to the total X^2, i.e., X^2 is not additive. This becomes more of a problem with a larger number of factors, and higher-order associations. One way round this is to use G^2, the likelihood ratio, which has an advantage over X^2 for modelling multivariate data, since it is additive under certain conditions.

With our bivariate association between profession and job satisfaction we find that:

$$G^2_{\text{Total}} = G^2_{\text{profession}} + G^2_{\text{satisfaction}} + G^2_{\text{profession,satisfaction}} \qquad (5.3)$$

In other words the overall test of association, G^2_{Total}, is the sum of the main effect goodness-of-fit statistics, $G^2_{\text{profession}} + G^2_{\text{satisfaction}}$, together with the test of the association, $G^2_{\text{profession,satisfaction}}$. Thus, by using the likelihood ratio statistic, G^2, one can test for the main effects, as well as the higher order associations, with the advantages of additivity of the test statistic, and the likelihood of Type I error kept at a reasonable level. One cannot use X^2 in this fashion to breakdown the contribution of each component to the overall model statistic. This becomes of considerable importance when examining three-way, or higher, interactions between factors, and we will return to the issue when considering loglinear techniques. Note that when speaking of relationships amongst these categorical variables, we follow the convention of using the term *association* to refer to a relationship between two factors, whilst the term *interaction* is used for three or more factors.

Adjusted Residuals

The goodness-of-fit statistics gives us an overall summary of the strength of our hypothesis in comparison to the null hypothesis, H_0. By examining the cell residuals one can look at the pattern of the fit across the cells of the table. Note that as the size of the expected frequency gets larger there is a tendency for the difference between the expected and obtained cell counts to be larger. Therefore, we use *adjusted residuals* because these give us a measure of the difference between the observed and expected values for each cell, one that is independent of the size of the expected frequencies. Adjusted residuals can be calculated using Equation 5.4.

$$\frac{o_{ij} - e_{ij}}{\sqrt{e_{ij}(1 - p_{i+})(1 - p_{+j})}} \tag{5.4}$$

where p_{i+} is the column marginal proportions, given by the total observed counts of that column divided by the overall observed total,

and p_{+j} is the row marginal proportions, given by the total observed counts of that row divided by the overall total.

Positive residuals indicate higher values in that cell than expected from the null hypothesis, whilst negative residuals indicate fewer than expected. When the absolute value of the adjusted residual, i.e., ignoring its sign, is more than about 1.96 this suggests a lack of fit of the null hypothesis in that cell. Adjusted residuals can be generated as part of the output of most statistical software. Sometimes they are called *studentized residuals*, and a refined version of these are the *studentized deviance residuals* which are more accurate (See Francis, Greene and Payne (1994), for corresponding formulae and description). For comparison, we provide both forms of adjusted residuals in the tables of this chapter.

Returning to our example of job satisfaction amongst doctors and dentists, Table 5.2 gives the expected values of the independence model, together with the adjusted residuals for each cell of the contingency table. All the residuals are greater than 1.96 in their absolute magnitude, indicating a poor fit of the independence model, H_0. In addition, the sign of the adjusted residuals supports the association model since dissatisfied doctors and satisfied dentists are both fewer in number than would be expected by chance, as indicated by the negative sign of their adjusted residuals, whilst satisfied doctors and dissatisfied dentists are both more than would be expected by chance, indicated by the positive adjusted residuals.

Table 5.2: Data Matrix of Job Satisfaction for Doctors versus Dentists

Job	Satisfaction	Count	Fitted Value	Studentized Residual	Studentized Deviance Residual
1	1	293	277.14	2.595	2.571
1	2	98	113.86	−2.595	−2.659
2	1	223	238.86	−2.595	−2.625
2	2	114	98.14	2.595	2.530

5.1.3 Modelling with Sample Odds Ratios

One can use the cell counts in the observed data to model likely outcomes for further samples drawn from the population of interest. With two factors this can be useful, though with three or more factors we may want to simplify the model to exclude some of the factors or the interactions between them, otherwise our models will lack parsimony and tend to be too closely tied to the original sample.

Consider the data earlier presented in Table 5.2, examining the association between profession, doctors and dentists, and the binary classification of job satisfaction. As with the data presented in the chapter on logistic regression, one can express the degree of association between two factors in terms of an odds ratio. The obtained frequencies are represented as a *data matrix*, where each row represents a different combination of the factors with a column representing the obtained counts for each of these rows. This differs from a row×column representation of the data, i.e., a cross tabulation, but has advantages in that it is the format used by many statistical packages and makes the entry and reading of data with many factors more straightforward. In this chapter we present tables of data, first as contingency tables and then in data matrix form, for the purposes of comparison.

Now we shall look at calculating the sample odds ratio, which is obtained from examining the sample cell counts and provides a useful description of the obtained data. When both of the factors can be considered as explanatory variables, then the odds ratio is defined as in Equation 5.5.

$$\hat{\theta} = \frac{n_{11}n_{22}}{n_{12}n_{21}} \tag{5.5}$$

where $\hat{\theta}$ represents the maximum likelihood estimate of the true odds ratio, and n is the count obtained in each cell.

The calculated sample odds ratio for the data described above is thus ($\frac{293 \times 114}{98 \times 223}$ = 1.528). This states that the odds of being satisfied compared to dissatisfied are 1.528 times higher for the doctors compared to the dentists. One can also calculate odds for the first factor at each level of the second, n_{11}/n_{12} and n_{21}/n_{22}, giving values of $293/98 = 2.990$ and $223/114 = 1.956$, i.e., the odds of being satisfied compared to dissatisfied are 2.99 for doctors and 1.956 for dentists. Calculating the odds of the second factor at each level of the first, n_{11}/n_{21} and n_{12}/n_{22}, gives values of $293/223 = 1.314$ and $98/114 = 0.860$, i.e., the odds of being a doctor compared to a dentist are 1.314 for the satisfied level of job satisfaction, and 0.860 for the dissatisfied level of job satisfaction.

The odds and odds ratios can be used to make predictions for other samples drawn from the population, but ideally we would like to know the range of possible values our predictions might be likely to take on, a reflection of the size of the original sample — a wide range of likely values will not be of much use in making predictions. For this purpose we calculate confidence intervals, and the next section illustrates how this can be done.

Confidence Intervals

Through the calculation of confidence intervals for the odds ratio, one can specify the likely range of values that it lies between, for the original population. Wide confidence intervals indicate poor predictive capability, whilst narrow confidence intervals indicate that more useful predictions may be made.

In order to calculate confidence intervals, one first calculates the standard error, known as the *asymptotic standard error* (ASE). It is calculated for a two-by-two table using Equation 5.6.

$$\text{ASE} (\log \hat{\theta}) = \sqrt{\frac{1}{n_{11}} + \frac{1}{n_{12}} + \frac{1}{n_{21}} + \frac{1}{n_{22}}} \tag{5.6}$$

where $\hat{\theta}$ is the estimate of the true odds ratio from equation 5.5.

The data from Table 5.1 gives the following value for the ASE:

$$\sqrt{\frac{1}{293} + \frac{1}{98} + \frac{1}{223} + \frac{1}{114}} = 0.164$$

Taking the log transform of the odds ratio provides us with a distribution that approximates the Normal distribution for large samples, from which we can estimate the confidence intervals of the odds ratio. One initially calculates the confidence interval on the log scale for $\log \theta$ using Equation 5.7.

$$\text{confidence intervals for } \log \theta = \log \hat{\theta} \pm z_{\alpha/2} \text{ASE}(\log \hat{\theta}). \qquad (5.7)$$

With the present data, from earlier we calculated $\hat{\theta} = 1.528$, and the ASE for $\log \hat{\theta} = 0.164$. The 95% confidence intervals for $\log \hat{\theta}$ are therefore $\log(1.528) \pm 1.96(0.164)$, i.e., confidence intervals of 0.103 and 0.745 on the log scale. These values can then be converted to obtain confidence intervals on the original scale by taking the exponents of the confidence intervals of $\log \hat{\theta}$ in order to obtain the confidence intervals directly in terms of $\hat{\theta}$, the odds ratio. Thus, the confidence intervals for the present sample's odds ratio are $e^{0.103}$ and $e^{0.745}$, i.e., 1.108 and 2.106 compared to the predicted value of $\hat{\theta}$ of 1.528. Note that $\hat{\theta}$ does not lie midway between the two endpoints because we have converted the confidence interval calculated on a distribution approximating Normality to that of the odds-ratio of the two factors which is skewed positively — on the original scale it cannot be less than zero and yet its upper limit is unbounded. It is this 'trick' of using the transformed scale that allows us to obtain confidence intervals for the odds ratio when its sampling distribution is not itself Normally distributed. This is often used to advantage with generalized linear models that do not use an identity link. To summarize the analysis above, the odds of being satisfied compared to dissatisfied are 1.528 times higher for doctors compared to dentists, and we can say with 95% confidence that the population value lies between 1.108 and 2.106.

5.2   Loglinear Models

Throughout this text there has been an emphasis on moving away from the traditional hypothesis testing framework using goodness-of-fit significance tests, towards one of model building. The development of generalized linear models allows the modelling sophistication found in ordinary least-squares regression to be made available for binary data, as described in the logistic regression chapter, and for frequency data, using loglinear models. Models which provide a good fit for the data offer several advantages over the use of significance tests. One can examine patterns of association and interaction between the factors by studying residuals and estimating odds ratios that describe the associations. The contribution of each effect can be evaluated by examining the estimated model parameters, and the predicted model values provide a smoothing of the original data and a greater degree of parsimony since irrelevant or weak effects can be removed from the model (McCullagh and Nelder, 1989).

5.2.1   The Loglinear Equation

Data collected for categorical variables can be described in terms of a count of the number of instances which occurred for each combination of variables. Generalized Linear Models for count data assume that the random component will follow a *Poisson* distribution (See, for example, Agresti, 1996; Lindsey, 1995). This distribution provides us with an estimate of the probability of a response variable and can therefore be used to make predictions about the likelihood of obtaining a value in each cell of the contingency table. Frequency variables have the property of being positively skewed, since the upper limit is unconstrained whilst the lowest value is zero (one cannot have a count of less than zero). For this reason one uses a log link between the random component and the linear model of the systematic component, in an analogous fashion to the logit link used for binary data in logistic regression. The use of a log link helps minimize the skew whilst preserving an additive relationship between the explanatory variables, required for the linear systematic component of the model. Thus, the generalized linear model for data with assumed Poisson errors uses a log link and for a model with j explanatory variables takes the form:

$$\log \mu_j = \alpha + \beta_1 x_1 + \beta_2 x_2, \ldots, \beta_j x_j \qquad (5.8)$$

where μ_j is used to denote the expected frequency generated by a particular combination of the explanatory variables,

α is the constant,

and β_1 to β_j are the unknown parameters for each explanatory variable, x_1 to x_j, that are estimated from the data.

Generalized linear models with a log link are known as *loglinear* models, making the link to the linear systematic component explicit. Loglinear analysis involves the generation of tables containing the possible combinations of the factors and a model of the expected frequencies of each combination, followed by the generation of statistical values that allow one to examine the significance of each factor and the goodness-of-fit of the model. The analysis typically begins with all the associations and interactions possible between a set of factors being represented and then proceeds to eliminate those which can be, whilst retaining a reasonable fit between the expected cell frequencies generated by the model, and the obtained frequencies.

As discussed in Chapter 2 on Data Screening, choosing a *log* link gives us a generalized linear model where the variance of the probability distribution for the response variable is a fixed function of the mean, as is the case with logistic regression. It is recommended that the reader check any good-fitting model for over/underdispersion, which results when the sample variability departs from that expected from the theoretical distribution. Cases of moderate departure from the expected variance can be compensated for by adjusting the standard errors using the method outlined in Chapter 2. This will have the effect of altering the range of the 95% confidence intervals for the estimated parameters.

5.2.2   A Bivariate Example

Consider our previous two-way association model for profession and job satisfaction from Table 5.2. The association model provided in Equation 5.3 is said to be *saturated* since it includes main effects for each of the factors, plus an interaction term. Saturated models provide an exact fit for the observed cell counts and do not offer any simplification or smoothing of the data, and since the observed values are the same as the expected ones we cannot obtain any goodness-of-fit statistics. In model building, one aims to build a simpler description of the data through the inclusion of only some of the factors and their combinations.

In keeping with the conventions for representing loglinear models, we use a notation involving the symbol lambda (λ) for the model equations. The saturated model for a two-way association is represented by Equation 5.9.

$$\log \mu_{ij} = \lambda + \lambda_i^X + \lambda_j^Y + \lambda_{ij}^{XY} \qquad (5.9)$$

where the letters X and Y are simply variable labels and do not raise λ to the *power* of X or Y.

For our model of job satisfaction we obtain:

$$\log \mu_{ij} = \lambda + \lambda_i^{\text{Profession}} + \lambda_j^{\text{Satisfaction}} + \lambda_{ij}^{\text{Profession,Satisfaction}} \qquad (5.10)$$

In loglinear models the data consist of contingency tables of categorical explanatory variables, that are either nominal or ordered categories, and which are used to predict the response variable — the frequency count of each cell of the table. The changes in the cell count, as one moves from one level of an explanatory variable to another, are the *effects* of that factor. The effects are estimated by the parameters obtained from running a loglinear model.

In the manner of dummy coding, one specifies the effects parameters so that the first row and column are set to zero, or the last row and column. This is known as *aliasing* and corresponds to the practice of choosing a reference category for OLS and logistic regression (see Sections 3.3.7 and 4.3.6). Each method will generate a different set of parameters, but the log odds ratio generated by the combination of the parameters will be the same in each case. This invariance of the log odds ratio is convenient, since one can always state how the odds of obtaining a case in one of two levels of a first factor will change across two levels of a second factor. Table 5.3 presents the parameter estimates and standard errors for the saturated model, aliasing level 2 of each factor, i.e., Job (Dentist) and Satisfaction (no). Values are only available for Factor levels which are non-aliased, i.e., those which have not been defined as the reference category.

Table 5.3: Parameter estimates of Job Satisfaction for Doctors versus Dentists

Parameter	Estimate	s.e.
Intercept	4.736	0.094
Prof(1)	−0.151	0.138
Satis(1)	0.671	0.115
Prof(1)×Satis(1)	0.424	0.164

$$\log \mu_{ij} = \lambda + \lambda_i^{\text{Profession}} + \lambda_j^{\text{Satisfaction}} + \lambda_{ij}^{\text{Profession,Satisfaction}}$$

One obtains fitted counts for the model depicted in Table 5.3 by adding in the successive parameters for each cell, as it deviates from the level of the reference category, and exponentiating the corresponding total. Thus, the cell with the two levels of the reference category, in this case Prof(2),Satis(2), has a fitted count of $e^{4.736}$, which equals 114. For the remaining cells we include the parameters that represent the additional count for the new factor levels. The counts for each cell can be derived using the equations:

$$\text{Prof(2),Satis(2)} = e^{4.736} = 114$$

$$\text{Prof(1),Satis(2)} = e^{4.736+(-0.151)} = 98$$

$$\text{Prof(2),Satis(1)} = e^{4.736+0.671} = 223$$

$$\text{Prof(1),Satis(1)} = e^{4.736-0.151+0.671+0.424} = 293.$$

The association parameters for the four cells of the contingency table can also be combined to obtain the log odds ratio using Equation 5.11.

$$\log \hat{\theta} = \log \left(\frac{n_{11}n_{22}}{n_{12}n_{21}} \right) = \hat{\lambda}_{11}^{XY} + \hat{\lambda}_{22}^{XY} - \hat{\lambda}_{12}^{XY} - \hat{\lambda}_{21}^{XY} \qquad (5.11)$$

We have set the reference category to level 2, but since the odds ratio is invariant to the chosen reference category, for our example the odds ratio can be calculated using Equation 5.12.

$$\log \hat{\theta} = \hat{\lambda}_{11}^{\text{Prof,Satis}} + \hat{\lambda}_{22}^{\text{Prof,Satis}} - \hat{\lambda}_{12}^{\text{Prof,Satis}} - \hat{\lambda}_{21}^{\text{Prof,Satis}} \qquad (5.12)$$

Inserting the relevant parameter estimates we obtain:

$$
\begin{aligned}
\log \theta \;&=\; (4.736 - 0.151 + 0.671 + 0.424) + \\
&\quad (4.736) - \\
&\quad (4.736 - 0.151) - \\
&\quad (4.736 + 0.671) \\
&=\; 0.424.
\end{aligned}
$$

Exponentiating this gives us an odds ratio of 1.528 for job satisfaction versus dissatisfaction, with doctors compared to dentists. Since the fitted counts for a saturated model are the same as the observed counts, we note that fitted odds ratio is the same as the sample odds ratio calculated in Section 5.1.3. A more direct estimate of the odds ratio is given by the association parameter between the two factors. Taking the exponent of the parameter estimate for Prof(1)×Satis(1) ($e^{0.424}$) we obtain $\theta = 1.528$, with confidence intervals equivalent to:

$$95\% \text{ confidence intervals for } \log \theta = 0.424 \pm (1.96 \times 0.164) \qquad (5.13)$$

giving lower and upper values of 0.103 and 0.745, which after exponentiation correspond to odds ratio limits of 1.108 and 2.106. Thus, the saturated model again has the same values as those obtained from the sample odds ratio. For small samples one would use the exact t-value rather than the large sample approximation of 1.96. Note that whilst we may have *a priori* explanatory assumptions when considering the association between profession and job satisfaction, this is not a formal part of the loglinear model, since one is simply modelling how the predicted cell counts change across each combination of the measured factors.

Computer software will usually have a default specification governing the generation of the effects parameters. Some generate the individual parameter estimates, whilst other packages directly output the log odds ratios. The net result, however, is identical. With multicategory data and more complex models, one examines the local odds ratio for various sets of four adjacent cells. For such cases, we are interested in how the local odds ratio changes as additional factors are examined. In other words, is the odds ratio between four neighbouring cells of two factors constant as a third factor changes, or is there an interaction between the three factors? In the case of such a three-way interaction we can state how the local odds ratio between the first two factors will change as the level of the third factor changes.

5.2.3 A Multivariate Example

As an initial multivariate example of a loglinear analysis, consider a three-way model between age, profession, and job satisfaction. The saturated model consists of the interaction between all the factors, age, profession and job satisfaction, three two-way associations consisting of age with profession, age with job satisfaction, and profession with job satisfaction, the three main effects for each of the factors, plus the intercept of the model. The saturated model for our three-way example is as follows:

$$
\begin{aligned}
\log \mu_{ij} \;=\; & \lambda + \lambda_i^{\text{Age}} + \lambda_j^{\text{Profession}} + \lambda_k^{\text{Satisfaction}} \\
& \lambda_{ij}^{\text{Age,Profession}} + \lambda_{ik}^{\text{Age,Satisfaction}} + \lambda_{jk}^{\text{Profession,Satisfaction}} + \\
& \lambda_{ijk}^{\text{Age,Profession,Satisfaction}}
\end{aligned}
$$

The analysis considers the significance of the three-way interaction and examines the effect of eliminating it from the model. It then proceeds to examine and eliminate if possible each of the two-way associations and the main-effects. In this way a model is built up that is a sub-set of all the possible combinations of factors, which provides an adequate fit to the observed data. The course of the analysis is similar to multiple ordinary least-squares regression where one tries to achieve parsimony of explanation through the development of a model adequately summarizing the observed data with a relatively small number of explanatory variables. We shall go into the detail of model building and parameter estimates in the sections below.

5.2.4 Model Notation

First we will introduce some common notation to indicate hierarchical models and their explanatory variables. Suppose a model (call it Model 2) with three variables (A, B and C) includes the associations $A \times B$ and $B \times C$, and the main effects A, B and C. Such a model is represented using the notation AB, AC and is shown in Figure 5.1. Another model (call it Model 1) includes the association $A \times B$ and the main effects A and B. Such a model is represented using the notation AB and is also shown in Figure 5.1. Both models are said to be *hierarchical*, which means that each term includes all lower order terms.

For example, if the association $B \times C$ is present, then the lower order main
effects of B and C are also present.

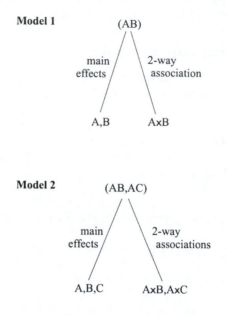

Figure 5.1: Examples of two-way hierarchical models

For the example above, Model 1 can be said to be *nested* within Model
2 as all the terms which appear in this model also appear in Model 2. Put
another way, Model 1 is a subset of Model 2.

Figure 5.2 shows an example of another hierarchical model (Model 3) represented by the notation ABC (this is a saturated model depicting the entire
hierarchy) and a non-hierarchical model (Model 4) represented by the notation
$A, B, C, A.B.C$. Model 4 shows a model which contains all of the main effects
and a three-way interaction term, but no two-way associations.

Hierarchical models are particularly useful since models that are nested
within the same hierarchy can be compared statistically. When one wishes to
compare models to find out the best one, a hierarchical analysis is, therefore,
usually the better option. It should be noted, however, that when the highest
order interaction is significant, then the hierarchical model is saturated and the
fit with the observed data is perfect (see Model 3). Since we are interested in
parsimony of explanation, and obtaining a model that smooths the data, one
may have to adopt a non-hierarchical approach for nominal categorical data
by excluding at least one of the lower order effects. For models which include

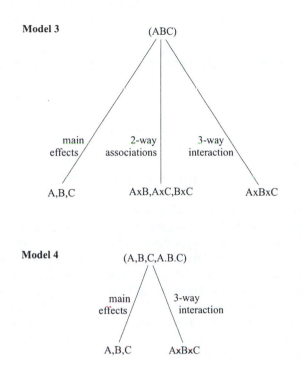

Figure 5.2: Examples of three-way hierarchical and non-hierarchical models

ordered categorical data, there is the possibility of using a linear×linear model
to examine higher-order associations that would otherwise be saturated for a
nominal treatment of the variables (see Section 5.2.7).

In this book we will restrict our discussion to hierarchical models since
they offer a straightforward method of comparison and evaluation using G^2.
The G^2 statistic allows a simple comparison to be made of nested models
and enables answers to questions such as whether the simpler sub-hierarchy
of Model 1 is sufficiently good at predicting the observed cells, or whether
the more complex Model 2 is significantly better. The balance is between
parsimony of explanation and goodness-of-fit of the model.

5.2.5 Model Building

Loglinear methods involve an initial screening of the data, the selection of
an optimal model, followed by its evaluation in terms of the degree-of-fit to
the data set. Given that the data depart significantly from an independence

model one can examine the reliability of the main-effects, two-way associations, three-way interactions, and so on. In some cases these results provide clear implications, perhaps only one or two associations are significant and the researcher can then discuss the topic of interest in the light of these findings. Sometimes particular models will be suggested by theoretical considerations, on other occasions one is simply interested in a parsimonious model for prediction purposes, in which case an automated model selection procedure such as a stepwise or backward elimination model selection might be used (See Section 3.3.9 for a further explanation of automated model selection methods). When the picture arising from data screening is of a number of significant associations, then the implications of the data are usually not so clear, and the goal then becomes to find a parsimonious model for predicting the cell frequencies.

As mentioned above, when all possible combinations of factors, i.e., all possible effects, are included in a loglinear analysis, then the model is said to be saturated. We will consider a hypothetical data set examining the associations between three factors, race, quality of housing and a measure of illness. If, as we would expect, there is an association between housing and illness then we can see if the odds ratio for housing and illness is independent of our control variable, race, or conditional upon it. If the association between housing and illness is independent for each level of race, then we can say that housing and illness are *conditionally independent* given race. The saturated model for this example is shown in Equation 5.14.

$$
\begin{aligned}
\log \mu_{ijk} \;=\; & \lambda + \lambda_i^{\text{Race}} + \lambda_j^{\text{Housing}} + \lambda_k^{\text{Illness}} + \\
& \lambda_{ij}^{\text{Race,Housing}} + \lambda_{ik}^{\text{Race,Illness}} + \lambda_{jk}^{\text{Housing,Illness}} + \\
& \lambda_{ijk}^{\text{Race,Housing,Illness}}
\end{aligned}
\tag{5.14}
$$

Equation 5.14 states that for every cell ijk, the natural logarithm of the expected frequency μ is an additive summation of the λ effect parameter for each factor, plus the constant λ. For any single cell the expected frequency derives from a different combination of the effect parameters. In this example we will treat all the variables as nominal, later in this chapter we will illustrate how the additional power available from ordered categorical variables can be analysed. A saturated model provides a perfect fit for the data, i.e., the expected frequencies equal the observed frequencies. The rationale behind generating a model is to obtain an *unsaturated* model with the fewest effects, but which still approximates the observed frequencies sufficiently well.

One tests the goodness-of-fit of an unsaturated model by calculating G^2 for that model, along with its significance. For a model to be a good approximation of the data one looks for a *non-significant* G^2, because we are looking for models in which the expected frequencies generated by the model are not significantly different from the observed cell frequencies. This is an important point, which is in contrast to the common practice of looking for *P*-values of 0.05 or less, and *significant* differences. In a loglinear model we are testing the difference between the expected counts from the model and the actual data, rather than comparing a model of independence with the observed counts as one would do in a traditional Chi-squared test.

When a range of non-significant, i.e., good-fitting models, have been generated, then one often wishes to compare the models. Hierarchical models can be compared statistically for how good the fit is between the generated expected frequencies and the observed cell frequencies, and this information can be made use of, when deciding upon a choice amongst several good-fitting models. However, non-hierarchical models allow no such comparison, since there are no statistical criteria for distinguishing between them.

One straightforward technique for making comparisons between models is to choose a number of hierarchical models from those which have non-significant G^2 values and evaluate them by examining the difference in their G^2 values. This is possible with hierarchical models because the difference between their G^2 values is also a G^2 value, thus when Model 1 is a subset of Model 2 the difference between the models can be determined using Equation 5.15.

$$G^2_{\text{Comparison}} = G^2_{\text{Model 1}} - G^2_{\text{Model 2}} \qquad (5.15)$$

where Model 1 is nested within Model 2.

$G^2_{\text{Comparison}}$ performs a similar function to partial-F in OLS regression and $-2LL_{\text{diff}}$ in logistic regression (see Sections 3.3.5 and 4.3.4). All techniques provide an indication of the significance of the difference in deviances between models and can be used as a basis for model building.

5.2.6   Goodness-of-fit Statistics and Residuals

In order to compare the two models, one subtracts the higher-order model's G^2 value from the lower-order, nested model's G^2 value, as in equation 5.15, and tests for significance with the χ^2 distribution using $df_{\text{comparison}}$ equal to the difference between the degrees of freedom for each of the two models. If the *difference* in G^2 between the two models turns out to be non-significant, then we can reject the more complex model in favour of the more parsimonious one. Note that whilst one looks for non-significance of G^2 to see if an individual model is a good fit of the observed frequencies, when comparing models one is looking for a *significant* $G^2_{\text{Comparison}}$ value to evaluate if one model is better than the other.

We shall return to our housing example, making use of the notation and methods of comparing hierarchically nested models. Table 5.4 provides hypothetical data for an examination of the associations between race (coded as 1 for *white* and 2 for *non-white*), housing, and illness (both coded into 3 ordered categorical variables). We shall illustrate a nominal treatment of the data here and return later to look at modelling with ordered categories. Amongst the many good-fitting models, one set of models we might wish to examine are those which test whether housing and illness are significantly associated once the associations between race and illness, and race and housing have been allowed for. In other words, we are examining whether the association between housing quality and illness is *conditionally independent*, given race.

Table 5.4: Contingency Table of Race, Housing and Illness

| | | Illness Category | | |
Race	Housing Quality	Low	Medium	High
White	poor	16	33	11
White	adequate	14	46	13
White	good	9	25	16
Non-White	poor	9	9	7
Non-White	adequate	11	20	10
Non-White	good	5	21	11

To examine the association between housing quality and illness, one compares a model with the housing and illness association term (HI, RH, RI) to a model which has the HI term removed (i.e., (RH, RI)). The statistics for the goodness-of-fit of these models are:

$$\text{model}(RH, RI): \quad G^2(RH, RI) = 10.155$$
$$df = 8, P = 0.254$$

$$\text{model}(HI, RH, RI): \quad G^2(HI, RH, RI) = 3.293$$
$$df = 4, P = 0.510$$

We compare the models to see if model (HI, RH, RI) provides a significant improvement over (RH, RI). This comparison is represented using the notation: $G^2[(RH, RI)|(HI, RH, RI)]$. For this example, $G^2_{\text{Comparison}}$ equals:

$$G^2[(RH, RI)|(HI, RH, RI)] = \quad 10.155 - 3.293 = 6.862$$
$$df = 8 - 4 = 4, \ P = 0.143.$$

Thus, for the sample chosen, one can conclude that there is support for the hypothesis that the association of housing and illness is conditionally independent, given race, since the model improvement obtained by including the HI term is not significantly different from the simpler (RH, RI) model. Agresti (1996, 1990) gives more discussion of models of conditional independence, and alternative comparisons with the saturated model.

Table 5.5: Data Matrix of Race, Housing and Illness

Race	Housing	Illness	Count	Fitted Value	Studentized Residual	Studentized Deviance Residual
1	1	1	16	12.787	1.235	1.189
1	1	2	33	34.098	−0.349	−0.351
1	1	3	11	13.115	−0.806	−0.829
1	2	1	14	15.557	−0.574	−0.584
1	2	2	46	41.486	1.376	1.352
1	2	3	13	15.956	−1.080	−1.116
1	3	1	9	10.656	−0.671	−0.689
1	3	2	25	28.415	−1.143	−1.168
1	3	3	16	10.929	2.035	1.902
2	1	1	9	6.068	1.571	1.464
2	1	2	9	12.136	−1.441	−1.511
2	1	3	7	6.796	0.105	0.105
2	2	1	11	9.951	0.492	0.483
2	2	2	20	19.903	0.039	0.039
2	2	3	10	11.146	−0.518	−0.528
2	3	1	5	8.981	−1.905	−2.080
2	3	2	21	17.961	1.248	1.215
2	3	3	11	10.058	0.435	0.428

$$\log \mu_{ijk} = \lambda + \lambda_i^{\text{Race}} + \lambda_j^{\text{Housing}} + \lambda_k^{\text{Illness}} + $$
$$\lambda_{ij}^{\text{Race,Housing}} + \lambda_{ik}^{\text{Race,Illness}} + \lambda_{jk}^{\text{Housing,Illness}}$$

Fitted values are provided by software packages and it is not necessary to calculate them manually from the parameter estimates. Table 5.5 gives the fitted values, studentized residuals and studentized deviance residuals for the (RH, RI) model. One can look to see which combinations of levels of the factors lead to large residuals, i.e., the cells that are outliers. This process is made easier by the use of these adjusted residuals, as in the bivariate example. Adjusted residuals larger than 1.96 in absolute magnitude indicate a poor model fit for that cell of the table, whilst the sign indicates the direction of the discrepancy. Negative values indicate expected values lower than observed, and positive values indicate expected values that are larger than the observed count for that cell. In this case, the cell for $R(2)H(3)I(1)$ appears to be around

-2 in value and is an indication that the model is underestimating occupants in this combination of factors. Cell $R(1)H(3)I(3)$, on the other hand, has a value of around 2, suggesting overestimation of occupants from this combination.

As discussed earlier, the adequacy of each particular model is tested by looking for a non-significant G^2 value. However, there can arise a problem reflecting the effect of sample size on the power of the test. For with large samples an alpha level of 0.05 may lead to models which are significantly different from the observed cell frequencies but which still provide a 'good fit'. This is because with large samples slight discrepancies can produce significant differences at $\alpha = 0.05$. Conversely with small samples, major discrepancies can still fail to produce a significant result, even if one chooses a higher criterion of $\alpha = 0.25$. The choice of alpha level becomes a matter of judgement, with smaller levels chosen for large samples, and larger levels chosen for small samples. Consideration of the parsimony of the model and the accuracy of the fitted counts can help in making such judgements. Where a non-standard *alpha* level is used, it is wise to explicitly state this alongside any reported results.

5.2.7   Explanatory Variables with Ordered Categories

When the variables in an analysis form ordered categories then one can test to see if there is a linear trend in the data, this can often produce a better fitting model than simply treating the variables as unordered categories. One does this by assigning scores to each level of a factor, so that each increasing level is given a higher score, the scale is then said to be *monotone*, i.e., non-decreasing.

Table 5.6 presents hypothetical data for a study of dopamine activity and ratings of psychosis for schizophrenic patients treated with neuroleptic medications, based on a research design by Sternberg, Van Kammen and Bunney (1982). Dopamine b-hydroxylase levels were measured in the cerebral spinal fluid of each patient, whilst the ratings of psychosis came from health professionals working with the patients. The dopamine levels have been grouped into five levels, between 0.01 and 0.35 dopamine units[2], and are treated as lying on an ordered categorical scale. Continuous variables, such as drug dosage, must be grouped in order to generate the contingency table required for the loglinear analysis. For this example we shall use five levels of drug dose and analyse the data using ordinal methods. One straightforward method of generating scores for the drug dose variable is to use the mean value on the original continuous scale for each level of the grouped ordered categories. We shall demonstrate the use of two additional scoring methods which can be used where the original continuous scale is unknown.

---

[2]The units of Dopamine b-hydroxylase are expressed in terms of $nmol/(ml)(hr)/(mg)$ of *protein*.

Table 5.6: Contingency Table of Dopamine Dosage and Psychosis

Dopamine	Psychosis	
	yes	no
0.010–0.015	46	26
0.015–0.020	35	28
0.020–0.025	39	35
0.025–0.030	28	35
0.030–0.035	26	32

Scoring Ordered Categorical Variables

The two scoring methods presented are *integer* scores in which the levels are assigned integers from 1 through to 5, giving equally spaced scores, and *midranks* in which the total count of each level of dopamine is used to generate a score based on the rank of the middle value. Integer scores are very easy to calculate and will not be described here (Table 5.7 shows dopamine scored using an integer method). To calculate the midranks, one begins by adding up the total counts for each ascending level of dopamine concentration, as follows:

0.01–0.015 $46 + 26 = 72$

0.015–0.02 $35 + 28 = 63$

0.02–0.025 $39 + 35 = 74$

0.025–0.03 $28 + 35 = 63$

0.03–0.035 $26 + 32 = 58$

The corresponding midranks are then calculated, using these totals, by adding the starting rank to the finishing rank of a particular level and then dividing by 2, giving us the following midranks

0.01–0.015 $(1 + 72)/2 = 36.5$

0.015–0.02 $((1 + 72) + (72 + 63))/2 = 104$

0.02–0.025 $((1 + 72 + 63) + (72 + 63 + 74))/2 = 172.5$

0.025–0.03 $((1 + 72 + 63 + 74) + (72 + 63 + 74 + 63))/2 = 241$

0.03–0.035 $((1+72+63+74+63)+(72+63+74+63+58))/2 = 301.5$

Integer scores and midranks are both straightforward to generate and provide us with simple means of running a *sensitivity analysis* to see if a statistical finding is robust across the scoring methods used for the ordered categorical variable. Other scoring methods may be produced by the researcher on the basis of theoretical considerations of the area of investigation, for additional comparison. A sensitivity analysis involves the comparison of the model statistics obtained when the data are coded in each of a number of different ways.

If the statistical values remain similar for each scoring method, then we can be confident that inferences and predictions made from our model are not just artifacts of the particular scoring method used. Through the judicious assignment of scores to the ranks, one obtains a monotonic scale which allows us to describe the nature of any association between factors, without assuming that the chosen numbers directly quantify an underlying scale of measurement. By making use of pre-assigned scores, one can estimate a single parameter for the associations between levels of the factors, rather than parameters for each combination of level of the factors. Thus, fewer degrees of freedom are needed and the test is more powerful at detecting associations in the data.

Bivariate Example with Explanatory Variables having Ordered Categories

Once Dopamine usage has been scored, we generate scores for the presence and absence of psychosis by dummy coding it as 0 and 1. Having assigned scores to two ordered categorical variables, one creates an additional term in the model reflecting the *linear* × *linear* association ($L \times L$) between these variables, known as $u_i v_j$. This is a covariate created by multiplying the scores of each variable together to obtain a value for each cell of the table. In Tables 5.7 and 5.8, we see two different sets of uv values representing the two scoring methods used for dopamine. The model for the linear×linear association is shown in Equation 5.16.

Table 5.7: Data Matrix for the Linear×Linear Model of Dopamine Dosage and Psychosis, using Integer Scores

Dopamine	Score	Psychosis	Count	Fitted Value	Studentized Residual	Studentized Deviance Residual
1	1	0	46	44.82	0.463	0.461
1	1	1	26	27.18	−0.463	−0.466
2	2	0	35	36.15	−0.344	−0.346
2	2	1	28	26.85	0.344	0.342
3	3	0	39	38.74	0.069	0.069
3	3	1	35	35.26	−0.069	−0.069
4	4	0	28	29.78	−0.541	−0.547
4	4	1	35	33.22	0.541	0.537
5	5	0	26	24.51	0.601	0.596
5	5	1	32	33.49	−0.601	−0.606

$$\log \mu_{ij} = \lambda + \lambda_i^{\text{Dopamine}} + \lambda_j^{\text{Psychosis}} + \beta u_i v_j$$

The term $\beta u_i v_j$ in Equation 5.16 represents the departure of the model from independence, and the value of β, its confidence intervals and associated

$$\log \mu_{ij} = \lambda + \lambda_i^{\text{Dopamine}} + \lambda_j^{\text{Psychosis}} + \beta u_i v_j \qquad (5.16)$$

Table 5.8: Data Matrix for the Linear×Linear Model of Dopamine Dosage and Psychosis, using Midrank Scores

Dopamine	Score	Psychosis	Count	Fitted Value	Studentized Residual	Studentized Deviance Residual
1	36.5	0	46	44.91	0.432	0.430
1	36.5	1	26	27.09	−0.432	−0.434
2	104.0	0	35	36.18	−0.354	−0.356
2	104.0	1	28	26.82	0.354	0.352
3	172.5	0	39	38.66	0.089	0.089
3	172.5	1	35	35.34	−0.089	−0.089
4	241.0	0	28	29.62	−0.496	−0.501
4	241.0	1	35	33.38	0.496	0.492
5	301.5	0	26	24.62	0.544	0.539
5	301.5	1	32	33.38	−0.544	−0.548

$$\log \mu_{ij} = \lambda + \lambda_i^{\text{Dopamine}} + \lambda_j^{\text{Psychosis}} + \beta u_i v_j$$

information, are produced as part of the output from software — one enters the two factors into the model along with the covariate. For integer scores we find that $\beta = 0.203$, with standard error of 0.080, and confidence intervals of $(0.05, 0.36)$. The goodness-of-fit statistic G^2 is 0.531, with $df = 3$ and $P = 0.912$. For midrank scores we obtain $\beta = 0.0031$, with a standard error of 0.001, and confidence intervals of $(7.05E - 04, 5.413E - 03)$. The goodness-of-fit statistic G^2 is 0.468, with $df = 3$ and $P = 0.926$. Note that the value of β differs in both cases, reflecting the different scale used for dopamine, but that the goodness-of-fit statistics are similar. The independence model (i.e., the model (D, P) with no association term) gives $G^2 = 7.044$, with $df = 4$ and $P = 0.137$, demonstrating a poorer fit.

The model for equally spaced scores is tested for a significant improvement in fit by taking its G^2 and degrees-of-freedom away from that of the model with independent main effects, the independence model (D, P), i.e.,

$$
\begin{aligned}
G^2(D, P | D, P, L \times L) &= G^2(D, P) - G^2(D, P, L \times L) \\
&= 7.044 - 0.531 \\
&= 6.513.
\end{aligned}
$$

with $df = 4 - 3 = 1$, giving $P = 0.011$, a statistically significant improvement. Similarly, for midranks we obtain $G^2(D, P|D, P, L \times L) = 7.044 - 0.468 = 6.576$, with $df = 4 - 3 = 1$, and $P = 0.010$, again, including the linear×linear term leads to a statistically significant improvement over the independence model (D, P). Note how one tests the fit for the linear×linear association model by comparing it to the independence model, in a similar fashion to comparing nested hierarchical models for nominal data. For integer scores, the estimated local odds ratio and confidence intervals are obtained by simply taking the exponent of β and its confidence intervals, i.e., e^β. Note how this approach allows one to examine associations with models that would otherwise be saturated if their nominal equivalents were used, i.e., the (XY) saturated model. There is a more straightforward interpretation of the odds ratios from integer scoring methods, one simply uses the parameter estimates directly. Therefore, if the goodness-of-fit statistics for the different scoring methods is similar, it makes good sense to use the integer scores (see Agresti, 1984 for further discussion of the interpretation of scoring methods with ordered categorical data).

5.2.8 Associations Between Nominal and Ordered Categorical Variables

When one of the factors is a multicategorical nominal variable and the other an ordered categorical variable, we have what is known as a *column-effects* model or *row-effects* model, depending upon the variable which has ordered categories. In this case one generates a covariate which is a copy of the scores used in the ordered categorical variable and enters this as an interaction term with the nominal variable. The variate with its model coefficient is referred to as βu for row-effects and βv for column-effects, reflecting the fact that only u or v scores are used in the model, unlike the βuv of the linear×linear. For a bivariate model the design consists of the terms,

$$\text{Constant} + X + Y + (X \times v)$$

where Y has ordered categories and v is the covariate representing its scores. Instead of one parameter for βuv for the linear×linear association model, one obtains one parameter for each level of X with the interaction term of X×v. This model retains the advantage of an interaction term that is unsaturated, unlike the (XY) model for nominal variables.

Consider the data presented in Table 5.9 from a study by McLean and Hakstian (1979). This is a study of four treatments of depression and patients' subsequent scores on the Beck Depression Inventory (B). The treatment factor (T) is nominal and has four levels, psychotherapy, relaxation therapy, drug therapy, and behaviour therapy, whilst the B scores are grouped into three

Table 5.9: Contingency Table of Treatment and Depression

	Beck's Depression Inventory		
Treatment	Low	Medium	High
Psychotherapy	11	20	13
Relaxation training	12	23	8
Drug therapy	12	27	10
Behaviour therapy	21	18	3

levels, giving an ordered categorical variable. If the B categories form the table column, then this is known as a column-effects model. The corresponding design is

$$\text{Constant} + T + B + (T \times v).$$

In Tables 5.10 and 5.11 two scoring methods have been used for B, integer scores and midranks, allowing a sensitivity analysis of the scoring method.

Table 5.10: Data Matrix for the Column-Effects Model of Treatment and Depression, using Integer Scores

Treatment	B Level	Score	Count	Fitted Value	Studentized Residual	Studentized Deviance Residual
1	1	1	11	9.601	0.991	0.968
1	2	2	20	22.799	−0.991	−1.012
1	3	3	13	11.601	0.991	0.972
2	1	1	12	12.436	−0.313	−0.314
2	2	2	23	22.127	0.313	0.311
2	3	3	8	8.436	−0.313	−0.315
3	1	1	12	12.800	−0.548	−0.554
3	2	2	27	25.400	0.548	0.543
3	3	3	10	10.800	−0.548	−0.555
4	1	1	21	21.163	−0.137	−0.137
4	2	2	18	17.674	0.137	0.137
4	3	3	3	3.163	−0.137	−0.138

$$\log \mu_{ij} = \lambda + \lambda_i^{\text{Treatment}} + \lambda_j^{\text{Depression}} + \beta u_i v_j$$

The column-effects model for integer scores of B gives $G^2 = 1.014$, with $df = 3$ and $P = 0.798$, and for midranks we obtain $G^2 = 1.187$, with $df = 3$

and $P = 0.756$, both of which provide similar model fits. In comparison, the independence model (T, B) has the design Constant $+ T + B$ and gives $G^2 = 12.830$, with $df = 6$ and $P = 0.046$, indicating a poor fit with the data. The inclusion of the association term $T \times v$ therefore appears to have improved the model fit (a demonstration of how to derive these figures from software is given in Section 5.4).

Table 5.11: Data Matrix for the Column-Effects Model of Treatment and Depression, using Midrank Scores

Treatment	B Level	Score	Count	Fitted Value	Studentized Residual	Studentized Deviance Residual
1	1	150.5	11	9.597	1.085	1.060
1	2	78.5	20	23.060	−1.085	−1.110
1	3	17.5	13	11.344	1.085	1.060
2	1	150.5	12	12.396	−0.312	−0.314
2	2	78.5	23	22.136	0.312	0.310
2	3	17.5	8	8.468	−0.312	−0.315
3	1	150.5	12	12.680	−0.511	−0.516
3	2	78.5	27	25.518	0.511	0.506
3	3	17.5	10	10.802	−0.511	−0.518
4	1	150.5	21	21.327	−0.306	−0.307
4	2	78.5	18	17.286	0.306	0.304
4	3	17.5	3	3.386	−0.306	−0.312

$$\log \mu_{ij} = \lambda + \lambda_i^{\text{Treatment}} + \lambda_j^{\text{Depression}} + \beta u_i v_j$$

It is interesting to note the representation of the relationship between T and B scores for nominal, column-effects and linear$\times$linear models. Treating both variables as nominal, the association term is represented by six terms, with B treated as ordered and T as nominal, the association is represented by three terms, and if both are treated as ordered (linear$\times$linear), then the association is represented by one term. Representing the association between the variables using fewer parameters enables non-saturated models to be constructed and the resulting reduction in the degrees of freedom allow for more parsimony.

Siegal and Castellan (1988) present an analysis of these data using Pearson's X^2 test, and it is worth the reader comparing their hypothesis testing approach. They obtain a value of $X^2 = 12.80$ with $df = 6$ and $P \leq 0.05$, supporting rejection of the null hypothesis of independence between treatment and depression. The column-effects model, developed here within the loglinear framework, has the advantage that one obtains parameter estimates and odds ratios, which also take into account the ordinality of the depression score groupings, as well as 95% confidence intervals for the parameter estimates —

the final result is a model which can be used for prediction, not just testing departures from independence in the manner of the traditional Pearson X^2 test.

5.2.9   Homogeneous Linear×Linear Associations

A variety of models exist which allow for linear×linear associations involving three or more factors, most of which are beyond the scope of this book, however we consider a useful case of two ordered categorical variables and a third nominal variable. The first two factors might correspond to the association we are interested in with the third factor being a control variable, such as the setting or region of the sample. An association between the two ordered categorical variables that is constant across the levels of the control variable is known as a *homogeneous* linear×linear association, i.e., the nature of linear relationship is the same regardless of the level of the control variable. The model that only considers the factors as nominal would be (XY, XZ, YZ), giving the model:

$$\log \mu_{ijk} = \mu + \lambda_i^X + \lambda_j^Y + \lambda_k^Z + \lambda_{ij}^{XY} + \lambda_{ik}^{XZ} + \lambda_{jk}^{YZ} \qquad (5.17)$$

A more parsimonious model is achieved by replacing the λ_{ij}^{XY} with the linear×linear term $\beta u_i v_j$, giving the model:

$$\log \mu_{ijk} = \mu + \lambda_i^X + \lambda_j^Y + \lambda_k^Z + \beta u_i v_j + \lambda_{ik}^{XZ} + \lambda_{jk}^{YZ} \qquad (5.18)$$

The addition of the $\beta u_i v_j$ results in an increase in parsimony because the model states that the departures from independence are captured within the single linear×linear term rather than the multi-parameter λ_{ij}^{XY}.

As an example, we return to the data presented in Table 5.5, investigating the association between housing, illness and race. Earlier we compared the model with the housing and illness term (HI, RH, RI) to that of H-I conditional independence (RH, RI), with nominal loglinear models. Recall that we obtained

$$G^2[(RH, RI)|(HI, RH, RI)] \;=\; 10.155 - 3.293 = 6.862$$

$$df = 8 - 4 = 4, P = 0.143$$

indicating that no significant improvement is obtained by using the more complex model. In the present case we will include a linear×linear term for the

H-I association, since housing and illness both have ordered categories. For simplicity of illustration we use integer scores — ideally one would also generate the midranks for each, and any other relevant scoring method, to test the sensitivity of the model to scoring method, however, testing combinations of each variable with the different scoring methods would require a number of analyses. Where one scoring method provides a great improvement in the fit of the model over the others, then we have to take into account theoretical considerations about whether such an improvement makes sense, given what we know about the phenomenon. Agresti (1996) gives a nice example from the ethology literature with some data from the social behaviour of horseshoe crabs. In this case the colour of their shells can either be coded with ordered categories for light to dark (1, 2, 3, 4), or in a binary fashion (1, 1, 1, 0) for light versus dark. The latter binary coding arises from his examination of the data, collapsing the first three levels together. Both scoring methods support a hypothesis that female dark coloured crabs are less likely to have male crabs residing nearby than their lighter coloured counterparts. This might lead an ethologist to consider the adaptive significance of lighter coloured female crabs — perhaps a greater degree of camouflage and protection from predation.

The design for the homogeneous linear×linear association model, with our three variables of housing, illness and race, becomes:

$$\text{Constant} + R + H + I + uv + RH + RI$$

which consists of the three main effects, R, H and I, the uv covariate representing the association between housing and illness, and the two-way association terms RH and RI. Using computer software we find that:

$$G^2[(RH, RI)|(L \times L, RH, RI)] \quad = 10.155 - 5.166 = 4.989$$

$$df = 8 - 7 = 1, P = 0.026.$$

By modelling the association between health and illness with a linear×linear term we have obtained a model which is a significant improvement over the *H-I* independence model ($P = 0.026$), compared to the non-significant improvement of the nominal (HI, RH, RI) model over that of *H-I* independence ($P = 0.125$). Thus one can see that by taking into account the ordinality of housing and illness a more powerful model is obtained which is sensitive to the association between housing quality and illness. Using a strictly nominal approach, this significant relationship in the data would have been missed.

5.2.10   Logit Analysis — Evaluating a Binary Response Variable

So far we have considered the case where the cell frequencies for each combination of explanatory variables are treated as the response variable. In this case the research question is one of assessing the degree of association of the explanatory variables in accounting for an obtained pattern of cell frequencies. However, there are many examples in the social sciences where one particular variable is of interest, measured across several levels, and it is the cell frequencies in each of these levels that we are interested in predicting. For example, one might wish to predict choice of radio station by teenage listeners on the basis of various measures of programmed content, gender of presenter, ratio of talk to music, etc.

Already in this book we have outlined how a regression analysis may be carried out with a dichotomous response variable using a logit link between the random component and the systematic, linear component of the model — the logistic regression technique. The logistic regression procedure has the advantage that continuous as well as categorical explanatory variables can be included in the model, but has the drawback that ordered categorical variables must either be treated as continuous, or as nominal with some loss of information. In addition, most commonly available computer software only allows for two levels of a categorical response variable in a logistic regression[3]. When all the variables are categorical, or the response variable has more than two levels, then a variant of the loglinear procedure with a logit link can be used with readily available software, though less conveniently than with software capable of running multicategory logistic regressions.

Let us consider a model of undergraduate social science course choices, psychology versus politics, with age, gender, and ethnic origin as explanatory variables. Our response variable is the frequency with which each category of social science is chosen for each combination of explanatory variables — this is readily expressed in terms of the odds of doing psychology versus politics. For this example we have treated age as a factor with four unordered levels, noting the consequent loss of information by this recoding of the data. When considering models with a logit analysis, one is always looking for the combinations of variables that include the response variable as part of each effect. Thus, to examine the effect of age upon course choice one examines the social science×age association. This is because it is the *change* in the probability of a student choosing each category of social science, as we move across the levels of the factor age, that is our concern. If we are interested in the interaction between age and gender as they affect course choice then it is the social science×age×gender interaction which we look at. The higher level interaction between age, gender, and ethnic origin upon course choice is examined by

---

[3]A model suitable for logistic regression with a response variable having ordered categories is the proportional odds model. Details of this model are given in Agresti (1996) and McCullagh and Nelder (1989), though it is only available in some software packages.

looking at the social science×age×gender×ethnic origin interaction. In other words you look at one level of association higher than the combination of explanatory variables you are interested in — the association with the added response variable term. In addition one adds in a general interaction term for just the relationships amongst the explanatory variables which fixes the values of the explanatory variables to those observed, resulting in a regression analysis. This additional term results in a loglinear model that has the same fit as a logit model. The logit model has fewer terms since the associations between the response variable and the explanatory variables are not made explicit.

Here are formal loglinear representations of main effects logit models for 3, 4 and 5 explanatory variables $(A–E)$, and one response variable (Y):

$$3 \text{ explanatory variables} \qquad (AY, BY, CY, ABC)$$

$$4 \text{ explanatory variables} \qquad (AY, BY, CY, DY, ABCD)$$

$$5 \text{ explanatory variables} \qquad (AY, BY, CY, DY, EY, ABDCE)$$

Note the final addition of a term for the interaction amongst just the explanatory variables which gives us numerically equivalent results to the corresponding logit regression models.

5.2.11 Multicategory Response Variables with Nominal and Ordered Categories

Nominal Response Variables: Baseline Category Logits

As we mentioned before, most computer software for logistic regression only allow binary response variables, with just a few packages offering the sophistication of allowing the analysis of multicategory response variables. One can get around this limitation for data with explanatory variables having nominal or ordered categories by using the equivalence of certain loglinear and logit models. From the example above, to evaluate a main-effects logit model of three explanatory variables and one response variable, one can use a loglinear model with four factors:

$$(AY, BY, CY, ABC)$$

where Y is the response variable and A, B and C are nominal explanatory variables. One defines a baseline, or reference, category, and obtains the odds of each category compared to the baseline. Some software packages assume a default category such as the largest coded category, or the first or last category, in which case one may need to recode the categories to obtain the baseline category of interest. In the case of multicategory nominal response variables, there is no natural ordering to aid in this, so the choice remains somewhat arbitrary. However, sometimes theoretical considerations allow one to make a sensible choice, perhaps setting the reference category to the 'control' response, e.g., response variables with a comparison of the odds of each of three methods of birth control compared to a baseline category of 'none', or perhaps choice of beer, wine, spirit, compared to 'soft drink'. In such cases the model is a straightforward extension of the loglinear version of the logit analysis with an interpretation in terms of odds of each category of the response variable relative to the baseline category.

Ordered Response Variables

Earlier in this book we considered the issue of ordered categorical response variables which could be pre-assigned scores and treated as continuous variables within the ordinary least-squares framework (See Chapter 3). That was with the proviso that the scores could be seen as representing some kind of underlying continuum, and were measured at a sufficient number of levels to assess Normality and constant variance. When this is not the case, one can use a baseline category logit model, ignoring the ordinality of the data. By developing linear×linear association models, one can extend this framework to deal with ordered variables having more than two categories. However, a further technique is to use a model that deals with the response variable within a *cumulative* framework, considering each rank in relation to those that precede (or follow) it. A number of sophisticated models are available for this purpose, but not many are readily available in standard software. For this reason we present a model which is calculated as a series of binary logits, where the statistical terms are then combined, making use of the additive property of G^2. This technique, known as a *continuation ratio* logit, makes use of the extra information provided by the ordinality of the response variable, but does not require the pre-assignment of scores to the ranks. This is particularly useful where the response measure is ordered, but score assignment is not obvious, e.g., undamaged, repairable, destroyed, for a variable measuring the status of packages arriving from a parcel delivery company. Logistic regression software could also be used for this analysis, but here we use a loglinear approach to constructing the logits. We will now compare the two approaches for modelling the ordinality of two variables in a bivariate example, firstly using a linear×linear association model outlined earlier, and secondly a continuation ratio model.

Table 5.12 gives results of a hypothetical study into the effect of alcohol consumption upon self-reports of the level of reduction in sexual libido in male drinkers. For the purposes of illustration, alcohol is grouped into three levels of

Table 5.12: Contingency Table of Alcohol Consumption and Libido

Alcohol	Libido		
	Low	Medium	High
0–30	1	10	12
31–60	4	13	7
≥ 61	5	15	7

0–30, 31–60, 61 or more units[4] in the seven days week, whilst the self-reports of libido are recorded on a categorical scale of low, medium and high. It is not clear what scoring method is appropriate for libido, though it obviously has an order. We shall initially try equally spaced scores for both variables in a linear×linear model, before trying a continuation ratio model which makes use of ordinality, but is unaffected by the spacing between the scores. The linear×linear model is shown in Equation 5.19,

$$\log \mu_{ij} = \lambda + \lambda_i^{\text{Alcohol}} + \lambda_j^{\text{Libido}} + \beta u_i v_j \qquad (5.19)$$

with the $u_i v_j$ term representing the covariate produced by multiplying the scorings of each level of the two variables (See Table 5.13). Using computer software (see Section 5.4) we obtain $G^2 = 1.040$, with $df = 3$, giving $P = 0.792$, which indicates a good fit. An examination of the adjusted residuals in Table 5.13 confirms this with the most discrepant cell containing a residual of 0.83, well below the level of 2 in absolute magnitude which indicates a significant discrepancy. Thus, we can conclude that the data support the linear×linear model of an association between alcohol consumption and libido.

Having confirmed that the model for a linear×linear association provides a good fit, we can use the parameter estimates from the model to make predictions about local odds ratios — how the odds change as one moves across adjacent cells in the contingency table. These parameter estimates are provided as part of the output from standard statistical software. The parameter β directly gives us the exponent of the local odds ratio, $\beta = -0.476$, with a standard error of 0.231 (β is the parameter associated with the linear×linear term $u_i v_j$). This allows us to calculate the local odds ratio of $\hat{\theta}$, which equals 0.622 (i.e., $e^{-0.476}$), and the confidence intervals are given by calculating $-0.476 \pm 1.96(0.231)$, i.e., -0.929, -0.023 on the log scale. Confidence intervals for the local odds ratios are calculated as being 0.394 and 0.977 ($e^{-0.929}, e^{-0.023}$).

With the continuation ratio model, one begins by collapsing the data into binary response variables, each pair representing one step along the ordered

---

[4]1 unit = 8–10 grams ethanol, e.g., 1/2 pint beer, 1 glass of wine, or 1 measure of spirits.

Table 5.13: Data Matrix for the Linear×Linear Model of Alcohol Consumption and Libido, using Integer Scores

Alcohol	Libido	Count	Fitted Value	Studentized Residual	Studentized Deviance Residual
1	1	1	1.483	−0.551	−0.585
1	2	10	10.324	−0.183	−0.184
1	3	12	11.193	0.631	0.624
2	1	4	2.911	0.832	0.787
2	2	13	12.598	0.202	0.201
2	3	7	8.490	−0.784	−0.809
3	1	5	5.606	−0.528	−0.538
3	2	15	15.078	−0.040	−0.040
3	3	7	6.316	0.578	0.568

$$\log \mu_{ij} = \lambda + \lambda_i^{\text{Alcohol}} + \lambda_j^{\text{Libido}} + \beta u_i v_j$$

scale, to model a series of logits. When comparing each level to those above, we obtain the following logits:

$$\log \left(\frac{\pi_1}{\pi_2 + \cdots + \pi_j} \right), \log \left(\frac{\pi_2}{\pi_3 + \cdots + \pi_j} \right), \ldots, \log \left(\frac{\pi_{j-1}}{\pi_j} \right) \qquad (5.20)$$

where π refers to the probability of an event happening.

Table 5.14 gives the collapsed response variable with the frequency count indicating a comparison of low libido with a collapsing of the counts in categories 2 and 3, i.e., either medium or high libido. The model $\log \mu_{ij} = \lambda + \lambda_i^{\text{Alcohol}} + \lambda_j^{\text{Libido}} + \beta u_i v_j$, using these categories gives us $G^2 = 0.750$, $df = 1$, $P = 0.386$.

Table 5.14: Contingency Table for First Cut-Point of Continuation Ratio Model of Alcohol Consumption and Libido, Low versus Medium or High

Alcohol	Libido	
	Low	Medium or High
0–30	1	22
31–60	4	20
≥ 61	5	22

In Table 5.15, the comparison is between the higher two levels of libido (medium and high). The model $\log \mu_{ij} = \lambda + \lambda_i^{\text{Alcohol}} + \lambda_j^{\text{Libido}} + \beta u_i v_j$, using these two categories gives us $G^2 = 0.345, df = 1, P = 0.557$.

Table 5.15: Contingency Table for Second Cut-Point of Continuation Ratio Model of Alcohol Consumption and Libido, Medium versus High

Alcohol	Libido	
	Medium	High
0–30	10	12
31–60	13	7
≥ 61	15	7

Having calculated individual logits for each of the continuation ratios one can then combine them to obtain an overall value of G^2 for the model using Equation 5.21.

$$
\begin{aligned}
G^2_{\text{Total}} &= G^2_{1vs23} + G^2_{2vs3} \\
&= 0.750 + 0.345 = 1.095 \\
df &= 1 + 1 = 2, P = 0.578
\end{aligned}
\tag{5.21}
$$

where G^2_{1vs23} is the value of G^2 comparing groups 1 with 2 and 3, and G^2_{2vs3} is the value of G^2 comparing groups 2 with 3.

The significance of the overall G^2 value ($P = 0.578$) indicates a reasonable fit for the overall continuation ratio model. An examination of the adjusted residuals for each logit, given in Tables 5.16 and 5.17, indicates no discrepant cells with all values well under 2 in absolute magnitude.

The parameter β provides the values for the exponent of the local odds ratio, one for each logit analysis carried out. For the level 1 versus 2, 3 comparison we obtain $\beta = -0.637$, with a standard error of 0.456, giving a local odds ratio, $\hat{\theta}$, of $e^{-0.637} = 0.529$, with confidence intervals of $-1.530, 0.256$ ($-0.637 \pm 1.96(0.456)$) on the log scale. The confidence intervals for the local odds ratios are 0.217, 1.291 ($e^{-1.530}, e^{0.256}$), compared to the predicted value of $\hat{\theta} = 0.529$. With the level 2 versus 3 comparison we obtain $\beta = -0.481$, with a standard error of 0.316, giving a local odds ratio, $\hat{\theta}$, of $e^{-0.481} = 0.618$, with confidence intervals of $-1.100, 0.138$ ($-0.481 \pm 1.96(0.316)$) measured on the log scale. The confidence intervals of the local odds ratios for this logit are 0.333, 1.149 ($e^{-1.100}, e^{0.138}$), against a predicted value of $\hat{\theta} = 0.618$. The wide confidence intervals for the continuation ratio model, either side of 1.0, suggest a non-significant improvement over the no-association model for the

Table 5.16: Data Matrix for First Cut-Point of Continuation Ratio Model of Alcohol Consumption and Libido, Low versus Medium or High

Alcohol	Libido	Count	Fitted Value	Studentized Residual	Studentized Deviance Residual
1	1	1	1.554	−0.870	−0.931
1	2	22	21.446	0.872	0.869
2	1	4	2.892	0.873	0.825
2	2	20	21.108	−0.874	−0.882
3	1	5	5.554	−0.874	−0.889
3	2	22	21.446	0.872	0.869

$$\log \mu_{ij} = \lambda + \lambda_i^{\text{Alcohol}} + \lambda_j^{\text{Libido}} + \beta u_i v_j$$

new contingency tables incorporating the cut-points (see Section 5.4 to see how all the above statistics can be generated using software).

As noted above, the continuation ratio logit does not require the use of pre-assigned scores for the level of the response variable in making use of the extra information provided by the ordinality of the data. This is useful when there is no clear way to assign scores to response variable, yet one still obtains odds ratios and confidence intervals that reflect this ordinality. However, continuation ratio logit models result in a local odds ratio for each separate logit analysis so they are less parsimonious than the single local odds ratio obtained with a linear×linear association model. In addition, the confidence intervals for the local odds ratio of the linear×linear model are considerably narrower, 0.394, 0.977 compared to 0.217, 1.293 and 0.333, 1.374, reflecting its utilization of the additional information available in scoring the ordered categorical response scale.

Table 5.17: Data Matrix for Second Cut-Point of Continuation Ratio Model of Alcohol Consumption and Libido, Medium versus High

Alcohol	Libido Reduction	Count	Fitted Value	Studentized Residual	Studentized Deviance Residual
1	1	10	10.527	−0.585	−0.590
1	2	12	11.473	0.585	0.580
2	1	13	11.947	0.585	0.576
2	2	7	8.053	−0.585	−0.598
3	1	15	15.527	−0.585	−0.588
3	2	7	6.473	0.585	0.577

$$\log \mu_{ij} = \lambda + \lambda_i^{\text{Alcohol}} + \lambda_j^{\text{Libido}} + \beta u_i v_j$$

We shall now summarize the predictions obtained by calculating the local odds ratios and their 95% confidence intervals. The linear×linear model tells us that the odds of reporting a lower libido category compared to the next higher libido category are in the ratio of 0.394–0.977 as one compares a lower alcohol intake to alcohol intake in the next higher category. The single local odds ratio is reflected in the generality of the prediction, it is the same whether one compares the odds of low libido to medium libido whilst looking at low versus medium drinkers, or whether one compares medium libido to high libido for medium versus high drinkers. The predictions arising from the continuation ratio logit models are more specific (though wider in 95% confidence intervals) since two separate logits are calculated. The first logit analysis predicts that the odds of low libido versus medium or high libido are in the ratio of 0.217–1.293 as one compares a lower alcohol intake to the next higher alcohol intake category. Whilst the second logit analysis predicts that the odds of medium libido versus high libido are in the ratio of 0.333–1.374 comparing a lower alcohol intake to the next higher alcohol intake. Since the 95% confidence intervals of the local odds ratios from the continuation ratio logit analyses are either side of 1.0 in value, one cannot reliably predict the direction of the ratio of the odds. This is not the case with the linear×linear model which has narrower intervals that are both below 1.0 in value, suggesting a consistent fall in the odds of reporting a higher libido versus a lower libido, when one compares a lower level of alcohol intake with the next higher level of alcohol intake, i.e., libido level decreases as alcohol consumption increases.

This example has focused on a two-variable model, however it is possible to extend the approach to multiple variables. For example, three-way interactions can be explored using a variety of models that extend the linear×linear model to three ordered categorical variables. One such model is shown in Equation 5.22.

$$\log \mu_{ijk} = \lambda + \lambda_i^X + \lambda_j^Y + \lambda_k^Z + \lambda_{ij}^{XY} + \lambda_{ik}^{XZ} + \lambda_{jk}^{YZ} + \beta u_i v_j w_k \qquad (5.22)$$

Whenever, i, j or k have more than two levels, the model is unsaturated. The variables holding the scores for each factor are multiplied together to generate a new variable for the term $u_i v_j w_k$, in a manner analogous to the $u_i v_j$ term in the linear×linear model. The three-way interaction term is then entered along with the main-effects, and the two-way association terms, into the statistical software to obtain the corresponding parameters estimates and model-fit statistics. If the model is a good fit, and significantly better than the two-way association model, then we can say that the local odds ratio across any two of the variables changes linearly across the level of the third variable. This, together with other ordinal models for investigating interactions and associations with three factors, are described in Agresti (1990). Fienberg (1980) gives considerable coverage of continuation ratio models.

5.3 Summary

Loglinear statistical methods provide a model-building approach to the analysis of frequency data and are of particular utility with multivariate data. Certain classes of loglinear model are equivalent to logit models, where one of the measured factors is designated the response variable and a model is built of its relationship to the explanatory variables. Unlike most software for logistic regression, loglinear software packages are not restricted to binary response variables and allow multicategory logit models to be developed, providing that the data can be reasonably grouped into a contingency table. Disadvantages over the logistic regression methods are the increased number of parameters generated in the output, and the possibility of sparse tables when grouping continuous variables.

By using a logarithmic link between the random component of the response variable and the model's systematic component, the linear structure of the explanatory variables, we remove the assumptions of Normality and constant variance of the response variable. Instead we generate linear models that predict values upon the logarithmic scale and convert them to the original frequency scale by taking their exponents. Odds ratios between adjacent cells of a contingency table are obtained in a similar fashion. By highlighting the distinction between the linear model of the systematic component, and a separate link function to the random component, we have sought to demonstrate how categorical nominal and ordered categorical data can be analysed within the same framework as ordinary least-squares regression, i.e., generalized linear models. By this means we have a much more sophisticated analytic technique than traditional bivariate methods, that allows both the significance testing of hypotheses, as well as the generation of predictive models with their confidence intervals.

Traditionally, nominal categorical data have been analysed in the social sciences with bivariate methods such as Pearson X^2 for independent samples, and Fisher's exact test. Whilst ordered categorical variables have tended to be analysed with non-parametric tests such as the Wilcoxon matched-pairs signed-ranks test and the Mann–Whitney U test, or justifications have been found for their inclusion in linear parametric methods, usually on the grounds of the purported test's robustness to violations of assumptions. Now that sophisticated methods are available for the multivariate analysis of categorical data we recommend a pragmatic approach: if the data are derived from the summation, or combination of a series of ordered categorical scales, then the number of discrete points is quite large and these combined values can be given numbers and treated as continuous data, screened as such, and entered into models requiring linear parametric assumptions, e.g., ordinary least-squares regression, factor analysis, etc. When the number of categories is fewer, then the alternative is to use the extensions to the categorical models for variables with ordered categories. Through the extension of loglinear models to examine linear×linear associations, the additional information available in ordered categorical variables can be utilized, whilst mixtures of nominal and ordered categorical variables can be examined through row and column-effects models. These are straightforward for bivariate data, though rapidly increase in complexity as more variables with ordered categories are added.

5.4   Statistical Software Commands

5.4.1   SPSS

Detailed discussions of the SPSS procedures outlined in this section can be found in the appropriate SPSS manuals (see, for example, SPSS Inc., 1996b).

Bivariate Methods

Input the first three columns of data from Table 5.2 exactly as shown. Weight cases using the commands:

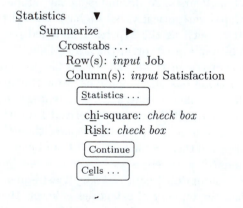

The values of the count variable are used as case weights. For example, a case which has a value of 10 for the count variable will represent 10 cases in the weighted data file. Following this, one can proceed with computing the traditional bivariate examples outlined in this chapter. The following commands can be used to obtain Pearson X^2, G^2, the studentized residuals[5] and the odds ratio and associated confidence intervals.

<u>S</u>tatistics   ▼
    S<u>u</u>mmarize   ▶
        <u>C</u>rosstabs ...
            R<u>o</u>w(s): *input* Job
            <u>C</u>olumn(s): *input* Satisfaction
                            <u>S</u>tatistics ...
                c<u>h</u>i-square: *check box*
                R<u>i</u>sk: *check box*
            Continue
            C<u>e</u>lls ...

---

[5]SPSS calculates *adjusted standardized residuals* which are identical to the *studentized residuals* referred to in the text.

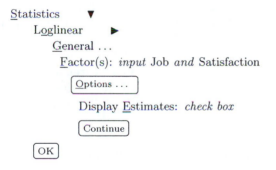

Adj. standardized: *check box*

Continue

OK

It should be noted that due to rounding error there may be some minor discrepancies between the statistics output by SPSS and those quoted in the chapter.

Loglinear Analysis

SPSS for Windows offers three versions of Loglinear analysis: General, Logit, and Model Selection. Model Selection offers a restricted analysis for hierarchical models with nominal explanatory variables, and Logit allows a simplified input for building logit models within a loglinear framework. For reasons of clarity, all the examples will be discussed with input suitable for the General Loglinear procedure, since it can deal with all of the situations described in this chapter.

A Saturated Model

To obtain the results shown in Table 5.3, input the data from Table 5.2 as above, remembering to weight the cases.

Statistics   ▼
    Loglinear   ▶
        General ...
            Factor(s): *input* Job *and* Satisfaction
                Options ...
                    Display Estimates: *check box*
                        Continue
    OK

Each parameter in the model is defined in the output and statistics are provided for the estimate and standard errors. You will note that the values computed by SPSS are very close but are not identical to those in the table, as SPSS uses a slightly different procedure for calculating values for saturated models than does GLIM — the package used to derive the values quoted in the text[6].

---

[6]You will note that SPSS adds 0.5 to the cell counts for saturated models to enable initial approximations. This default value can be overridden by changing the Delta criterion in the Options menu (SPSS Inc., 1996b).

Loglinear Analysis: an Unsaturated Model

Input the first four columns of data from Table 5.5. Remember to weight the
cases using the variable Count. To obtain the fitted values and the studentized residuals (adjusted residuals) for the model (RH, RI), use the following
commands:

Statistics   ▼
  Loglinear   ►
   General ...
    Factor(s): *input* Housing, Illness *and* Race
     | Save ... |
      Adjusted residuals: *check box*
      Predicted values: *check box*
      | Continue |
     | Model ... |
      Custom: *check box*
      Build term(s):
       Main effects: *input* Housing, Illness *and* Race
       Interaction: *input* Housing*Race *and* Illness*Race
      | Continue |
  | OK |

The fitted values and adjusted residuals for the model are presented in the
output and also saved to the data file as variables pre_1 and adj_1. The value
of G^2 for the model is also provided as the likelihood ratio statistic. For the
model (RH, RI), $G^2 = 10.155, df = 8, P = 0.254$.

It is a simple matter to run the model (HI, RH, RI) by repeating the analysis
above, but also adding the interaction term (HI). If we do this we obtain
the following statistics — $G^2 = 3.293, df = 4, P = 0.510$. These are identical
statistics to those obtained in the text.

Bivariate Example with Explanatory Variables having Ordered Categories

Input the first three columns of data from Table 5.7. Remember to weight the
cases using the variable Count. To generate the equally-spaced linear×linear
interaction term, $\beta u_i v_j$, compute a new variable which is the product of Score
(for Dopamine) and Psychosis. Call the new variable *uveq*. The model using
equally-spaced categories can be derived using the commands:

Statistics   ▼
  Loglinear   ►
   General ...

      Factor(s): *input* Dopamine *and* Psychosis
      Cell covariate(s): *input uveq*

        | Model ... |

          Custom: *check box*
          Build term(s):
            Main effects: *input* Dopamine *and* Psychosis
            Interaction: *input uveq*

          | Continue |

  | OK |

The above commands generate the same statistics as are provided in Table 5.8. The model has a G^2 value of 0.531 with $df = 3$ and $P = 0.912$. A similar method to this can be used to generate the statistics for the midrank coding method (see Table 5.8).

Associations Between Nominal and Ordered Categorical Variables

This example will demonstrate how a column-effects model can be calculated on data using midranks. Input the first four columns of data as shown in Table 5.11. Weight cases using the variable Count. To obtain the model described in the text, use the commands:

Statistics   ▼
    Loglinear   ▶
        General ...
        Factor(s): *input* Treatment *and* Depression
        Cell covariate(s): *input* Score

          | Model ... |

            Custom: *check box*
            Build term(s):
              Main effects: *input* Treatment *and* Depression
              Interaction: *input* Treatment*Score

            | Continue |

    | OK |

Using the above model, the association between Treatment and Depression (T and B) is represented as three terms in the model. If we were to run a saturated model (i.e., treat both variables as nominal), then six parameters are used to represent the association.

Ordered Response Variables

Input the first three columns of data from Table 5.13. Weight the cases using the Count variable. Compute a new variable showing the linear×linear term Alcohol×Libido. Call this variable *uv*. The statistics for the linear×linear model can now be obtained using the commands:

<u>S</u>tatistics   ▼
    L<u>o</u>glinear   ▶
        <u>G</u>eneral ...
            <u>F</u>actor(s): *input* Alcohol *and* Libido
            <u>C</u>ell covariate(s): *input uv*
                <u>O</u>ptions ...
                  Display <u>E</u>stimates: *check box*
                  Continue
                <u>M</u>odel ...
                  <u>C</u>ustom: *check box*
                  Build term(s):
                      Main effects: *input* Alcohol *and* Libido
                      Interaction: *input uv*
                  Continue
       OK

The above commands provide the values for G^2, the fitted values, studentized residuals, and the parameter β for the linear×linear association term $u_i v_j$.

For calculating the continuation ratio model, enter the first three columns data from either Table 5.16 or 5.17 exactly as shown. Weight cases using the variable Count. Compute a new variable, *uv*, which is the product of alcohol and libido (this provides the linear×linear association term). The fitted values, residuals and associated statistics described in the text can be generated using the commands:

<u>S</u>tatistics   ▼
    L<u>o</u>glinear   ▶
        <u>G</u>eneral ...
            <u>F</u>actor(s): *input* Alcohol *and* Libido
            <u>C</u>ell covariate(s): *input uv*
                <u>M</u>odel ...
                  <u>C</u>ustom: *check box*
                  Build term(s):
                      Main effects: *input* Alcohol *and* Libido
                      Interaction: *input uv*
                  Continue
       OK

For the data in Table 5.16, $G^2 = 0.75, df = 1, P = 0.386$, and for the data in Table 5.17, $G^2 = 0.345, df = 1, P = 0.557$. From these statistics it is a simple matter to calculate G^2_{Total} using Equation 5.21.

5.4.2   GLIM

In order to run the GLIM examples presented below, type in the following command from within GLIM: `$INPUT 'FILENAME.EXT'$`, replacing `FILENAME.EXT` with that of each example file. To aid the reader, we have commented the commands extensively within each file. All macros which have been used are included at the end of this section.

Bivariate Methods: Loglinear Analysis

```
$echo on $
!       Example from the data set in Table 5.2.
!       First input required macros.
$input %plc 80 dres $
$input 'loglin.mac' $
$echo on $
!       Read in the data set, declaring the factors and setting
!       the reference categories to the upper level of each factor.
$slen 4 $
$gfactor J 2 S 2 $
$factor J 2 (2): S 2 (2) $
$data Count
$read
293 98
223 114
!       Set the response variable to the variable containing the
!       cell counts.
$yvar Count $
!       Set the error term to Poisson errors.
$error p $
!       First simple hypothesis tests using the Pearson Chi Squared
!       and the G Squared statistic.
$fit J+S $
$num pval $
$calc pval=1-%chp(%x2,%df) $
$pr 'X Squared ='%x2' df '%df' P ='pval; $
$calc pval=1-%chp(%dv,%df) $
$pr 'G Squared ='%dv' df '%df' P ='pval; $
!       Display fitted values, studentized residuals and studentized
!       deviance residuals.
$use studres $
$accu 4 3 $ $look j s count %fv ssrs ssdr $ $pr; $ $accu $
!       Fit the saturated model and display parameter estimates.
$fit J+S+J.S $
$dis e $
!       Display the conversion of the parameter estimates to fitted
!       cell counts for the saturated model
```

```
$extr %pe %se $
!       J(2) S(2) fitted count.
$calc %exp(%pe(1)) $
!       J(1) S(2) fitted count.
$calc %exp(%pe(1)+%pe(2)) $
!       J(2) S(1) fitted count.
$calc %exp(%pe(1)+%pe(3)) $
!       J(1) S(1) fitted count.
$calc %exp(%pe(1)+%pe(2)+%pe(3)+%pe(4)) $ $pr ; $
!       Calculate the odds ratio and large sample 95% CI's.
$num logitlo logithi or orlo orhi $
$calc logitlo=%pe(4)-1.96*%se(4) $
$calc logithi=%pe(4)+1.96*%se(4) $
$calc or=%exp(%pe(4)): orlo=%exp(logitlo): orhi=%exp(logithi) $
$pr 'Odds ratio ='or' with 95% CI of ('orlo','orhi')'; $
$return $
```

Loglinear Analysis; an Unsaturated Model; Homogeneous Linear×Linear Associations

```
$echo on $
!       Example from the data set in Table 5.4.
!       First input required macros.
$input %plc 80 dres $
$input 'loglin.mac' $
$echo on $
!       Read in the data set, declaring the factors and setting
!       the reference categories to the upper level of each factor.
$slen 18 $
$gfactor R 2 H 3 I 3 $
!       Set reference category to correspond with SPSS for Windows
$factor R 2 (2): H 3 (3): I 3 (3) $
$data Count
$read
16 33 11
14 46 13
9  25 16
9  9  7
11 20 10
5  21 11
!       Set the response variable to the variable containing the
!       cell counts.
$yvar Count $
!       Set the error term to Poisson errors.
$error p $
!       Fit the model to be tested.
$fit R+H+I+R.I+R.H+H.I $
!       call macro to set G Squared and df for fitted model.
$use gsqdf1 $
!       Remove the tested model term.
$fit -H.I $
!       call macro to set G Squared and df for reduced model.
$use gsqdf2 $
```

```
!        Call macro to calculate G Squared test.
$use gsqtest $
!        Display fitted values, studentized residuals and studentized
!        deviance residuals.
$use studres $
$accu 4 3 $ $look r h i count %fv ssrs ssdr $ $pr; $ $accu $
!        Examine the later Ordinal model for linear*linear
!        H.I association.
!        Calculate covariates holding integer scores.
$calc XH=H: XI=I $
!        Test the linear*linear H.I association.
$fit R+H+I+R.I+R.H+XH.XI $
$use gsqdf1 $
$fit -XH.XI $
$use gsqdf2 $
$use gsqtest $
!        Refit model of interest and display parameter estimates.
$fit +XH.XI $
$dis e $
!        Calculate the odds ratio and 95% CI's.
$num logitlo logithi or orlo orhi $
$num td95 $
$extract %pe %se $
$calc or=%exp(%pe)
$calc logitlo=%pe(11)-1.96*%se(11) $
$calc logithi=%pe(11)+1.96*%se(11) $
$calc or=%exp(%pe(11)): orlo=%exp(logitlo): orhi=%exp(logithi) $
$pr 'Odds ratio ='or' with 95% CI of ('orlo','orhi')' $
$return
```

Bivariate Example with Explanatory Variables having Ordered Categories

```
$echo on $
!        Example from the data set in Tables 5.6 and 5.7.
!        First input required macros.
$input %plc 80 dres $
$input 'loglin.mac' $
$echo on $
!        Read in the data set, declaring the factors and setting
!        the reference categories to the upper level of each factor.
$slen 10 $
$gfactor D 5 PS 2 $
$factor D 5 (5): PS 2 (2) $
$data Count
$read
46 26
35 28
39 35
28 35
26 32
!        Set the response variable to the variable containing the
!        cell counts.
```

```
$yvar Count $
!        Create covariate to hold dummy codes for PS.
$calc XPS=PS-1 $
!        Create covariate to hold integer scores for D.
$calc XDEQ=D $
!        Read in the midrank scores for D.
$data XDMR
$read
36.5   36.5
104.0  104.0
172.5  172.5
241.0  241.0
301.5  301.5
!        Set the error term to Poisson errors.
$error p $
!        Examine the linear*linear association with integer scores for D.
$fit D+PS+XDEQ.XPS$
$use gsqdf1 $
$fit -XDEQ.XPS $
$use gsqdf2 $
$use gsqtest $
!        Display fitted values, studentized residuals and studentized
!        deviance residuals for the no association model.
$use studres $
$accu 4 3 $ $look D XPS count %fv ssrs ssdr $ $pr; $ $accu $
!        Refit model of interest and display parameter estimates.
$fit +XDEQ.XPS $
$dis e $
!        Display fitted values, studentized residuals and
!        studentized deviance residuals
$use studres $
$accu 4 3 $ $look D XDEQ XPS count %fv ssrs ssdr $ $pr; $ $accu $
!        Calculate the odds ratio and 95% CI's.
$num logitlo logithi or orlo orhi $
$num td95 $
$extract %pe %se $
$calc or=%exp(%pe)
$calc logitlo=%pe(7)-1.96*%se(7) $
$calc logithi=%pe(7)+1.96*%se(7) $
$calc or=%exp(%pe(7)): orlo=%exp(logitlo): orhi=%exp(logithi) $
$pr 'Odds ratio ='or' with 95% CI of ('orlo','orhi')' $
!        Examine the linear*linear association with midrank scores for D.
$fit D+PS+XDMR.XPS$
$use gsqdf1 $
$fit -XDMR.XPS $
$use gsqdf2 $
$use gsqtest $
!        Refit model of interest and display parameter estimates.
$fit +XDMR.XPS $
$dis e $
!        Display fitted values, studentized residuals and
!        studentized deviance residuals.
$use studres $
```

```
$accu 4 3 $ $look D XDMR XPS count %fv ssrs ssdr $ $pr; $ $accu $
!        Calculate the odds ratio and 95% CI's.
$extract %pe %se $
$calc or=%exp(%pe)
$calc logitlo=%pe(7)-1.96*%se(7) $
$calc logithi=%pe(7)+1.96*%se(7) $
$calc or=%exp(%pe(7)): orlo=%exp(logitlo): orhi=%exp(logithi) $
$pr 'Odds ratio ='or' with 95% CI of ('orlo','orhi')' $
$return $
```

Associations between Nominal and Ordered Categorical Variables

```
$echo on $
!        Example from the data set in Tables 5.10 and 5.11.
!        First input any macros that we require.
$input %plc 80 dres $
$input 'loglin.mac' $
$echo on $
!        Read in the data set, declaring the factors and setting
!        the reference categories to the upper level of each factor.
$slen 12 $
$gfactor T 4 D 3 $
$factor T 4 (4): D 3 (3) $
$data Count
$read
11 20 13
12 23 8
12 27 10
21 18 3
!        Create covariate to hold integer scores for D .
$calc XDEQ=D $
!        Read in the midrank scores for D.
$data XDMR
$read
150.5  78.5 17.5
150.5  78.5 17.5
150.5  78.5 17.5
150.5  78.5 17.5
$
$yvar Count $
$error p $
!        Fit the column effects model with integer scores for D.
$fit T+D+T.XDEQ $
$use gsqdf1 $
$fit -T.XDEQ $
$use gsqdf2 $
$use gsqtest $
!        Refit model of interest.
$fit +T.XDEQ $
!        Display fitted values, studentized residuals and studentized
!        deviance residuals.
$use studres $
$accu 4 3 $ $look T D XDEQ count %fv ssrs ssdr $ $pr; $ $accu $
```

```
!        Fit the column effects model with midrank scores for D.
$fit T+D+T.XDMR $
$use gsqdf1 $
$fit -T.XDMR $
$use gsqdf2 $
$use gsqtest $
!        Refit model of interest.
$fit +T.XDMR $
!        Display fitted values, studentized residuals and studentized
!        deviance residuals.
$use studres $
$accu 4 3 $ $look T D XDMR count %fv ssrs ssdr $ $pr; $ $accu $
!        Refit the column effects model with integer scores for D.
$fit T+D+T.XDEQ $
!        Display the parameter estimates.
$dis e $
!        Calculate the odds-ratio and 95% Confidence Intervals.
$extract %pe %se $
!        Set the parameters for comparison.
$num prm1 prm2 $
$calc prm1=7: prm2=8 $
!        Call macro for odds ratios and large sample CI's with row
!        or column effects models.
$use orcirow $
!        Repeat for each pair of column-effect parameters.
$calc prm1=7: prm2=9 $
$use orcirow $
$calc prm1=7: prm2=10 $
$use orcirow $
$calc prm1=8: prm2=9 $
$use orcirow $
$calc prm1=9: prm2=8 $
$use orcirow $
$calc prm1=8: prm2=10 $
$use orcirow $
$calc prm1=9: prm2=10 $
$use orcirow $
$return $
```

Ordered Response Variables

```
$echo on $
!        Example from the data set in Table 5.13.
!        First input any macros that we require.
$input %plc 80 dres $
$input 'loglin.mac' $
$echo on $
!        Read in the data set, declaring the factors and setting
!        the reference categories to the upper level of each factor.
$slen 9 $
$gfactor A 3 L 3 $
$factor A 3 (3): L 3 (3) $
$data Count
```

```
$read
1 10 12
4 13 7
5 15 7
!        Create covariates to hold integer scores for A and L.
$calc  XA=A: XL=L $
$yvar Count $
$error p $
!        Examine the linear*linear association model.
$fit A+L+XA.XL$
$use gsqdf1 $
$fit -XA.XL $
$use gsqdf2 $
$use gsqtest $
!        Refit model of interest.
$fit +XA.XL $
!        Display the parameter estimates.
$dis e $
!        Display fitted values, studentized residuals and studentized
!        deviance residuals.
$use studres $
$accu 4 3 $ $look A L count %fv ssrs ssdr $ $pr; $ $accu $
!        Calculate the odds ratio and large sample 95% CI's.
$num logitlo logithi or orlo orhi $
$extract %pe %se $
$calc or=%exp(%pe)
$calc logitlo=%pe(6)-1.96*%se(6) $
$calc logithi=%pe(6)+1.96*%se(6) $
$calc or=%exp(%pe(6)): orlo=%exp(logitlo): orhi=%exp(logithi) $
$pr 'Odds ratio ='or' with 95% CI of ('orlo','orhi')' $
!        Correct for any over/under-dispersion.
$calc seadj=%se*%sqrt(%dv/%df) $
!        Calculate the odds ratio with the adjusted large sample
!        95% CI's.
$calc or=%exp(%pe)
$calc logitlo=%pe(6)-1.96*seadj(6) $
$calc logithi=%pe(6)+1.96*seadj(6) $
$calc or=%exp(%pe(6)): orlo=%exp(logitlo): orhi=%exp(logithi) $
$pr 'Odds ratio ='or' with 95% CI of ('orlo','orhi')' $
$return $

$echo on $
!        Example from the data set in Table 5.15 and 5.17.
!        First input any macros that we require.
$input 'loglin.mac' $
$input %plc 80 dres $
$echo on $
!        Read in the data set, declaring the factors and setting
!        the reference categories to the upper level of each factor.
$slen 6 $
$gfactor A 3 L 2 $
$factor A 3 (3): L 2 (1) $
!        Read in first cut point of continuation ratio logit.
```

```
$data Cnt1vs23
$read
1 22
4 20
5 22
$yvar Cnt1vs23 $
$calc  XA=A $
!       Create a variate with Dummy codes for L.
$calc XL=L-1$
$error p $
!       Examine the Linear * Linear model with the binary factor L.
$fit A+L+XA.XL$
$use gsqdf1 $
!       Save first G Squared and DF for the Combined values of
!       the cut points.
$num cut1gsq1 cut1df1 cut1gsq2 cut1df2 $
$calc cut1gsq1=%dv: cut1df1=%df $
$fit -XA.XL $
$use gsqdf2 $
!       Save second G Squared and DF for the Combined values of
!       the cut points.
$calc cut1gsq2=%dv: cut1df2=%df $
$use gsqtest $
!       Refit model of interest.
$fit +XA.XL $
!       Display the parameter estimates.
$dis e $
!       Display fitted values, studentized residuals and studentized
!       deviance residuals.
$use studres $
$accu 4 3 $ $look A L Cnt1vs23 %fv ssrs ssdr $ $pr; $ $accu $
!       Calculate the odds ratio and large sample 95% CI's.
$num logitlo logithi or orlo orhi $
$num td95 $
$extract %pe %se $
$calc or=%exp(%pe)
$calc logitlo=%pe(5)-1.96*%se(5) $
$calc logithi=%pe(5)+1.96*%se(5) $
$calc or=%exp(%pe(5)): orlo=%exp(logitlo): orhi=%exp(logithi) $
$pr 'Odds ratio ='or' with 95% CI of ('orlo','orhi')' $
!       Read in second cut point of continuation ratio logit.
$data Cnt2vs3
$read
10 12
13 7
15 7
$yvar Cnt2vs3 $
$calc  XA=A $
!       Create a variate with Dummy codes for L.
$calc XL=L-1$
!       Examine the Linear * Linear model with the binary factor L.
$fit A+L+XA.XL$
$use gsqdf1 $
```

```
!         Save first G Squared and DF for the Combined values of
!         the cut points.
$num cut2gsq1 cut2df1 cut2gsq2 cut2df2 $
$calc cut2gsq1=%dv: cut2df1=%df $
$fit -XA.XL $
$use gsqdf2 $
$use gsqtest $
!         Save second G Squared and DF for the Combined values of
!         the cut points.
$calc cut2gsq2=%dv: cut2df2=%df $
!         Refit model of interest.
$fit +XA.XL $
!         Display the parameter estimates.
$dis e $
!         Display fitted values, studentized residuals and studentized
!         deviance residuals.
$use studres $
$accu 4 3 $ $look A L Cnt2vs3 %fv ssrs ssdr $ $pr; $ $accu $
!         Calculate the odds ratio and large sample 95% CI's.
$num logitlo logithi or orlo orhi $
$num td95 $
$extract %pe %se $
$calc or=%exp(%pe)
$calc logitlo=%pe(5)-1.96*%se(5) $
$calc logithi=%pe(5)+1.96*%se(5) $
$calc or=%exp(%pe(5)): orlo=%exp(logitlo): orhi=%exp(logithi) $
$pr 'Odds ratio ='or' with 95% CI of ('orlo','orhi')' $
!         Combine G Squared and DF for the two cut points.
$num combgsq1 combdf1 combgsq2 combdf2 $
$calc combgsq1=cut1gsq1+cut2gsq1: combdf1=cut1df1+cut2df1$
$calc p=1-%chp(combgsq1, combdf1) $
!         The ordinal terms only just reach a good model fit.
$pr 'Model 1:' $
$pr 'Overall G Squared ='combgsq1' with 'combdf1' df and P ='p ;$
$calc combgsq2=cut1gsq2+cut2gsq2: combdf2=cut1df2+cut2df2$
$calc p=1-%chp(combgsq2, combdf2) $
$pr 'Model 2:' $
$pr 'Overall G Squared ='combgsq2' with 'combdf2' df and P ='p ;$
$num diffgsq diffdf $
$calc diffgsq=combgsq2-combgsq1: diffdf=combdf2-combdf1 $
$calc p=1-%chp(diffgsq, diffdf) $
$pr 'Change in combined G Squared ='diffgsq' with '
        diffdf' df and P ='p ;$
$return $
```

Macros for use in Loglinear Chapter

```
$mac studres
!         Calculates studentized residuals and studentized deviance
!         residuals, the results are stored in the variates ssrs and ssdr.
$arg dres dr $
$use dres $
$extr %lv $
```

```
$calc ssrs=%rs/%sqrt(%sc*(1-%lv)) $
$calc ssdr=dr/%sqrt(%sc*(1-%lv)) $
$endmac $


$mac cior
!       Produces a table of LARGE SAMPLE 95% CI's for the model parameters
!       and corresponding exponentiated values.
$extract %pe %se $
$calc or=%exp(%pe)
$calc pelo=%pe-(1.96*%se)
$calc pehi=%pe+(1.96*%se)
$calc orlo=%exp(pelo) $
$calc orhi=%exp(pehi) $
$acc 4 3 $ $look %pe %se pelo pehi or orlo orhi $ $pr $ $acc $
$delete pelo pehi or orlo orhi $
$endmac $


$num gsq1 gsq2 df1 df2 df21 s2 gsq21  p $


$mac gsqdf1 $assign gsq1=%dv: df1=%df $ $endmac $


$mac gsqdf2 $assign gsq2=%dv: df2=%df $ $endmac $


$mac gsqtest
!       Calculates G Squared Tests for Goodness-of-fit and
!       change in G Squared.
$calc p=1-%chp(gsq1, df1) $
$pr 'Goodness-of-fit' $
$pr '   first model:  G Squared ='
        gsq1' df=' df1' P =' p $
$calc p=1-%chp(gsq2, df2) $
$pr '   second model: G Squared ='
        gsq2' df=' df2' P =' p $
$calc gsq21=gsq2-gsq1: df21=df2-df1 $
$calc p= 1-%chp(gsq21, df21) $
$pr 'Change in G Squared  ='gsq21' with 'df21' df and P ='p ;$
$endmac $


$macro orcirow
!       Calculate odds ratios and LARGE SAMPLE 95% CI's from a
!       row or column effect model.
$num or orlo orhi$
!       Note that aliased parameters generate warnings in
!       calculating lo and hi, but are harmless.
$calc lo=%exp(%pe-1.96*%se) $
$calc hi=%exp(%pe+1.96*%se) $
$calc or=%exp(%pe(prm2)-%pe(prm1)) $
$calc orlo=%exp(%log(lo(prm2))-%log(hi(prm1)))
$calc orhi=%exp(%log(hi(prm2))-%log(lo(prm1)))
$pr    'With adjacent ordered catagories, '
        'the odds ratio and large sample CI''s';
        'for parameter 'prm1' versus 'prm2
        ' of the unordered factor are:';
```

```
        'Odds ratio =' or ' with 95% C.I. of ('orlo','orhi')'; $
$del lo hi $
$endmac $

$return $
```

Chapter 6

Factor Analysis

One of the problems that sometimes occurs when computing generalized linear models (GLMs) is the presence of multicollinearity which is caused by strong interrelationships amongst the explanatory variables (refer to Section 3.3.6). High levels of multicollinearity affect the reliability of the regression parameters and make it difficult to accurately interpret the results. One of the suggested methods for dealing with this is to collapse those variables which appear to be indicators of the same underlying concept into a single composite variable. Whilst this technique can be applied to a small number of variables where the interrelationships in the data are fairly obvious and easy to interpret, it is not a practical method to use on larger data sets which tend to have more complex patterns of interrelationships. In such cases a collection of techniques which go under the heading of *factor analysis* can be useful in collapsing variables to reduce the level of multicollinearity and thereby enable GLMs to be more successfully applied to the data.

Factor analysis is a technique which is quite different to those described in earlier chapters as the aim is not to explicitly model variables but to represent a number of them in terms of a smaller number of *factors*, or *latent variables* as they are often referred to. It should be noted that the term 'factor' as it is used here is different to earlier chapters and this can be the source of some confusion. In this chapter, a factor is a continuous latent variable which is assumed to account for relationships in the data, whereas in previous chapters, it referred to a categorical explanatory variable. This is an unfortunate overlap in terminology, however, the term factor will be used in this chapter to refer to a continuous latent variable as this is the form commonly used in the literature.

The identification of factors is important for at least two reasons. Firstly, it can provide useful theoretical insights into underlying relationships and patterns in the data, and secondly, it can enable data containing highly correlated variables to be modelled using GLMs. Whilst the identification and interpretation of factors is important in its own right, the aim of this chapter is not to describe factor analysis as a primary analytic tool, but to describe the procedures and practicalities of using it in conjunction with GLMs.

A distinction can be made between two different types of factor analysis — *exploratory* and *confirmatory*. The two techniques are related in as far as they both deal with latent variables, however, they are distinct techniques and serve different purposes. Exploratory factor analysis identifies relationships among variables which are often far from obvious in the original data. The purpose is to summarize and concisely describe the data by grouping correlated variables together. Typically, one would conduct an exploratory factor analysis and attempt to interpret the meaning of the factors once they have been identified. The factors are only of use if a meaningful description can be applied to them. Confirmatory factor analysis, on the other hand, uses carefully selected variables to reveal factors which are hypothesized to exist. It enables one to test whether relationships expected on theoretical grounds actually appear in the data and allows these to be modelled. Confirmatory factor analysis is a technique for modelling data using already identified latent variables, whereas exploratory factor analysis is a technique for the initial identification of the latent variables. This discussion deals exclusively with the use of exploratory factor analysis as a technique to reduce problematic levels of multicollinearity.

It has been said that exploratory factor analysis is a technique which is often used to 'save' poorly conceived research (see, for example, Tabachnick and Fidell, 1996). Whilst we would agree that the use of factor analysis to reduce high levels of multicollinearity is not a preferred option (it would be better to carefully select variables at the design stage of a study so that such problems do not occur), it is often necessary to analyse data from poorly designed, or exploratory studies and studies which have been primarily designed for different purposes. The use of exploratory factor analysis can enable such data to be usefully analysed using GLMs and can also provide insights into the existence of underlying processes which are also of use when model-building.

6.1   Overview

Factor analysis is based on the assumption that relationships between variables are due to the effects of underlying factors. It is assumed that factors may represent the *causes* of relationships in the data and that observed correlations are the result of variables sharing common factors. For example, the existence of certain attitudes can be inferred from answers which are given to a number of questions. Answers of "agree" or "strongly agree" to questions such as "It is important to preserve one's culture", "I am prepared to die for my country" and "It is good to take part in our traditional festivals" may lead one to conclude that the 'patriotism' factor is present. Here, patriotism is not a single measurable entity but is a construct which is derived from the measurement of other variables (more specifically, it represents the observed correlations between the subjects' answers to a number of questions). Hypothesizing the existence of something called 'patriotism' explains some of the relationships between the variables, can simplify the description of the data and help in our understanding of the complex relationship between answers to numerous and varied questions.

Consider the hypothetical correlation matrix presented in Table 6.1 which shows student performance in a number of subjects. A visual inspection of the matrix suggests that the six subjects might usefully be categorized into two groups. Maths, Physics and Computing are closely related and constitute one group, whilst Art, Drama and English which are also closely related constitute the other. The matrix also suggests that these two groups of subjects are not highly correlated with each other. For these data a factor analysis should clearly show two factors which can be meaningfully interpreted as representing the different skills required by the subject groups.

Table 6.1: Correlation Matrix Suggesting Two Factors

	Maths	Physics	Computing	Art	Drama	English
Maths	1.00					
Physics	0.80	1.00				
Computing	0.78	0.73	1.00			
Art	0.12	0.14	0.15	1.00		
Drama	0.04	0.21	0.13	0.68	1.00	
English	0.24	0.15	0.07	0.91	0.79	1.00

Describing a data set in terms of factors is useful as it can help in the identification of the underlying processes which may have determined the correlations among the original variables. In the example above, the marks obtained by the children might be better understood as a function of whether the subject requires logical or creative skills rather than skills specific to each individual subject. Using these two factors, a description of the children's academic performance can now be given in terms of two latent variables as opposed to six directly measured variables and this results in a simpler interpretation.

As well as providing some theoretical insight into school performance (i.e. that performance might usefully be explained in terms of underlying competencies as opposed to achievement in individual subjects) factor analysis enables these data to be modelled using GLMs. It is not appropriate to enter the six variables in Table 6.1 directly into a regression analysis due to the strong relationship between maths, physics and computing, and between art, drama and English. However, it might be appropriate to enter the two latent variables identified using factor analysis as these are not highly correlated with one another and are therefore unlikely to show problematic levels of multicollinearity.

6.2   Factor Analysis Equations

To appreciate more fully the process of defining factors it is useful to look at some equations, which in order to maintain some continuity are couched in terms similar to those used in previous chapters. Each *variable* in a data set can be expressed as a linear combination of *factors* which are not actually observed (these are the latent variables which are assumed to account for the correlations between variables). For example, a student's examination result in mathematics is not only dependent upon mathematical competence, but is also likely to be dependent on such things as experience with taking examinations, communicative and writing ability. These factors are not directly observed (i.e., they are not variables which have been measured) but are inferred from the data on the basis of correlations between the examination results.

We can see from Equation 6.1 that a student's test score depends, at least to some extent, on the three factors.

$$\text{Maths Score} = \beta_1 \text{Communicative Competence} + \beta_2 \text{Experience} +$$
$$\beta_3 \text{Writing Competence} + U_{\text{Maths Score}} \qquad (6.1)$$

where 'Maths Score' is the observed variable,

Communicative Competence, Experience and Writing Competence are unobserved factors,

$U_{\text{Maths Score}}$ represents the portion of the variable 'Maths Score' which is not accounted for by the factors,

and β_1 to β_3 are weightings which indicate the strength of association between each factor and the variable.

The importance of each of these factors in determining the test score is indicated by the weights which are associated with them (β_1 to β_3). $U_{\text{Maths Score}}$ is called a *unique factor*, since it represents the part of the student's maths score that cannot be explained by the factors (that is, it is unique to that variable). Any number of variables can be represented in a similar fashion, using equations where each variable is described in terms of the same factors as shown in Equations 6.2a to 6.2c overleaf, where k variables are described in terms of three factors, communicative competence, experience and writing competence. These factors are called *common factors*, since all variables are expressed as functions of them.

$$\text{Variable 1} = \quad \beta_{1(1)}\text{Communicative Competence} + \beta_{2(1)}\text{Experience} +$$
$$\beta_{3(1)}\text{Writing Competence} + U_{\text{test score}(1)} \quad (6.2\text{a})$$

$$\text{Variable 2} = \quad \beta_{1(2)}\text{Communicative Competence} + \beta_{2(2)}\text{Experience} +$$
$$\beta_{3(2)}\text{Writing Competence} + U_{\text{test score}(2)} \quad (6.2\text{b})$$

$$\text{Variable } k = \quad \beta_{1(k)}\text{Communicative Competence} + \beta_{2(k)}\text{Experience} +$$
$$\beta_{3(k)}\text{Writing Competence} + U_{\text{test score}(k)} \quad (6.2\text{c})$$

where k is the number of variables,
and $\beta_{1(k)}$ to $\beta_{3(k)}$ are weights which indicate the strength of association between each factor and variable k.

Similar equations to these can be used to represent the *factors* in terms of *variables*. Equations 6.3a to 6.3c show three factors which are represented as a combination of six variables.

$$\text{Factor 1} = \beta_{1(1)}\text{Maths} + \beta_{2(1)}\text{Physics} + \beta_{3(1)}\text{Computing} + \cdots + \beta_{6(1)}\text{English}$$
$$(6.3\text{a})$$

$$\text{Factor 2} = \beta_{1(2)}\text{Maths} + \beta_{2(2)}\text{Physics} + \beta_{3(2)}\text{Computing} + \cdots + \beta_{6(2)}\text{English}$$
$$(6.3\text{b})$$

$$\text{Factor 3} = \beta_{1(3)}\text{Maths} + \beta_{2(3)}\text{Physics} + \beta_{3(3)}\text{Computing} + \cdots + \beta_{6(3)}\text{English}$$
$$(6.3\text{c})$$

where Factor 1 to Factor 3 are factors derived from the data,
Maths, Physics, Computing and English are variables,
and $\beta_{1(k)}$ to $\beta_{6(k)}$ are weights which indicate the strength of association between each variable and factor k.

The three factors represent three different patterns of correlation in the data which are unrelated to one another. Although we have only included three factors above, in practice we could identify k factors, where k is equal to the number of variables.

6.3 Preliminary Analyses

Before running a factor analysis it is important to be aware of some of the assumptions made by the techniques and determine which variables should be included, whether any of them should be transformed, and also how good the overall analysis is likely to be.

6.3.1   Data Assumptions

Factor analysis makes a few assumptions about the data, most notably with regards to the underlying distribution and the sample size needed for a 'robust' solution.

Continuous Data and Ordered Categorical Data

Factors are determined on the basis of the Pearson correlation coefficient, r, which requires data to be measured on a continuous scale. In practice, however, this requirement is often relaxed so that ordered categorical data can be included (data from Likert scales, for example). The relaxation of the requirement for continuous data can be justified for exploratory factor analysis as the usefulness of the procedure is based purely on the interpretability of the factors. Factor analysis is therefore only a useful technique (at least in the context of this chapter) if it manages to produce meaningful results and meaning may be obtained from ordered categorical data in much the same way as it can be from continuous data.

Sample Size

Factor analysis is based on correlation coefficients, which tend to be most reliable when computed for large samples. Comrey and Lee (1992) recommend that for a 'good' factor analysis solution a data set should contain at least 300 cases. However, solutions which have a few highly correlated 'marker variables' (as would be the case if we were using factor analysis in an attempt to reduce the degree of multicollinearity) may require fewer cases (Tabachnick and Fidell, 1996, estimate that about 150 cases are required for a 'good' solution). It should be noted, however, that these recommendations are for studies designed specifically to investigate underlying processes and that factor analysis may be usefully applied to much smaller samples (see the example presented in Section 6.7). One should always keep in mind, however, that computing factors on small samples can be problematic and the solutions variable.

6.3.2   Data Screening

As with other techniques covered in this book, it is important to screen data and transform any variables which violate the assumptions of the test. As indicated above, exploratory factor analysis can be applied to relatively small data sets where the use of careful data screening and transformation procedures is particularly important. Here we will deal briefly with investigating Normality, linearity and outliers (refer to Chapter 2, for more detailed information on these topics) and suggest ways in which the data may be transformed to improve the solution.

Factor analysis assumes that variables are Normally distributed — the inclusion of variables which are not will degrade the analysis. Ideally, multivariate Normality should hold for the data, but as the tests for this can be overly sensitive, checking for Normality among single variables is often adequate. Univariate Normality can be assessed using skewness and kurtosis statistics and one should consider transforming those variables which deviate significantly.

Factors are determined using Pearson correlations and are therefore based on linear relationships. If these relationships depart markedly from linearity, the analysis will be degraded. Non-linear relationships therefore need to be identified (using scatter plots, for example) and, if possible, the appropriate variables transformed.

The presence of outliers can also degrade a factor analysis as correlations between variables can be adversely affected by a small number of 'unusual' influential cases. As outliers can have a disproportionate effect on the identification of factors, their influence needs to be limited. This can be achieved by, for example, amending the value of the outlier to reduce its influence, or by eliminating the case completely (refer to Chapter 2 for options on dealing with outliers). It should be emphasized that extreme care is needed before data are removed or amended as outliers can indicate a misspecified model.

The use of data screening procedures and transformations is an important part of factor analysis and can greatly improve the solution. As we are advocating the use of factor analysis with relatively small samples and for studies which were not primarily designed to identify latent variables, violations of the test assumptions can have particularly serious consequences. To maximize the power and reliability of the factor analysis we therefore advise that data are screened and appropriate transformations applied if it proves necessary.

6.3.3   Examining Correlations

As the identification of factors is based on correlations between variables it follows that, for a good solution, groups of variables need to be correlated. Variables that do not appear to be related to other variables will not easily form factors and should be removed from the analysis. If variables which are not related to others are retained in the analysis they tend to form factors on their own and hinder the efficient running of the analysis. A first check on the appropriateness of including variables in a factor analysis is to investigate the correlation matrix and remove those variables which are not correlated with any others. Studying the correlation matrix can also prove useful in identifying some of the more obvious patterns in the data and provide a basis for model-checking and building.

Table 6.2 shows a correlation matrix computed for seven variables. From the information in this table we can see that variable 2 is not strongly related to any of the other variables (the maximum correlation is below 0.3) and is a candidate for removal. Although there is no strict recommendation as to the minimum size of correlation needed for a variable to be retained, it appears quite obvious that a factor analysis on this data might benefit from the removal of variable 2 as it does not appear to be part of any underlying factor.

Table 6.2: Correlation Matrix

	Var 1	Var 2	Var 3	Var 4	Var 5	Var 6	Var 7
Var 1	1.0000						
Var 2	0.0320	1.0000					
Var 3	0.6513	0.2475	1.0000				
Var 4	0.3678	0.1552	0.3608	1.0000			
Var 5	0.5484	0.2895	0.3471	0.4065	1.0000		
Var 6	0.5335	0.0065	0.3295	0.6577	0.7567	1.0000	
Var 7	0.7074	0.2968	0.7722	0.3805	0.4326	0.4015	1.0000

6.3.4   Measures of Sampling Adequacy

A useful method for determining the appropriateness of running a factor analysis is to compute a measure of sampling adequacy. Such measures have been
proposed by Kaiser (1970) and are based on an index which compares correlation and partial correlation coefficients (these measures of sampling adequacy
are also known as Kaiser–Meyer–Olkin, or KMO statistics). KMO statistics
can be calculated for individual and multiple variables using Equations 6.4a
and 6.4b.

$$\text{KMO for individual variables} = \frac{\sum_{i \neq j} r_{ij}^2}{\sum_{i \neq j} r_{ij}^2 + \sum_{i \neq j} a_{ij}^2} \tag{6.4a}$$

$$\text{KMO for multiple variables} = \frac{\sum \sum_{i \neq j} r_{ij}^2}{\sum \sum_{i \neq j} r_{ij}^2 + \sum \sum_{i \neq j} a_{ij}^2} \tag{6.4b}$$

where r_{ij} is the simple correlation coefficient between variables i and j,
and a_{ij} is the partial correlation coefficient between variables i and j.

The KMO statistic for an individual variable is the sum of the squared
correlation coefficients between this variable and all other variables (but not
with itself, hence the $i \neq j$ term) divided by this value added to the sum
of the squared partial correlation coefficients. The KMO statistic for multiple
variables is the sum of these statistics computed for all variables in the analysis.
Similar to correlations, KMO statistics take values between 0 and 1. High
values (approaching 1) are obtained if the sum of the correlation coefficients

are relatively large compared to the sum of the partial correlation coefficients. In this case there are likely to be patterns of correlation in the data indicating that a factor analysis might be an appropriate technique to use. If, on the other hand, the sum of the partial correlation coefficients is relatively large compared to the correlation coefficients, the relationships in the data are likely to be quite diffuse making it unlikely that the variables will form distinct factors. Table 6.3 suggests how KMO statistics might be interpreted (Kaiser, 1974).

Table 6.3: Interpretation of the KMO Statistics

KMO statistic	Interpretation
in the .90's	marvelous
in the .80's	meritorious
in the .70's	middling
in the .60's	mediocre
in the .50's	miserable
below .50	unacceptable

Most statistical software provides KMO statistics for the overall data set and for individual variables. In SPSS, the overall KMO value is provided as a single statistic, whilst KMO values for individual variables are derived from the anti-image correlation matrix (a full description of the anti-image correlation matrix at this point is not necessary, however, information about its use can be found in Norušis, 1994, and SPSS 1996c). Table 6.4 shows a hypothetical anti-image correlation matrix with the KMO statistics for individual variables provided on the diagonal (the KMO statistic for variable 1 is 0.9474 and for variable 5, 0.8959). Variable 2 has an individual KMO score of only 0.4352 (which, to use Kaiser's terminology, is unacceptable) and would be considered as a candidate for removal from the factor analysis. It is advisable to remove variables one at a time and then recalculate the statistics since the KMO scores for the other variables in the analysis will change along with the overall KMO

Table 6.4: Anti-image Correlation Matrix

	Var 1	Var 2	Var 3	Var 4	Var 5	Var 6	Var 7
Var 1	0.9474						
Var 2	0.0093	0.4352					
Var 3	−0.0255	−0.0722	0.9247				
Var 4	0.0884	−0.0763	−0.1633	0.8487			
Var 5	−0.0260	0.1447	0.0858	−0.1535	0.8959		
Var 6	−0.0820	−0.0703	0.0486	0.0372	−0.3764	0.9273	
Var 7	−0.1107	−0.0183	−0.2444	0.0801	−0.0376	0.0771	0.9484

Note: Measures of sampling adequacy for individual variables are shown on the diagonal.

statistic when each variable is removed. The procedure to derive the overall and individual KMO statistics in SPSS is described in Section 6.9.

6.4 Factor Extraction

Once the variables to be used in the factor analysis have been screened and selected, the factors needed to represent the data can be determined. Here, factor extraction is demonstrated using a hypothetical data set showing the performance of 1000 children on 10 different tasks (for a list of these tasks see Table 6.6). Each task was assessed using a standard instrument and scores of between 1 and 5 were assigned to indicate performance (1 = very poor and 5 = very good). For the purposes of illustration, it can be assumed that these data have been screened for outliers, Normality and non-linear relationships, and that the KMO figures for the overall data set and individual variables are within acceptable limits.

Although there are several methods which can be used to extract factors from a data set, only one will be described here as we are more concerned with the general theory behind factor extraction and interpretation than with the advantages and disadvantages associated with individual techniques (for detailed information on these see, for example, Kim and Mueller, 1994, and Tabachnick and Fidell, 1996). The factor extraction technique discussed here is Principal Components Analysis, which is perhaps the most popular and is implemented in a number of statistical software packages.

6.4.1 Principal Components Analysis

Before we discuss the use of principal component analysis it is important to differentiate between this technique and factor analysis. The objective of principal components analysis is to select the components which explain as much of the variance in the sample as possible. The objective of factor analysis, on the other hand, is to explain the interrelationships among the original variables. Kim & Mueller differentiate between the two in the following way:

> ... factor analysis represents the covariance structure in terms of a hypothetical causal model, whereas components analysis summarizes the data by means of a linear combination of the observed data. The choice between the two will depend on the researcher's overall objectives. The explanation of the correlation in terms of a smaller number of factors is achieved by an imposition of a hypothetical model. The mathematical representation of the linear combination of observed data does not require imposing what some may consider a questionable causal model, but it does not reveal any underlying causal structure, if such a structure exists.

> Kim and Mueller (1994), pp. 87–88

Principal components analysis is used here as a first step in factor analysis to identify the factors which may explain the relationships within the data. Although there are differences between components and factors, for our purposes, they are both used to identify underlying relationships in the data and the terms are used more or less interchangeably throughout the remainder of this chapter (for more detailed discussions of the differences between components and factors see Afifi and Clarke, 1996; Dunteman, 1994).

In principal component analysis, linear combinations of the observed variables are formed. The first principal component is the weighted linear combination of variables that accounts for the largest amount of variance in the sample. For a set of k variables, principal component 1 can be defined using Equation 6.5.

$$\text{Principal component 1} = \beta_{1(1)}\text{Variable 1} + \beta_{2(1)}\text{Variable 2} +$$

$$\beta_{3(1)}\text{Variable 3} + \ldots + \beta_{k(1)}\text{Variable } k \quad (6.5)$$

The second principal component is the weighted linear combination of the variables that is *uncorrelated* with the first principal component and accounts for the maximum amount of the remaining total variation in the data. Principal component 2 is formed from the residual correlations left over after principal component 1 has been identified. For a set of k variables, principal component 2 can be defined using Equation 6.6.

$$\text{Principal component 2} = \beta_{1(2)}\text{Variable 1} + \beta_{2(2)}\text{Variable 2} +$$

$$\beta_{3(2)}\text{Variable 3} + \ldots + \beta_{k(2)}\text{Variable } k \quad (6.6)$$

Successive principal components explain progressively smaller portions of the total sample variance, and are all uncorrelated with each other. This procedure produces a unique mathematical solution and, essentially, transforms a set of correlated variables into a set of uncorrelated principal components. For our data set which looks at children's competencies, a total of 10 principal components can be identified from the 10 original variables.

Table 6.5 shows 10 principal components and the amount of variance in the sample each of these components accounts for. As each variable in the analysis is standardized to have a mean of 0 and a standard deviation of 1, the total variation in the sample is equal to 10. The *eigenvalue* shows the amount of this variance explained by each principal component with the sum of the eigenvalues equalling the number of variables (i.e., 10). The first principal

Table 6.5: Variance Accounted for by the Principal Components

Component	Eigenvalue	% of Variance	Cumulative %
1	5.238	52.384	52.384
2	1.328	13.275	65.659
3	1.166	11.657	77.316
4	0.481	4.811	82.128
5	0.463	4.629	86.756
6	0.384	3.840	90.596
7	0.303	3.025	93.622
8	0.245	2.451	96.072
9	0.200	1.996	98.068
10	0.193	1.932	100.000

component has an eigenvalue of 5.238 and accounts for 52.38% of the variability in the entire sample. The second principal component has an eigenvalue of 1.328 and accounts for 13.28% of the variability in the sample. Principal components 1 and 2 together account for 65.66% of the variability in the sample. Successive principal components have progressively smaller eigenvalues and account for smaller and smaller proportions of the overall variability in the data. The 10 principal components shown in Table 6.5 account for all of the variance in the sample. The 10 variables are therefore perfectly accounted for by the 10 principal components.

The cumulative percentages in Table 6.5 show that a large proportion of the data can be accounted for by a relatively small number of principal components. It may be possible, therefore, to model the 10 variables quite closely using just a few components. The problem for the analyst is to decide how many components are needed to adequately describe the data whilst ensuring that the components are interpretable.

Selecting the Number of Factors

There are numerous methods of choosing the number of factors which are needed to adequately describe the data. The easiest and most commonly used method is to select any component with an eigenvalue greater than 1.0. For the example above, three components would be retained if this method were used. Table 6.5 shows that these three components account for over 77% of the variability in the data. It should be noted, however, that this method only provides a rough estimate of the optimal number of factors which can be used to describe the data.

Scree plots which show eigenvalues plotted against component number have also been proposed as a method of identifying the number of factors required (Cattell, 1966). The important thing to note from these plots is the discontinuity between the slope of the line linking the later principal components (components which account for little variance) and the slope linking the earlier, more important components. From Figure 6.1 it can be seen that components 4 to 10 fall roughly on a straight line and that components 1 to 3 depart from this line. This discontinuity suggests that the first three components might be interesting with regards to the amount of variance they account for and should, therefore, be retained in the analysis. The interpretation of the scree plot is, however, not always so clear cut and can be open to differing interpretations. As with the eigenvalues, it can only be used as a rough guide as to the optimal number of factors required to describe the data.

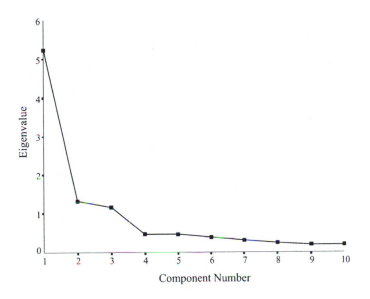

Figure 6.1: Scree Plot

There are no hard and fast rules which can determine the optimum number of factors to retain in an analysis. If there are many factors included in the solution, it may be difficult to interpret them all and make it difficult to justify their inclusion in a GLM. Alternatively, if too few factors are retained, the data might not be adequately described and important information about distinct factors left out. A balance needs to be struck between the amount of variance in the sample which is accounted for and the number of interpretable factors. We recommend that eigenvalues and scree plots be used to provide a first indication of the number of factors needed to adequately describe the data, but also recommend that analyses are repeated using different numbers of factors if there is any doubt about the optimal number to include. The number of factors included in an analysis will ultimately depend on the interpretability of the factors and the objectives of the research.

6.4.2   Interpreting the Initial Factors

As a first step in interpreting the results, it is useful to look at the proportion of variance for each variable which is accounted for by the retained factors (in this case, these have been calculated using principal components analysis). This statistic is known as the *communality* and is shown in Table 6.6 for both a 10-factor (the maximum number of components) and a 3-factor model (retaining the components having eigenvalues greater than 1.0 and those recommended by a scree plot).

Table 6.6: Communalities for 10 and 3-Factor Models

Variable	10-Factor Model	3-Factor Model
Articulation	1.000	0.741
Attention	1.000	0.852
Comprehension	1.000	0.789
Coordination	1.000	0.847
Drawing	1.000	0.826
Memory	1.000	0.742
Motor Skill	1.000	0.644
Sentence Completion	1.000	0.620
Temperament	1.000	0.872
Writing	1.000	0.798

It can be seen in Table 6.6 that the 10-factor model accounts for all of the variance in the data. The communalities for each variable are therefore 1.000. The 3-factor model, on the other hand, does not account for all of the variance in the data (this model only explains 77.3% of the total variance, see Table 6.5) and the communalities are therefore less than 1.000. For example, the three factors account for 74.1% of the variance in the variable 'articulation', 87.2% of the variance in the variable 'temperament', and only 62% of the variance in the variable 'sentence completion'. These data provide some clues as to the power of the model in relation to particular variables and also provide some indication as to which variables may be omitted from the analysis. Those variables which show particularly low communalities may be removed on the basis that they are unlikely to form a major part of any of the proposed factors.

If the factors are to be given some substantive meaning, their relationship with each variable needs to be quantified. For the 3-factor model derived above, these relationships are shown in Table 6.7. The values provided in this table are the correlations between the variables and the factors, and are commonly known as *factor loadings*. These loadings show the contribution made by each factor to the communality score. In fact, the communalities for each variable is equal to the sum of the squared correlation coefficients between the variable and each factor. For example, the variable 'articulation' has a communality of 0.741 which is equal to $0.641^2 + 0.379^2 + (-0.432^2)$. Similarly, the amount of variance in the sample which is explained by each factor (the eigenvalue) can be calculated by summing the squared factor loadings for that factor. For example, factor 1 accounts for $0.641^2 + 0.615^2 + 0.766^2 + \cdots + 0.540^2 + 0.796^2 = 5.238$ (see Table 6.5).

Table 6.7: Factor Loadings for the 3-Factor Model

Variable	Factor 1	Factor 2	Factor 3
Articulation	0.641	0.379	−0.432
Attention	0.615	0.451	0.520
Comprehension	0.766	0.253	−0.371
Coordination	0.824	−0.391	0.123
Drawing	0.815	−0.384	0.115
Memory	0.769	0.188	−0.340
Motor Skill	0.673	−0.431	0.076
Sentence Completion	0.741	0.194	−0.181
Temperament	0.540	0.444	0.619
Writing	0.796	−0.399	0.071

The factors can be interpreted by identifying the variables they are highly related to. For example, if factor 1 is strongly related to the variables, 'motor skill', 'drawing' and 'coordination', this could be interpreted as representing physical dexterity. Such a clear-cut identification of the three factors identified in Table 6.7 is not possible as they are related to many variables. The difficulty with providing interpretations for the factors in such circumstances is demonstrated graphically in Figure 6.2, where the first two factors from the 3-factor model identified above are shown in a simple two-dimensional scatter plot[1]. This graph suggests that there are two distinct factors in the data which are represented clearly as two clusters of points. The factors are represented as the axes of the graph and those points falling on or close to an axis indicate a strong relationship with that factor. We can see from the graph that the variables fall midway between the axes and are therefore related to both factors.

The presence of the two factors shown in Figure 6.2 is not obvious from the factor loadings of the initial factors (see Table 6.7) as the variables are

---

[1] In order to show this information in two dimensions, only the first two factors and those variables which form part of a two-factor solution are shown. The variables 'attention' and 'temperament' which form a third factor are omitted from this demonstration.

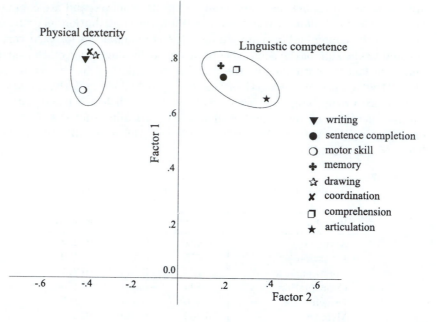

Figure 6.2: A graphical representation of the principal components

not exclusively related to one factor or the other. Attempting to interpret the factor loading scores obtained in a principal components analysis directly is therefore not an ideal method to identify distinct factors.

6.5   Factor Rotation

The technique of factor rotation discussed here enables a simpler interpretation of factors to be obtained and can be most easily understood with reference to the scatter plot shown in Figure 6.2. In this example, it was not easy to interpret the factors as the variables fell midway between the axes. A simple interpretation could have been obtained, however, if the clusters of points had fallen on or close to the axes. Graphically, this can be achieved simply by 'rotating' the axes of the graph relative to the data points in such a way that the clusters load highly on a particular factor.

Figure 6.3 shows what happens when the factors (the axes of the graph) are rotated for the example above. Two methods of rotation are demonstrated, an orthogonal rotation, where the axes are kept at right angles (this represents factors which are uncorrelated, similar to the principal components), and an oblique rotation, where the axes are not constrained to lie at right angles (in other words, the factors are allowed to correlate with one another). The choice of which rotation method to use is based on theoretical considerations about the nature of the factors and whether a degree of correlation between them might be expected.

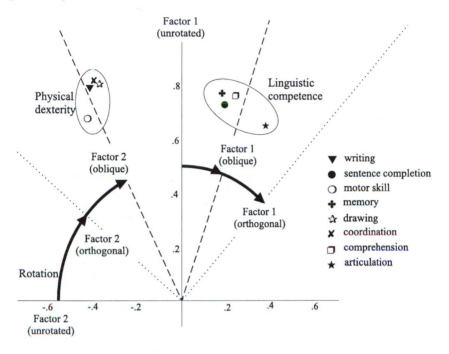

Figure 6.3: A graphical representation of factor rotation

It can be seen from Figure 6.3 that the rotated axes in the graph pass much closer to the clusters of points than do the principal component axes. The precise degree of rotation is determined using one of a number of algorithms available in most common statistical software packages. Popular methods include minimizing the number of variables which have high loadings to enhance the interpretability of the factors, and minimizing the number of factors which provides simpler interpretations of the variables (refer to Kim and Mueller, 1994, for a discussion of rotation techniques). Although there are many rotation techniques available, in practice, the different techniques tend to produce similar results when there is a large sample and the factors are relatively well defined (Fava and Velicer, 1992). The factor loadings for two rotation techniques, orthogonal and oblique, are shown in Table 6.8. In this example, the factors can be interpreted directly from the rotated factor loadings as variables tend to load highly on only one factor. For example, the variable 'attention', which correlated with all three of the principal components more or less evenly, only correlates highly with a single rotated factor (factor 3). A similar pattern can be seen for the other variables in Table 6.8. Software typically provides two matrices for obliquely rotated factors, a structure matrix and a pattern matrix. A structure matrix shows the correlations between each factor and each variable, whilst a pattern matrix shows the regression weights for the common factors where each observed variable is a linear combination of the factors (see Equations 6.2a to 6.2c). The factors are interpreted on the basis of the loadings in the pattern matrix.

Table 6.8: A Component Matrix showing Orthogonal and Oblique Rotation of Factors

Variable	Initial Factors			Rotated Factors					
				Orthogonal[†]			Oblique[‡]		
	1	2	3	1	2	3	1	2	3
Articulation	.641	.379	−.432	.843	.089	.149	.936	.154	−.011
Attention	.615	.451	.520	.231	.164	.879	.073	−.002	.890
Comprehension	.766	.253	−.371	.826	.274	.178	.857	−.062	−.007
Coordination	.824	−.391	.123	.259	.855	.221	.018	−.890	.052
Drawing	.815	−.384	.115	.261	.843	.215	.025	−.876	.047
Memory	.769	.188	−.340	.779	.327	.167	.789	−.138	−.019
Motor Skills	.673	−.431	.076	.179	.776	.102	−.032	−.836	−.050
Sent. Comp.	.741	.194	−.181	.660	.328	.276	.631	−.158	.123
Temperament	.540	.444	.619	.117	.134	.917	−.058	.007	.959
Writing	.796	−.399	.071	.273	.834	.167	.049	−.869	−.006

† Rotation technique = Equamax (see SPSS Inc., 1996c).
‡ Rotation technique = Oblimin; pattern matrix (see SPSS Inc., 1996c).

It should be noted that rotating the factors does not affect the goodness-of-fit of a factor solution. Although the factor matrix changes, the percentage of total variance explained for each variable (the communality) does not change. However, the percentage of variance accounted for by each of the factors does change. Rotation merely redistributes the explained variance. The communality of the variables and the eigenvalues of the factors can still be calculated from the component matrix of the orthogonally rotated factors as the axes remain at right angles. For example, the variable 'articulation', which had a communality of 0.741 can be obtained by calculating the sum of the squared factor loadings for that variable ($0.843^2 + 0.089^2 + 0.149^2 = 0.741$). The same cannot be said of the factor loadings for obliquely rotated factors as these values are correlated and no longer sum to 1.0 (for a solution with as many factors as variables). For example, the sum of the squared factor loadings for the variable 'articulation' is equal to 0.90 ($0.936^2 + 0.154^2 + (−0.011^2)$), which is considerably higher than the communality value of 0.741 shown in Table 6.6.

Unlike principal components analysis, where there is a unique mathematical solution, there is no mathematically unique solution to the application of rotations. In fact, there are an infinite number of rotations which can be applied, each accounting for the same amount of variance in the original data, but with this variance distributed differently among the factors. There are no objective criteria as to which rotation is best and researchers must decide which one to use on the basis of the interpretability of the results.

6.5.1   Interpreting the Rotated Factors

A first look at Table 6.8 suggests that the rotated factors are easier to interpret than the initial factors as the variables tend to load highly on only one factor. Table 6.9 shows all variables with factor loadings above 0.5 for the three factors using both orthogonal and oblique rotation techniques.

Table 6.9: Factor Loadings for Orthogonally and Obliquely Rotated Factors

	Orthogonally Rotated Factors	Obliquely Rotated Factors
Factor 1: Linguistic Competence		
Articulation	0.843	0.936
Comprehension	0.826	0.857
Memory	0.779	0.789
Sentence Completion	0.660	0.631
Factor 2: Physical Dexterity		
Coordination	0.855	−0.890
Drawing	0.843	−0.876
Writing	0.834	−0.869
Motor Skill	0.776	−0.836
Factor 3: Interactive Competence		
Temperament	0.917	0.959
Attention	0.890	0.890

Using Table 6.9 it is quite simple to interpret the factors. As the loadings are quite similar for the different rotation techniques, similar factors are obtained for both. Factor 1 is strongly related to the variables 'articulation', 'comprehension', 'memory' and 'sentence completion' and could be described as indicating linguistic ability. The relatively high loading associated with the variable 'memory' is theoretically interesting as it might not be immediately obvious that memory is such an important part of linguistic competence. Factor 2 is strongly related to the variables, 'coordination', 'drawing', 'writing' and 'motor skill', which suggests a physical dexterity factor. Factor 3 is strongly related to temperament and attention and can be interpreted as interactive competence.

It is important to realize that the sign of the factor loadings do not have any intrinsic meaning. We should not therefore infer anything from the fact that the orthogonally and obliquely rotated factor 2s have different signed loadings. However, differences between variables in the signs of the loadings for particular factors are important as they indicate the way in which variables are related to the factor relative to the other variables. It is also interesting to note that the obliquely rotated factors tend to have higher loadings. As oblique rotation does not impose any restrictions on the degree of rotation which can be applied, the loadings on particular factors can be maximized. If the factors themselves are unrelated to one another (that is, orthogonal) solutions of the different techniques of factor rotation will tend to converge.

For this example, in most cases the factor scores increase as variable scores increase — the higher the score on the variable (1 = poor, 5 = good) the higher the score on the factor. This provides an intuitive interpretation to the factors — a high score on the linguistic competence factor indicates a child who is relatively advanced linguistically. Such a straightforward interpretation is not always possible as the obliquely rotated factor 2 shows. Table 6.9 shows that the variables which are related to this factor have negative factor loadings which means that as the score on the original variables increases, the score on the factor decreases. A high score on the physical dexterity factor therefore indicates a child who is *not* advanced in this skill. As it is relatively easy to misinterpret the factor scores we suggest that a quick check is made on the correlations between the original variables and the factors. For the example above, the correlation between factor 1 and articulation equals 0.850, between factor 2 and coordination, −0.919, and between factor 3 and temperament, 0.932. Using this information it is easy to see that factors 1 and 3 show a positive relationship with the variables whilst factor 2 shows a negative one.

Table 6.10 shows the correlations between the factors for the orthogonal and obliquely rotated factors. We can see that the orthogonal factors are all uncorrelated with one another, whilst the oblique factors show significant relationships. Strong relationships between the obliquely rotated factors may be expected on theoretical grounds. For example, children who have relatively good linguistic competence are also likely to be relatively accomplished at writing (one of the components of the physical dexterity factor[2]). Similarly, those children who are quite interactive will also tend to be well-developed linguistically (they will tend to be more practiced and confident).

To summarize, the use of factor analysis has enabled the original 10 variables, which measured children's competencies in a number of related tasks, to be reduced to three factors. These factors have been interpreted as indicating

---

[2]The correlation between the factors as shown in Table 6.10 is negative since the factor loadings for physical dexterity are negative compared to the positive loadings for linguistic competence.

Table 6.10: Correlations Between Orthogonal and Obliquely Rotated Factors

	Linguistic Competence	Physical Dexterity	Interactive Competence
	Orthogonal Factors		
Linguistic Competence	1.000	0.000	0.000
Physical Dexterity	0.000	1.000	0.000
Interactive Competence	0.000	0.000	1.000
	Oblique Factors		
Linguistic Competence	1.000	$-0.524^{\dagger}$	$0.408^{\dagger}$
Physical Dexterity	$-0.524^{\dagger}$	1.000	$-0.382^{\dagger}$
Interactive Competence	$0.408^{\dagger}$	$-0.382^{\dagger}$	1.000

$\dagger = P < 0.0005$.

linguistic competence, physical dexterity and interactive competence. In this case, the factors appear to make theoretical sense and suggests that the factor analysis has been successful.

6.6   Including Factors in GLMs

Having determined that factors can be extracted from the data and that these are theoretically meaningful, it is possible to include them in Generalized Linear Models. Each case can be described in terms of factors as opposed to the original variables, and 'factor scores' can be computed and saved as new variables. Factor scores can basically be seen as estimates of the scores that subjects would have got on the factors had these been measured directly.

The procedure for calculating the factor scores is relatively simple, but is computationally demanding as scores have to be derived for each individual case. We know the score of each case for each variable (this is the raw data) and we also know the relationship between the factors and the variables (the factors are calculated on the basis of this relationship). Given these two pieces of information, it is possible to estimate the factor scores for each case. One of the most popular methods, of a number which are available to calculate factor scores, is the multiple regression technique. Equation 6.7 shows how to estimate the factor score that case 1 is likely to have got for factor 1.

$$\text{factor 1, case 1} = \hat{\beta}_1 x_1 + \hat{\beta}_2 x_2 + \hat{\beta}_3 x_3 + \ldots + \hat{\beta}_p x_p \qquad (6.7)$$

where $\hat{\beta}_p$ is the estimated factor score coefficient for variable p, and x_p is the pth observed variable.

Using similar formulas, factor scores for each case can be computed for every factor. The general form for this equation is given as:

$$\hat{F}_{ij} = \hat{\beta}_1 x_{i1} + \hat{\beta}_2 x_{i2} + \hat{\beta}_3 x_{i3} + \ldots + \hat{\beta}_p x_{ip} \qquad (6.8)$$

where F_{ij} is the estimated factor score for case i, for factor j,
and x_{ip} is the pth observed variable for case i.

Factor scores can be simply generated using statistical software — a procedure which is demonstrated in Section 6.7. Further information about how factor scores are generated can be found in Sharma (1996).

The inclusion of the original data (that is, the 10 variables) in a GLM would have been inappropriate as the variables are highly inter-related and would have demonstrated high levels of multicollinearity (these levels can be calculated using VIF and tolerance statistics; see Section 3.3.6). Factor scores can, however, usually be included (after they have been screened for outliers) as they are unlikely to show problematic levels of multicollinearity even when an oblique rotation has been used and the factors are significantly related (see Table 6.10. For the three oblique factors extracted in the example above, the maximum tolerance score is 1.482, which is well above the accepted score (an example of the calculation of tolerance scores for factors is given in the next Section).

6.7   A Worked Example of Factor Analysis

This example is primarily designed to demonstrate how factor analysis can be used in conjunction with GLMs. The data were collected as part of a project which investigated interviewing techniques used by practicing interviewers and the quality of young childrens' testimonies (see Hutcheson, Baxter, Telfer and Warden, 1995). Although these data have been adapted somewhat to enable a straightforward demonstration of factor analysis, the conclusions drawn here broadly concur with those found using the original data. Although this data set contains only 43 cases, which is below the sample size recommended in the text, it is sufficient for the purposes of this demonstration.

The data shown in Table 6.11 consist of 16 variables, 14 of which (Q1 to Q14) assess different aspects of the interview and two of which assess the quality of testimony using measures of completeness and accuracy. Variables Q1 to Q14 show the average scores provided by a panel of raters who assessed the interviews on a number of aspects of child and interviewer behaviour and overall impressions about the interviews. These behaviours were rated using a 5-point Likert scale and were averaged across a number of different raters, producing a continuous scale ranging in value from 1 to 5. The variables 'comp' and 'acc' are continuous variables which provide a measure of the completeness

Table 6.11: Child Witness Example Data Set

Subject	Q1	Q2	Q3	Q4	Q5	Q6	Q7	Q8
1	2.5	1.9	1.8	3.6	1.7	3.0	2.4	2.5
2	3.5	3.5	3.8	3.5	3.7	4.0	3.9	4.0
3	4.0	3.9	3.5	3.0	3.0	3.1	3.2	3.4
4	3.8	3.4	2.9	3.2	3.2	3.2	3.4	3.3
5	3.6	3.6	3.0	4.1	3.1	3.4	4.0	3.6
6	2.5	2.6	2.6	3.7	2.9	3.6	2.4	1.8
7	4.9	4.9	4.5	2.6	4.7	4.4	3.6	3.5
8	3.3	3.2	3.5	2.8	3.3	3.7	2.9	2.6
9	2.6	2.8	2.8	2.9	2.9	3.8	1.8	1.6
10	2.3	2.5	1.8	4.5	2.1	2.1	3.7	3.6
11	4.4	4.2	3.6	3.0	3.4	3.7	2.4	2.6
12	4.2	3.8	3.1	4.5	2.9	2.0	3.9	1.7
13	3.8	3.9	4.1	3.1	3.5	3.7	3.2	2.7
14	2.5	2.0	1.6	4.9	2.0	3.3	2.9	3.6
15	4.3	4.1	4.3	1.7	4.3	4.9	2.1	1.6
16	2.6	2.0	1.8	3.6	1.8	2.9	2.4	2.6
17	3.5	3.4	3.8	3.5	3.8	3.8	3.9	4.0
18	4.1	3.8	3.5	3.0	3.2	3.0	3.2	3.3
19	3.8	3.4	2.9	3.1	3.1	3.2	3.4	3.3
20	3.5	3.5	3.0	4.0	3.3	3.3	4.0	3.6
21	2.6	2.7	2.4	3.5	2.8	3.6	2.3	1.7
22	4.9	3.2	3.5	2.8	3.4	3.8	3.0	2.6
23	2.6	2.9	2.7	3.0	3.0	3.9	1.9	1.5
24	2.3	2.4	1.8	4.5	2.1	2.0	3.5	3.4
25	4.5	4.6	4.8	2.0	4.3	4.7	3.1	3.4
26	4.4	4.1	3.5	2.9	3.3	3.6	2.5	2.5
27	4.2	3.8	3.2	4.4	3.1	1.9	3.7	1.6
28	3.7	3.8	4.2	3.1	3.5	3.6	3.4	2.8
29	2.5	1.8	1.8	4.8	1.9	3.2	2.9	3.8
30	4.1	4.2	4.4	1.8	4.3	4.9	2.2	1.7
31	4.0	3.9	3.6	2.9	3.0	3.1	3.1	3.2
32	3.9	3.4	3.1	3.0	3.1	3.2	3.3	3.2
33	3.6	3.5	3.2	4.0	3.2	3.3	3.9	3.5
34	2.6	2.7	2.5	3.5	2.9	3.6	2.5	1.8
35	4.9	4.9	4.4	2.5	4.6	4.3	3.6	3.5
36	3.1	3.3	3.4	2.8	3.3	3.7	3.0	2.8
37	2.6	2.8	2.8	3.0	3.0	3.9	1.9	1.5
38	2.3	2.3	1.9	4.5	2.1	2.1	3.6	3.5
39	4.4	4.6	4.8	1.9	4.3	4.7	3.0	3.5
40	4.4	3.8	3.1	4.6	3.0	2.1	3.9	1.6
41	3.7	3.7	4.1	3.0	3.7	3.6	3.3	2.6
42	2.5	1.8	1.7	4.8	2.1	3.2	3.0	3.6

continued...

... continued

Subject	Q9	Q10	Q11	Q12	Q13	Q14	Comp.	Acc.
1	2.4	2.3	1.8	1.4	2.3	2.2	22.0	66.6
2	2.4	3.1	3.5	3.6	3.2	3.2	63.4	97.5
3	3.2	2.6	3.3	3.3	2.9	2.7	48.2	78.4
4	2.2	2.5	3.2	2.1	2.5	2.7	41.2	61.2
5	3.0	3.9	3.5	1.9	2.4	2.1	29.1	83.2
6	2.6	3.7	2.6	2.2	2.2	2.1	31.3	74.2
7	1.6	1.3	4.4	1.4	1.1	0.9	26.2	58.1
8	3.0	2.3	3.2	2.8	2.5	2.7	52.8	78.9
9	2.1	2.4	2.7	2.5	1.0	2.2	43.9	58.2
10	3.2	4.0	2.0	2.4	1.3	2.3	15.2	65.3
11	2.2	2.4	3.0	1.5	1.5	1.4	42.5	52.9
12	2.6	4.3	3.6	1.6	0.8	0.6	32.1	61.1
13	2.3	1.8	3.4	1.8	1.3	1.6	60.9	66.3
14	3.6	4.8	1.7	1.8	1.5	1.6	19.4	64.5
15	1.1	1.7	3.9	2.2	2.0	2.7	80.4	67.2
16	2.4	2.3	1.9	1.9	2.0	1.8	20.8	65.3
17	2.4	2.9	3.5	3.6	2.7	3.2	62.9	68.9
18	3.1	2.4	3.4	2.5	2.4	3.2	33.9	64.0
19	2.4	2.4	3.1	2.9	1.8	2.5	54.4	78.1
20	3.0	3.9	3.4	2.5	1.9	2.6	29.1	83.0
21	2.6	3.7	2.5	2.4	1.6	2.2	20.4	85.6
22	3.0	2.3	3.3	3.2	2.5	3.3	20.0	78.4
23	2.1	2.4	2.8	2.3	2.5	1.8	25.4	62.8
24	3.1	4.1	2.0	1.9	2.2	1.4	15.2	72.8
25	1.5	1.3	4.5	2.3	2.6	2.5	92.9	58.9
26	2.4	2.4	3.0	2.3	1.5	1.6	43.0	64.7
27	2.7	4.3	3.4	1.8	1.0	1.1	52.4	48.2
28	2.2	1.7	3.4	1.8	1.6	2.5	59.0	63.7
29	3.8	4.8	1.5	1.5	2.5	1.4	23.4	73.1
30	1.3	1.8	4.0	1.9	1.2	1.8	77.3	78.0
31	3.1	2.5	3.3	3.0	3.4	3.0	44.7	81.5
32	2.2	2.5	3.0	2.7	2.4	2.8	45.0	90.4
33	3.0	3.7	3.3	2.6	2.7	2.1	27.2	85.3
34	2.6	3.7	2.4	2.8	2.2	1.7	21.5	85.5
35	1.7	1.4	4.4	1.8	1.3	1.5	78.2	61.9
36	3.0	2.4	3.3	3.7	3.4	2.8	68.9	93.2
37	2.2	2.4	2.8	1.6	1.7	2.2	25.1	62.4
38	3.2	4.1	2.0	1.7	1.5	2.2	15.8	68.1
39	1.4	1.3	4.4	2.7	2.2	2.4	68.9	58.7
40	2.6	4.4	3.4	1.1	0.4	0.7	37.1	48.1
41	2.3	1.8	3.4	1.7	1.5	1.5	60.0	63.9
42	3.7⁻	4.8	1.6	1.8	1.8	2.0	25.7	58.2

and accuracy of the childrens' statements. Table 6.12 provides a key to the data and shows the original rating scale.

Table 6.12: Questions Used in the Child Witness Study

Variable	Description	Coding scheme
Q1	How authoritative was the interviewer?	5=very, 0=not at all
Q2	How business-like was the interviewer?	5=very, 0=not at all
Q3	How formal was the interview?	5=very, 0=not at all
Q4	How much like a normal conversation was the interview?	5=very, 0=not at all
Q5	How serious was overall atmosphere?	5=very, 0=not at all
Q6	How willing was child to participate?	5=very, 0=not at all
Q7	How easy was it for the child to follow the interview?	5=very, 0=not at all
Q8	How clear were the interviewer's objectives?	5=very, 0=not at all
Q9	To what extent was the child encouraged to talk freely?	5=a lot, 0=not at all
Q10	How much smalltalk did the interviewer engage in?	5=a lot, 0=none
Q11	How serious was the interviewer's manner?	5=very, 0=not at all
Q12	How coherent were the child's answers?	5=very, 0=not at all
Q13	How well did the child understand the purpose of the interview?	5=very, 0=not at all
Q14	How credible was the child's evidence?	5=very, 0=not at all
Comp.	How complete was the child's evidence?	percentage score
Acc.	How accurate was the child's evidence?	percentage score

The aim of this example is to model the quality of childrens' evidence and determine what effect, if any, interviewer style has. Models of statement quality can be calculated using OLS regression techniques with variables 'acc' and 'comp' as continuous response variables and 'Q1' to 'Q14' as explanatory variables. However, using the data as it stands is unlikely to provide a theoretically satisfying model as a number of the explanatory variables are likely to be strongly related to one another which suggests that multicollinearity could pose a problem. This is, in fact, the case as Table 6.13 illustrates. A number of variables show VIF values above 5 and tolerance values below 0.2, which indicate inappropriately high levels of multicollinearity. It is hardly surprising that such high levels are found as many of the variables measure similar things (for example, we would expect the degree to which interviews are perceived as 'serious' and 'formal' to be closely related). A factor analysis is computed on these data in an attempt to reduce the levels of multicollinearity and enable testimony quality to be modelled using OLS regression. In addition, it is important to identify latent variables which can be used to inform the model-building process and provide theoretical insights into child eyewitness testimony.

Table 6.13: Multicollinearity Statistics

Variable	Tolerance	VIF
Q1	0.077	13.069
Q2	0.022	45.542
Q3	0.042	24.035
Q4	0.019	52.453
Q5	0.023	43.150
Q6	0.048	20.757
Q7	0.039	25.518
Q8	0.123	8.123
Q9	0.165	6.062
Q10	0.061	16.328
Q11	0.029	34.701
Q12	0.261	3.835
Q13	0.297	3.373
Q14	0.220	4.550

Before computing a factor analysis, it is important to screen the data and transform any variables which violate the assumptions of the test. For this demonstration, however, we will assume that all of the variables are Normally distributed, that relationships between variables are linear and also that there are no significant outliers (refer to Chapter 2 for a detailed description of data screening and transformation procedures). The appropriateness of applying a factor analysis to these data can be determined by computing overall and individual KMO statistics. The overall KMO statistic for all 14 variables is 0.763, which, to use Kaiser's interpretation, is 'middling'. This statistic can be improved by screening out those variables which are not strongly related to any factors. These can be identified using the individual KMO statistics. Table 6.14 shows that on the basis of the smallest individual KMO statistics, two variables can be excluded from the analysis (Q7 and Q8[3]). We can see that the exclusion of these variables leads to an improvement in the overall KMO statistic to a value of 0.832, which, to use Kaiser's terminology is 'meritorious'. It would therefore appear to be appropriate to run a factor analysis on the 12 remaining variables.

The 12 correlated variables can now be converted into 12 uncorrelated components using principal component analysis (see Table 6.15). We can see

---

[3]These variables will not form a part of this factor analysis but can be entered into a GLM as separate explanatory variables.

Table 6.14: Removing Variables on the Basis of Individual KMO Statistics

Number of Variables	Overall KMO Statistic	Smallest Individual KMO Statistic	Variable Removed
14	0.763	0.313(Q8)	Q8
13	0.793	0.304(Q7)	Q7
12	0.832	0.646(Q12)	no variable removed

that the first three components all have eigenvalues above 1.0 and collectively account for 89.24% of the variance in the data. Eigenvalues above 1.0 suggests that three components should be used in the analysis[4].

Table 6.15: Variance Accounted for by the Principal Components

Component	Eigenvalue	% of Variance	Cumulative %
Q1	7.021	58.509	58.509
Q2	2.624	21.870	80.378
Q3	1.063	8.862	89.240
Q4	0.368	3.071	92.311
Q5	0.330	2.749	95.060
Q6	0.208	1.732	96.792
Q9	0.164	1.370	98.162
Q10	0.103	0.861	99.023
Q11	0.045	0.372	99.395
Q12	0.031	0.262	99.657
Q13	0.025	0.206	99.862
Q14	0.017	0.138	100.000

Table 6.16 shows the communalities and the loadings for a 3-factor model before and after rotation. From this Table we can see that all of the variables are well-described by the three factors (Over 80% of the variance in each variable is accounted for). It is however, difficult to interpret the initial factors since factor 1 loads highly on most of the variables whilst factor 3 does not load particularly highly on any. In order to achieve a better differentiation, the factors were rotated. The method of rotation used here is oblique rotation as it is reasonable to assume a degree of correlation between the factors.

Using the rotated loadings it is relatively easy to interpret the factors. From Table 6.17 we can see that the more serious, formal and business-like the interview, the higher the child scores on factor 1. The more coherent and

---

[4]A three component model is also suggested by an inspection of a scree plot for these data.

Table 6.16: Communalities and Factor Loadings for a 3-factor Model

Variable	Communality	Initial Factors[†] 1	2	3	Rotated Factors[‡] 1	2	3
Q1	.916	.815	−.301	.402	1.024	−.075	.123
Q2	.981	.899	−.233	.346	.994	−.024	.007
Q3	.956	.963	−.049	.162	.782	.089	−.267
Q4	.944	−.894	−.206	.319	−.145	−.154	.840
Q5	.933	.957	−.077	.110	.729	−.043	−.323
Q6	.810	.762	.206	−.431	−.059	.101	−.912
Q9	.872	−.809	.242	.398	−.132	.310	.842
Q10	.856	−.846	−.117	.355	−.100	−.050	.851
Q11	.955	.927	−.108	.290	.916	.077	−.088
Q12	.842	.211	.850	.274	.187	.927	.127
Q13	.802	.068	.886	.113	−.086	.891	−.001
Q14	.842	.214	.892	.017	−.102	.874	−.188

† Initial factors extracted using principal components analysis.
‡ Rotation method = Oblimin. Loadings taken from Pattern Matrix.

credible the child, and the more they understood the purpose of the interview (a measure of the child's ability to understand), the higher the child scores on factor 2. The more smalltalk engaged in, the more like a normal conversation the interview was and the more the child was encouraged to talk freely corresponds with a high score on factor 3. The willingness of the child to provide information is also related to factor 3. However, in this case, as the loading is negative, it is the children who were less willing to provide information who scored highly.

The three factors shown in Table 6.17 are theoretically meaningful and we propose the following interpretation:

Factor 1 = Interview atmosphere

Factor 2 = Child's task competence

Factor 3 = Conversational interaction

The interpretation of the first two factors is fairly straightforward, however, the interpretation of the third is a bit more complicated. This factor was identified as conversational interaction as it is related to the degree of conversation normality, amount of smalltalk and the degree to which children were encouraged to talk freely. It is also related (in the opposite direction) to how willing

Table 6.17: Interpreting the Obliquely Rotated Factors

		Rotated Factor Loadings
Factor 1		
Q1	Authoritative (interviewer)	1.024
Q2	Business-like (interviewer)	0.994
Q11	Serious (interviewer)	0.916
Q3	Formal (interviewer)	0.782
Q5	Serious Atmosphere	0.729
Factor 2		
Q12	Coherent (child)	0.927
Q13	Understand Purpose (child)	0.891
Q14	Credible (child)	0.874
Factor 3		
Q6	Willing to Participate (child)	−0.912
Q10	Amount of Smalltalk	0.851
Q9	Encouraged to Speak Freely (child)	0.842
Q4	Normal Conversation	0.840

the child was to provide information. On reflection, this is perhaps not too surprising as an unwilling child needs more encouragement, which typically involves the interviewer getting the child to speak by engaging in 'normal' conversation with more 'smalltalk'. Children who are willing to provide information, on the other hand, could be interviewed in a more formal manner with less encouragement and less smalltalk.

Using an oblique method for rotating the components we have derived three factors which are correlated and Table 6.18 shows a significant correlation between 'interview atmosphere' and 'conversational interaction'. This correlation is to be expected since the general atmosphere of the interview and the interviewer's behaviour will have a strong influence on the type of conversation. From the sign of the correlation, we can see that a very formal

Table 6.18: Correlation Between the Latent Variables

	Interview Atmosphere	Child's Task Competence	Conversational Interaction
Interview Atmosphere	1.000	0.001	−0.617[†]
Child's Task Competence	0.001	1.000	−0.169
Conversational Interaction	−0.617[†]	−0.169	1.000

† $P < 0.0005$.

atmosphere is related to an interview which does not appear to be much like a normal conversation and contains relatively little smalltalk. Calculating the degree of correlation between the factors is an important exercise as it provides information which can be of use when model-building using GLMs (see below).

Table 6.19: Multicollinearity

	Collinearity Statistics	
	Tolerance	VIF
Q7	0.190	5.272
Q8	0.490	2.445
Interview Atmosphere	0.214	4.667
Child's Task Competence	0.762	1.313
Conversational Interaction	0.189	5.297

Having determined that the factors are interpretable and make 'sense' they can be considered for entry into a regression model. First, one saves the factor scores as variables (see Section 6.9), and then enters these into a model along with other explanatory variables (Q7 and Q8). An initial look at these variables, however, indicates that it might not be advisable to input them directly into a model as there is a high level of multicollinearity present (see Table 6.19).

Table 6.20: Correlation Matrix

	Q7	Q8	Interview Atmosphere	Child's Task Competence	Conv. Interaction
Q7	1.000	$0.602^{\dagger}$	0.268	0.024	$0.413^{\dagger}$
Q8	$0.602^{\dagger}$	1.000	0.040	0.381^{*}	0.143
Interview Atmosphere	0.268	0.040	1.000	0.001	$-0.617^{\dagger}$
Child's Task Competence	0.024	0.381^{*}	0.001	1.000	-0.169
Conversational Interaction	$0.413^{\dagger}$	0.143	$-0.617^{\dagger}$	-0.169	1.000

$*$ $P < 0.05$.
$\dagger$ $P < 0.0005$.

Before we attempt to reduce the levels of multicollinearity in the data it is useful to look at the bivariate correlations between all of the explanatory variables. Table 6.20 shows highly significant relationships between the factors 'interview atmosphere' and 'conversational interaction', and between 'Q7' and 'Q8'.

As the two latent variables are theoretically distinct, for the present we will leave them in the analysis unchanged. The variable 'Q7' and 'Q8', on the other hand, are strongly related and could be considered to be measuring very similar interview attributes. 'How easy was it for the child to follow the interview (Q7)' and 'How clear were the interviewer's objectives (Q8)', might both be considered to be measures of clarity. It is reasonable, therefore, to amalgamate these two variables into a single index of clarity. This can be achieved by summing the two variables and then dividing by 2 (thus retaining a range of values similar to the original 5-point scale). By making up the composite variable 'clarity' from Q7 and Q8, the levels of multicollinearity between the explanatory variables reduces to within acceptable limits (see Table 6.21).

Table 6.21: Multicollinearity

	Collinearity Statistics	
Variable	Tolerance	VIF
Clarity	0.599	1.668
Interview Atmosphere	0.444	2.255
Child's Task Competency	0.781	1.280
Conversational Interaction	0.388	2.577

Using the three factors and the composite variable 'clarity' one can model statement quality using OLS regression. For interest, the regression models we derived are shown in Table 6.22 (for information on how to compute these models see Chapter 3 and the SPSS code in Section 6.9).

The two regression models in Table 6.22 provide some interesting information about the effect that interviewing styles have on the quality of childrens' testimonies. When we consider accuracy, we find that the child's task competency is the only variable which is significantly related. In this case, the greater the child's competence, the greater the accuracy of the statement. When we consider the completeness of the statement we find that it is 'interview atmosphere' and 'conversational interaction' which are important. In this case, the higher the atmosphere score (the more authoritative, business-like and serious the interviewer) and the lower the conversational interaction score (the less smalltalk engaged in with little encouragement to speak freely and the less like a normal conversation the interview appeared), the more complete the testimony. In order to ascertain the nature of the relationships more simply, the inspection of correlation matrices of the type used in Table 6.10 is suggested. These results suggest that there is little an interviewer can do to

Table 6.22: Models of Statement Quality

	Coefficient	s.e.	t	P
Accuracy				
Child's Task Competency	7.913	1.367	5.789	0.000
(constant)	69.737	1.351	51.625	0.000
Completeness				
Interview Atmosphere	10.838	2.570	4.217	0.000
Conversational Interaction	−8.003	2.570	−3.114	0.003
(constant)	42.737	1.999	21.376	0.000

increase the accuracy of a child's testimony as this appears to be determined by competencies of the child which are beyond the interviewer's control. The interviewer may, however, influence the completeness of the child's testimony by adopting an appropriate conversational style and promoting a certain interview atmosphere. A tentative recommendation which could be drawn from this analysis is that interviewers should be encouraged to concentrate on improving statement completeness rather than ensuring statement accuracy if overall statement quality is to be maximized.

6.8   Summary

This chapter has outlined how factor analysis can be used to represent a number of correlated variables as a smaller number of factors. The emphasis has been on the use of this procedure to reduce the level of multicollinearity in data sets and to provide information about theoretically interesting underlying patterns in the data which can inform the process of model-building. In particular, this chapter has demonstrated how factor analysis can be used in conjunction with GLMs. We present factor analysis here as a useful technique which can be used to improve the quality of GLM modelling, particularly with highly correlated, exploratory data sets.

6.9   Statistical Software Commands

Techniques for computing factor analyses are provided in SPSS, but not in GLIM. Software commands are therefore only provided for the SPSS package. Detailed discussions of the SPSS procedures outlined in this section can be found in the appropriate SPSS manuals (see, for example, SPSS Inc., 1996c).

6.9.1   SPSS

Calculating KMO Statistics

The overall and individual MKO statistics described in Section 6.3.4 can be derived using the following commands:

Statistics   ▼
    Data Reduction   ▶
        Factor ...
            Variables: *input variables*
                | Descriptives ... |
                    Correlation Matrix:
                        KMO and Bartlett's test of sphericity: *check box*
                        Correlation Matrix: Anti-image: *check box*
                | Continue |
           | OK |

The overall KMO statistic is provided in the output by SPSS and the KMO statistics for individual variables are shown on the diagonal of the anti-image correlation matrix.

Calculating VIF and Tolerance Values

Tolerance and VIF values can be calculated using the following commands (also see Section 3.3.6):

Statistics   ▼
    Regression   ▶
        Linear ...
            Dependent: *input response variable*
            Independent(s): *input explanatory variables*
                | Statistics ... |
                    Collinearity diagnostics: *check box*
                | Continue |
           | OK |

Calculating the Correlation between Factors and Individual Variables

Statistics   ▼
        Correlate   ▶
            Bivariate ...
                Variables: *input factors and variables*
      | OK |

Calculating the Factor Analysis from Section 6.7

Input the data shown in Table 6.11. Use the individual KMO statistics to identify variables Q7 and Q8 for removal. The following commands will compute
the statistics shown in Tables 6.15, 6.16 and 6.17 for a three-factor solution:

Statistics   ▼
    Data Reduction   ▶
        Factor ...
            Variables: *input all questions apart from Q7 and Q8*

Compute the overall and individual KMO statistics:

    Descriptives ...

        Correlation Matrix:
            KMO and Bartlett's test of sphericity: *check box*
            Correlation Matrix: Anti-image: *check box*

    Continue

Use principal components analysis to extract the components with eigenvalues
above 1.0:

    Extraction ...

        Method: Principal components
            Extract: Eigenvalues over 1

    Continue

Use the oblique method for rotating the factors:

    Rotation ...

        Method: Direct Oblimin: *check box*

    Continue

Save the rotated factor scores to the spreadsheet:

    Scores ...

        Save as variables: *check box*
            Method: Regression: *check box*

    Continue

    OK

Computing the OLS Regression Model Shown in Table 6.22

Construct a new variable (call it 'clarity') which is the average of the variables Q7 and Q8 (refer to Chapter 2 for a detailed account on computing new variables). The regression models can be computed using the factor scores, Fac1_1, Fac1_2, Fac1_3 (as computed using the commands outlined above), and clarity as explanatory variables and completeness and accuracy as response variables. All commands needed to obtain the models shown in Table 6.22 are shown below:

Statistics   ▼
    Regression   ▶
      Linear ...
        Dependent: *input* accuracy *or* completeness
        Independent(s): *input* Fac1_1, Fac1_2, Fac1_3 *and* clarity
        Method: Backward
      [OK]

Chapter 7

Conclusion

Throughout this book we have sought to demonstrate the underlying unity between a number of common statistical modelling methods and illustrate how they can be used to go beyond the traditional framework of Normal response errors, characterized by OLS regression and ANOVA. This unity provides a more coherent framework for both teaching and understanding statistics, as it is no longer necessary to adopt a 'cookbook' approach covering a range of seemingly disparate methods of data analysis. Through the development of a model-building approach to analysing data, it is hoped that there will be a move towards considering *substantive* significance, rather than just the simple criterion of *statistical* significance engendered by the traditional hypothesis testing approach. By this means, two frequent goals of science, explanation and prediction, can be accommodated in the social sciences. Whilst we have concentrated on large sample statistics, the main concepts dealt with in this book are often directly applicable to small samples through the use of exact methods.

In this book we have illustrated some of the main techniques in generalized linear modelling and hope that the reader, having read the text and perhaps tried out some of the examples, will feel confident enough to read more advanced level texts in their area of speciality. The remainder of this chapter will briefly address some of the areas we believe are worthy of further study, which for reasons of space, we have been unable to dwell on in any great detail. It should be noted that some of these techniques are difficult conceptually for the beginner, and the reader may therefore benefit from consulting a statistical specialist — using the concepts and language for talking about the problems which have been presented in this book.

7.1   Main Points of the GLM Framework

GLMs are a family of models where a fixed linear combination of explanatory variables, the systematic component, is mapped onto the fitted values of a model assumed to follow the probability distribution of the response variable. This scheme was originally developed by Nelder and Wedderburn (1972) and extended in McCullagh and Nelder (1989). GLMs emphasize a move away from the traditional approach of dealing with non-Normality, non-linearity, and non-constant variance by transforming the observed response variable, to one which incorporates this in the link between the linear predictor of the model and the fitted values. By using an appropriate link, one avoids trying to balance the sometimes conflicting transformations which can be used to optimize Normality, ensure constant variance and additivity of effects. With a GLM, one can tune the individual components separately, leaving the original scales of measurement unaltered, thereby aiding the interpretation of the model. Nelder (1997) makes the point that 25 years on researchers are still transforming their response variables when a GLM framework makes this largely unnecessary. In our experience, part of the problem is that not many existing software packages implement the full range of GLM features, and the user is left somewhere between making use of the new features which have been implemented, and falling back on traditional data transformation, where they have not. We consider this software issue further, below.

The measure of the goodness-of-fit of a GLM is the deviance, and this has a direct correspondence to the measures traditionally used for each probability distribution assumed of the response variable, e.g., least-squares for Normal errors, -2 log likelihood for logistic regressions, G^2 for loglinear models. Once one moves away from the identity link for Normal response errors, the common practice of testing the significance of parameters by evaluation with their standard errors, using a t-test, becomes no more than a rough guideline. Instead, the generalized way of testing the significance of a parameter is to evaluate the change in deviance when this term is present and absent from the model, whilst all other terms in the model remain the same. The use of deviance provides a coherent framework for model-building and model evaluation — one which is very similar for all the techniques covered in this book. The common theoretical basis for evaluating goodness-of-fit is a major attraction of GLMs as it greatly simplifies the techniques and provides an easier framework for teaching.

7.2   Sampling Assumptions and GLMs

An important assumption of GLMs is the randomness of the sampling method used to obtain the initial observations. In an experimental context this will be the random allocation of subjects to conditions. With surveys, the data may involve some form of stratified design. If a stratified design or weighted sample design is used where there is no clustering, then a standard GLM approach can be used for the analysis. Each stratified variable, e.g., gender, or socio-economic status, is simply entered into the model as a stratifying factor. This allows for the possibility of unequal numbers of each strata, since they will each have their own parameter estimate. Where no differences are found in the level of a stratifying variable, the variable can be omitted from the model (Aitkin, Anderson, Francis and Hinde, 1989). Factors can also be used for the representation of *blocks* in experimental designs. In each of these internally homogeneous units, the experimental treatment is repeated, with the allocation of the cases to the conditions being random within the block. Blocks may be different schools, countries, or professional groups, but the design within each block is made the same.

Where some form of *cluster* sampling is used, this tends to produce correlations between the observations in a cluster, violating the assumption of independent measurements in a GLM. The regression models outlined in this book are invalid when used with data from a clustered sampling scheme. Models have been developed for this purpose, together with software for the task, in an extension known as *multi-level* modelling (e.g., Goldstein, 1986; 1995). A software package allowing the multi-level modelling of clustered samples is MLn, whilst macros have been developed allowing the analysis of clustered data in GLIM, e.g., Aitkin and Francis (1995; in press).

As the reader can imagine, careful consideration to appropriate sampling at the design stage of an experiment or survey can make the analysis of the data much more straightforward. Avoiding cluster-sampling, snowball methods, or any technique that induces correlations within each sub-group of observations will allow a GLM analysis following the pattern of those in this book. Otherwise, considerable additional complexity is introduced into the analysis, and a multi-level modelling approach may be required. Further discussion of these issues is given in Aitken et al. (1989), and Fienberg (1980).

7.3   Measurement Assumptions of Explanatory Variables in GLMs

The variates fall into two classes, a single response variable, and one of several explanatory variables. The assumptions about each are different and affect the utility of the resulting model. The response variable is held to be a random variable whose probability distribution is one of the exponential family, e.g., the Normal, Poisson, binomial, or gamma, whilst the explanatory variables are held to be fixed variables with values that are known with little or no measurement error, and without missing values. Thus, there is assumed to be a fixed structure of explanatory variables, which together with the parameter estimates, forms the systematic component of the model. This assumption of the error being confined to a single response variable with known values of the explanatory variable underlies the generalized linear models developed in this book, and is an important point.

Measurement error is common in the explanatory variables often available to us in the social sciences, e.g., repeated measurements of the same subject often give different values for a particular variable. Within the GLMs outlined here it is not possible to allow for measurement errors in the explanatory variables, except in the case where repeated measurements are taken to give us replicate or 'parallel' measurements on an unreliable explanatory variable. Where replicates are unavailable, it is common to ignore the issue and run the analysis anyway. This may be fine for a descriptive model, but Aitken et al. (1989) caution against this for experimental designs in which causal inferences are to be made. Draper and Smith (1981) take the pragmatic line that from a real-world point of view it is rare that the explanatory variables are measured without error, but an analysis explicitly including such measurement errors is much more complicated. Therefore, they suggest that regression models are used in situations where the random variation is likely to be small in comparison to the *range* of an explanatory variable, such that we can effectively ignore it. The loglinear models are an exception to this in that they allow multiple categorical response factors, in the manner described in Chapter 5 — one models associations between factors entered into the right-hand side of the model equation, some of which can be treated as responses, by means of the fitted frequency counts. Fahrmeir and Tutz (1994) give an extensive discussion of discrete multivariate statistical models within the GLM framework.

For readers wishing to read more about modelling with explicit measurement error, Fuller and Hideroglou (1978) give a detailed analysis of the estimation of regression models with measurement errors present in the explanatory variables, whilst the LISREL statistical software package (Jöreskog and Sörbom, 1981) is able to fit many such models. Whittaker (1990), and Edwards (1995) provide alternative frameworks for the multivariate modelling of continuous and categorical variables, using graph theory. They introduce the MIM statistical package that allows graphical models with mixed continuous and discrete response variables.

7.4   Ordinal Variables

In a GLM framework, variates fall into the classes of continuous and categorical variables. Categorical response variables can be analysed with logit or log links, depending on the number of categories, whilst continuous variables can be analysed with an identity link. Categorical explanatory variables form dummy coded factors, whilst continuous explanatory variables are entered as single covariates. Ordered categorical data can be entered as either unordered categorical data, or if some assumptions are made about the scale of measurement, as grouped continuous variates. In addition, models which explicitly recognize the properties of ordered categorical response variables are available in some statistical packages. We have covered extensions of the loglinear framework to include the additional element of covariates with scores for the levels of each rank, e.g., the linear×linear and continuation ratio logit models. However, one very useful model which has only been implemented in a limited range of software packages is the *proportional odds* model (McCullagh and Nelder, 1989). A Macro is available for the GLIM software package, and this analysis is available as standard within GENSTAT, and the GENMOD module of SAS. The issue of modelling ordinal data is given extensive coverage in Agresti (1984).

7.5 GLM Variants of ANOVA and ANCOVA

Traditional parametric models in the social sciences include ANOVA and ANCOVA which both involve modelling a single continuous response variable. In the case of ANOVA, the explanatory variables are all categorical, whilst ANCOVA involves a mixture of continuous and categorical explanatory variables. The response variable is assumed to have Normal errors, with constant variance across the explanatory variables. The categorical explanatory variables are assumed to be uncorrelated, i.e., orthogonal to one another, and each combination is held to have an equal number of cases. This leads to the need for estimation procedures for any missing values, or more complex analyses for unbalanced designs. Both approaches can be modelled directly within the regression framework using dummy variables for the categorical explanatory variables, with the advantage of parameter estimates and confidence intervals for the effects.

A simple two-way ANOVA with two factors, gender and smoker, each with two levels, can be modelled as

$$\text{gender} + \text{smoker}$$

for a main effects model, or

$$\text{gender} + \text{smoker} + (\text{gender} \times \text{smoker})$$

for a model including a term for the interaction. Adding a covariate of age in years (a continuous variable) would give us a main effects ANCOVA model of

$$\text{gender} + \text{smoker} + \text{age}$$

whilst the model including all two-way interactions would be

The advantage of the GLM framework is that models with non-orthogonal factors, i.e., those with some degree of multicollinearity, can be built, and

$$\text{gender} + \text{smoker} + \text{age} +$$

$$(\text{gender} \times \text{smoker}) + (\text{gender} \times \text{age}) + (\text{smoker} \times \text{age}).$$

there is no requirement of equal cell sizes for each combination of the factors. A further extension allows the use of alternative link functions to develop corresponding analysis of deviance models for response variables having non-Normal errors, non-constant variance, or multiplicative rather than additive effects. This allows considerable scope in the type of data which can be analysed using the GLM extensions of the familiar techniques of ANOVA and ANCOVA, and is a useful way for those new to GLMs to develop their existing modelling skills. Draper and Smith (1981) illustrate how to use orthogonal dummy coding to obtain results in the traditional ANOVA form. Crawley (1993) demonstrates how to obtain parameter estimates of the means and mean-difference, together with confidence intervals, for each effect.

7.6   Repeated Measurements

A basic GLM assumption is that measurements are independent of one another. Therefore, if the same subject is measured on a number of occasions, allowance will have to be made for this since repeated measurements are unlikely to be independent. Consider a simple study measuring the strength of depression following a trauma, on the Beck Depression Inventory (BDI), analysed as a response variable with Normal errors, and treatment with cognitive-behaviour therapy, together with age as a covariate. Therapy/no-therapy and age form the explanatory variables, and we measure the BDI immediately before treatment, as well as 3, 6, 9 and 12 months afterwards, rounded to the nearest month. The study allows one to examine whether the change in the response variable over the period of assessment differs between the treatment groups, and whether there is an interaction between the therapy condition and the age of subject. Occasion of assessment forms a factor with five levels, we shall call occasion, and a factor for subject enables the subject differences to be allowed for in the analysis. We could have treated occasion as a single continuous variable measuring time, but since the variable has been rounded to the nearest month it is unlikely to be very accurate, therefore here we treat it as a factor with five levels. When the number of measurement occasions is small compared to the number of cases, one can include occasion as a factor in the model along with the other explanatory variables. The other factor in the analysis is therapy, and we have the covariate of age.

A package such as GLIM 4 allows 'nuisance' variables such as subject to be allowed for even though they are not entered explicitly in the model terms or described in the output through the use of the 'eliminate' command. If such a command is not available, the interactions between the subject and the other factors will have to be specified explicitly in the model. In this simple example we will assume the use of an eliminate facility to simplify the model specification.

Fitting an interaction term for *therapy * occasion* allows us to examine whether the within-subject differences in occasion differ from one therapy group compared to the other. The * symbol indicates the model hierarchy of an interaction and the corresponding main effects — in this case the model notation expands to *therapy + occasion + therapy × occasion*. By allowing for the *subject* factor with the eliminate command, the specified model will be *(therapy(subject) * age(subject)) * occasion*. The bracketed term *(subject)* identifies the model term which we have allowed for with the eliminate command. This model allows for differing patterns of change for each combination of *age * therapy*. If such differences are within the realm of chance variation then one can specify the simpler model that omits the *age × therapy* interaction: *(therapy + age)(subject) * occasion*. This example assumes there are no complicated patterns of correlations within the measurement occasions, and that we can therefore examine the within-subject trends in the BDI for treatment compared to no-treatment.

Designs using matched-pairs of subjects can be treated in the same manner as this example, by creating a separate factor for subject, though the utility of this will depend on how well matched the subjects are. A model including a grouping factor corresponding to within-group correlations allows one to treat the observations as if they are independent, when the within-group effects are eliminated from the model (McCullagh and Nelder, 1989). A more complex biomedical example using a number of covariates is provided in Francis, Green and Payne (1994). Loglinear models with repeated measures, or matched pairs, are considerably more complex and the reader is referred to Agresti (1996) for a discussion of models for categorical data. A comprehensive treatment of the analysis of repeated measures data is given by Lindsey (1994).

7.7   Time Series Analysis

Whilst one of the basic assumptions of GLMs is that the measurements are independent, as we have seen from the above section, in some cases it is possible to develop effective models in which the data are explicitly assumed to be correlated. Draper and Smith (1981) discuss the use of dummy coding to examine a response variable across a series of measurements made before and after a notable event. Two time trends are modelled, one might be a baseline containing pre-treatment observations, and the second a series of post-treatment observations. They discuss instances where the notable event — that is, the point of intersection of the two trend lines — is already known and also where it is unknown and must be inferred from the data. Examples of notable events might be employees going on a time-management course, or patients undergoing an operation. These authors develop the simple linear model using X_1 and X_2 to denote two dummy variables, one for before the notable event, and one for after the event:

$$\hat{Y} = \alpha + \beta_1 X_1 + \beta_2 X_2 \tag{7.1}$$

where $\alpha = $ the value of the linear predictor, $\hat{Y}$, at the point of intersection,

β_1 is the slope of the initial trend line,

and β_2 is the slope of the final trend line.

This approach generalizes in a straightforward manner to data with non-Normal response variables by means of an appropriate choice of link function, e.g., a logit link for proportions, and a logarithmic link for counts.

In autoregressive models, the strategy is to include conditional distributions or moments for the response variable, i.e., one models y_t given $y_{t-1}, \ldots, y_1$ together with the explanatory variables at each x_t. This approach has typically been applied to data with Normal errors, and is quite amenable to fitting within a GLM framework (Scallan, 1985). More recently, models for binary and multi-category response variables have been developed, e.g., whether it has rained on a given day with 2 levels of yes/no, or 3 levels of no/low/high, whilst count data can also be modelled, e.g., number of cases of a disease per month. Fahrmeir and Tutz (1994) discuss these autoregressive generalized linear models, whilst Lindsey (1992) demonstrates the analysis of stochastic processes with GLMs using the GLIM software package.

7.8 Gamma Errors and the Link Function: an Alternative to Data Transformation

OLS regression and other traditional linear models, such as ANOVA and AN-COVA, assume Normal response errors and constant variance, but data are often found in which the variance increases with the mean and the errors are highly skewed. One way around this problem is to transform the response variable using the procedure described in Chapter 2. However, as mentioned in Section 7.1, such a procedure has the disadvantage that a transformation to obtain constant variance may not lead to a distribution where other distributional aspects are also optimized (McCullagh and Nelder, 1989). A useful alternative within the GLM framework is to specify a model with a different distributional assumption and link function. A gamma distribution is appropriate when the standard deviation divided by the mean is constant, or the square root of the standard deviation divided by the mean is constant, as opposed to a model with Normal errors, which assumes that the standard deviation is constant. Such models are common in ecological modelling such as crop yield versus planting density. Some statistical packages, such as GLIM, offer the facility to specify Gamma errors, and a reciprocal link function is typically used for additive combinations of explanatory variables, whilst a log link is suitable when a multiplicative combination seems appropriate. A special case of the gamma distribution is the exponential distribution which is used in the analysis of survival data, discussed in the following section. Not many statistical packages offer the full range of GLM error distributions and link functions, so the researcher may be constrained to making transformations of the response variable. Aitken et al. (1989) discuss the data transformation approach versus the use of link functions in dealing with non-Normal errors, whilst Crawley (1993) provides some useful worked examples.

7.9   Survival Analysis

Survival analysis is a popular application of GLMs in the biomedical sciences, and involves modelling time until some key event, e.g., time to death given exposure to different levels of a toxin, time to reoffence for convicted offenders with and without a particular rehabilitation program, or the lifetime of components manufactured using different methods. For these models, gamma errors are typically assumed and one uses a special case of this — the exponential distribution. Whilst the chosen link function depends on the distributional form of the data, a common choice is the reciprocal, and log or identity links are other possibilities. If there is risk of fitted values being negative, then the log link may be a better choice, since you cannot have negative times to death. An example of this is survival durations for patients in a trial investigating treatment for a particular form of cancer. If we had also measured the patients' age, then the response variable would be the survival time, whilst the explanatory variables would be the treatment/no-treatment factor and the age covariate. Having set the gamma errors and reciprocal link in our statistical package we could try and fit the full interaction model: drug*age. The differences in deviance of this model compared to that of the main effects models: drug+age, drug alone, and age alone, would allow us to evaluate the significance of the model terms, following the pattern of modelling described in the present text.

Survival data are characterized by the occurrence of *censoring*. For the above examples, this is when the study terminated whilst the person was still alive, the ex-convict had not reoffended, or the component is still functioning, i.e., the exact failure time is unknown, and all we can say is that failure had not occurred by the end of the study. Another reason why censoring occurs is that some subjects may be lost from the study, e.g., through emigration. GLMs are available for the analysis of such censored data, whilst variations of these survival models are available for time-dependent covariates — explanatory variables which are non-constant over the duration of the study, e.g., measures of the physiological status of a patient. There is a large literature on survival analysis, and Crawley (1993) gives a useful introduction, whilst Aitken et al. (1989) provide further details.

7.10   Exact Sample and Sparse Data Methods

Recommendations for minimum sample sizes for regression methods vary, but as a guide Draper and Smith (1981) recommend at least 10 cases per variable. With the contingency tables of data used in loglinear methods the general rule of thumb, when there is more then 1 degree-of-freedom, is that not less than 20% of cells should have expected frequencies of less than 5, and no cell should have an expected frequency of less than 1. All these recommendations are based upon large sample approximations to the distributions of the test statistic used. With fewer cases than these, the usefulness of the large sample approximations begin to break down, though procedures exist for dealing with occasional zero cells (examples are given in Aitkin et al., 1989; Agresti, 1996 and Francis et al., 1994). One way around this is to use exact statistical methods, which, although computationally intensive, have been developed in recent years to the point where commercial software is readily available for the analysis of data with categorical response variables. This is particularly useful for complex multiway contingency tables where zero cell counts are not infrequent. StatXact offers a wide variety of exact tests for hypothesis testing, whilst LogXact offers exact tests for logistic regressions. These packages allow more reliable goodness-of-fit tests, parameter estimates, and confidence intervals than the large sample methods of standard GLM software.

Exact tests can also be of use when large sample methods generate an infinite parameter estimate. The exact methods allow one to calculate P values in such cases when *one* of the endpoints of the confidence intervals has a finite value. Consider a small hypothetical group of bank robbery victims in which half the sample subsequently received counselling, and the other half were controls. The response variable is whether the victims later suffered from post-traumatic stress disorder, or not. If the odds ratio of suffer/not-suffer for control:treatment has 95% confidence intervals $(3, \infty)$, this provides us with the useful information that subjects who received no counselling had, at least, three times the odds of developing post-traumatic stress disorder, compared to subjects who underwent counselling following such a trauma. Thus, we can still make useful inferences from data with large confidence intervals, provided one of the estimates has a finite value. This is of interest to applied researchers, such as clinical psychologists, who may have only a very limited sample of individuals with a rare condition. Agresti (1996) discusses sample size and power when modelling categorical data and gives some clear examples of exact methods, together with a discussion of StatXact and LogXact.

The program MIM (described in Edwards, 1995) provides exact tests of conditional independence in multi-way contingency tables.

7.11   Cross Validation of Models

One common occurrence when applying regression models for prediction is that the developed model is usually not as good at predicting new samples as it was with the original sample. One way to try and get a realistic idea of the predictive utility of the model is to do a *cross validation*. In studies with large samples one randomly splits the data set into two halves and fits the model to the first half, and then tests the predictions upon the second half. With smaller samples a method for data with Normal errors is to use a PRESS procedure (Prediction Sum of Squares) in which each case is omitted in turn and the model is fitted to the remaining observations, with a prediction made for each omitted case. Draper and Smith (1981) and Aitkin et al. (1989) give discussion of the PRESS method. Similar procedures for generalized linear models are given by Fahrmeir and Tutz (1994), and Stevens (1992) gives a discussion of the issue of Cross Validation for loglinear models, emphasizing the need for such procedures to reduce the likelihood of generating models that are too sample specific.

7.12   Software Recommendations

So far in this chapter we have pointed the reader to specific software that is ideally suited to solving particular problems. In this section we endeavour to discuss some popular general purpose statistical software to give some guidance through the hyperbole of the sales literature and the enthusiasm of the converts to each package. We shall begin by making one thing clear — as far as we are concerned there is *no* ideal software for carrying out GLM analyses, all have their drawbacks, either in terms of limited modelling features, or cryptic user-interfaces.

7.12.1   SPSS for Windows

We have chosen SPSS for Windows as one of the packages to illustrate this text since it is widely available, and has a familiar mouse-driven graphical user interface. This has advantages for teaching since the majority of students now learn their basic computing skills in a windowing environment and find the spreadsheet interface relatively familiar. Unfortunately, behind this gloss one finds a poorly structured menu set-up and a software kernel that appears years old, with only a limited implementation of GLMs. There is also little consistency in the application of techniques across various statistical methods. For example, automated dummy coding is available in logistic regression and loglinear models, but not in OLS regression. Prediction and confidence intervals for the response variable are provided in OLS regression, but not in logistic regression. Similarly the statistics for multicolinearity are provided in OLS regression, but not in logistic regression.

7.12.2   GLIM

The alternative package we have used to illustrate the text is GLIM, the statistical software developed by the Royal Statistical Society. GLIM has the disadvantage of an older style command-driven interface[1] in which the user types in commands at the keyboard, reading the results in a large output window. This seems confusing at first, but because the command language is built around the central concepts of GLMs it has a logic to it that, once mastered, helps in understanding the process of modelling. In addition to the main GLMs it has been considerably extended by macros written for new applications, and is still the state of the art facility for this class of models. It has a particularly useful model notation based on Wilkinson and Rogers (1973) that allows the specification of factors, without explicit dummy coding, as well as orthogonal polynomials, and arbitrary levels of interactions between explanatory variables. Whilst SPSS for Windows is suited for teaching newcomers to GLMs, GLIM is ultimately more useful as an on-going research tool. Since it deals with models of a single response variable, it does not offer factor analysis, and so needs to be used in conjunction with another package when this facility is required.

7.12.3   SAS

SAS is a general purpose package that works in the manner of older command-syntax batch systems, like the non-Windows versions of SPSS, such as SPSS-X. In contrast to SPSS, it has been continually improved through the implementation of a versatile range of GLMs in the CATMOD and GENMOD libraries. Its drawbacks are that it is expensive and lacks the friendliness of SPSS for Windows. However, it is popular amongst statisticians and has a wide base of users.

7.12.4   GENSTAT for Windows

A package that may one day fulfil the promise of a versatile GLM package with a friendly interface is GENSTAT for Windows. This is a mouse driven version of GENSTAT version 5 which is a general purpose statistical package of the SPSS-X and SAS ilk, with a long history, and offers a version of the powerful Wilkinson and Rogers model syntax, as implemented in GLIM. It has been updated with a spreadsheet interface, which seems appealing at first, but after a short period of time reveals some poor user interface design features, that lead one to question the wisdom of the whole exercise. The file operations in the spreadsheet are in a 'spreadsheet' menu, whilst the file operations in the 'file' menu apply to the data set held in the program kernel. This distinction between spreadsheet and kernel requires one to constantly choose the 'update-kernel' menu option every time a change is made to the spreadsheet. Unlike

---

[1]At the time of writing a Windows version is in preparation.

GLIM, the ANOVA menu entries are kept distinct from the regression menu, which reinforces the misconception that they are unrelated techniques. Only a subset of the version 5 features are implemented in the graphical interface and one is forced to learn and use the command syntax for anything more complicated. If the authors of this program can remove some of the quirks of the interface then this offers the possibility of a very useful teaching and research tool in one, but as it stands we cannot recommend it without reservation.

7.12.5   Overall

In conclusion, SPSS for Windows is friendly, but its limited facilities make it frustrating to use for dummy coding and building regression models with interactions. SAS is versatile, but it is expensive, resource-hungry and uses unfriendly command syntax. GLIM is conceptually well integrated, very versatile, but a pain to learn and students are repelled by its poor user-interface. However, once mastered it offers a convenient model building syntax that helps in specifying complex interaction models. GENSTAT for Windows offers a lot of GLIM's power in a windows environment, but poor user interface design, and many bugs, makes it a frustrating system to work with.

References

Afifi, A. A. and Clark, V. (1996). *Computer-Aided Multivariate Analysis.* (2nd edition). Chapman & Hall.

Agresti, A. (1984). *Analysis of Ordinal Categorical Data.* John Wiley & Sons, Inc.

Agresti, A. (1990). *Categorical Data Analysis.* John Wiley & Sons, Inc.

Agresti, A. (1996). *An Introduction to Categorical Data Analysis.* John Wiley & Sons, Inc.

Aitkin, M. A., Anderson, D. A., Francis, B. J. and Hinde, J. P. (1989). *Statistical Modelling in GLIM.* Oxford University Press.

Aitkin, M. and Francis, B. J. (in press). Fitting generalized linear variance component models by non-parametric maximum likelihood. *The GLIM Newsletter.*

Aitkin, M. and Francis, B. J. (1995). Fitting overdispersed generalized linear models by non-parametric maximum likelihood. *The GLIM Newsletter,* **25**, 37–45.

Barrett, J. P. (1974). The coefficient of determination — some limitations. *The American Statistician,* **28**, 19–20.

Berry, W. D. and Feldman, S. (1993). Multiple Regression in Practice. In M. S. Lewis–Beck (editor). *Regression Analysis.* International Handbooks of Quantitative Applications in the Social Sciences, Volume 2. Sage Publications.

Bishop, Y., Fienberg, S. E. and Holland, P. W. (1975). *Discrete Multivariate Analysis: Theory and practice.* MIT Press.

Box, G. E. P. and Cox, D. R. (1964). An analysis of transformations. *Journal of the Royal Statistical Society, B,* **26**, 211–252.

Box, G. E. P. and Jenkins, G. M. (1976). *Time Series Analysis: Forcasting and Control.* Holden-Day.

Cattell, R. B. (1966). The Scree-Test for the Number of Factors. *Multivariate Behavioural Research*, **1**, 245–276.

Clogg, C. C. (1982). Using association models in sociological research: some examples. *American Journal of Sociology*, **88**, 114–134.

Collett, D. (1991). *Modelling Binary Data*. Chapman & Hall.

Comrey, A. L. and Lee, H. B. (1992). *A First Course in Factor Analysis*. (2nd edition). Erlbaum.

Cook, R. D. and Weisberg, S. (1982). *Residuals and Influence in Regression*. Chapman & Hall.

Crawley, M. J. (1993). *GLIM for Ecologists*. Blackwell Science.

Crawshaw, J. and Chambers, J. (1984). *A Concise Course in A-Level Statistics* (3rd edition). Stanley Thornes Publishers Ltd.

Draper, N. and Smith, H. (1981). *Applied Regression Analysis*. (2nd edition). John Wiley & Sons.

Dunteman, G. D. (1994). *Principal Components Analysis*. In M. S. Lewis–Beck (editor). Factor Analysis and Related Techniques. International Handbooks of Quantitative Applications in the Social Sciences, Volume 5. Sage Publications.

Edwards, A. L. (1985). *Multiple Regression and the Analysis of Variance and Covariance*. (2nd edition). Freeman.

Edwards D. E. (1995). *Introduction to Graphical Modelling*. Springer-Verlag.

Elliason, S. R. (1993). *Maximum Likelihood Estimation: Logic and Practice*. Sage University Paper series on Quantitative Applications in the Social Sciences. Sage Publications.

Fahrmeir, L. and Tutz, G. (1994). *Multivariate Statistical Modelling based on Generalized Linear Models*. Springer-Verlag.

Fava, J. L. and Velicer, W. F. (1992). An empirical comparison of factor, image, component, and scale scores. *Multivariate Behavioral Research*, **27**, 301–322.

Fienberg, S. E. (1980). *The Analysis of Cross-Classified Categorical Data*. The MIT Press.

Francis, B., Green, M. and Payne, C. (1994). *GLIM 4: The Statistical System for Generalized Linear Interactive Modelling*. (2nd edition). Clarendon Press.

Fuller, W. A. and Hideroglou, M. A. (1978). Regression estimation after correcting for attenuation. *Journal of the American Statistical Association*, **73**, 99–104.

Goldstein (1986). Multilevel mixed linear model analysis using iterative generalized least squares. *Biometrika*, **73**, 43–56.

Goldstein, H. (1995). *Multilevel Statistical Models* (2nd edition). Edward Arnold.

Goodman, L. A. (1970). The multivariate analysis of qualitative data: interaction amongst multiple classifications. *Journal of the American Statistical Association*, **65**, 226–256.

Goodman, L. A. (1979). Simple models for the analysis of association in cross-classifications having ordered categories. *Journal of the American Statistical Association*, **74**, 537–552.

Hardy, M. A. (1993). Regression with Dummy Variables. In M. S. Lewis–Beck (editor). *Regression Analysis*. International Handbooks of Quantitative Applications in the Social Sciences, Volume 2. Sage Publications.

Hays, W. L. (1994). *Statistics* (5th edition). Harcourt Brace College Publishers.

Hosmer, D. W. and Lemeshow, S. (1989). *Applied Logistic Regression* Wiley Series in Probability and Mathematical Statistics. John Wiley & Sons.

Hutcheson, G. D., Baxter, J. S., Telfer, K. and Warden, D. (1995). Child witness statement quality: general questions and errors of omission. *Law and Human Behaviour*. **19**, 631–648.

Jaccard, J., Turrisi, R. and Wan, C. K. (1990). *Interaction Effects in Multiple Regression*. Sage University Paper Series on Quantitative Applications in the Social Sciences. Sage Publications.

Jöreskog, K. G. and Sörbom, (1981) *LISREL V: Analysis of Linear Structural Relationships by Maximum Likelihood and Least Squares Methods*. Department of Statistics, University of Uppsala.

Kaiser, H. F. (1970). A second-generation little jiffy. *Psychometrika*, **35**, 401–415.

Kaiser, H. F. (1974). An index of factorial simplicity. *Psychometrika*, **39**, 31–36.

Kim, J. and Mueller, C. W. (1994). *Factor Analysis: Statistical Methods and Practical Issues*. In M. S. Lewis–Beck (editor). *Factor Analysis and Related Techniques*. International Handbooks of Quantitative Applications in the Social Sciences, Volume 5. Sage Publications.

Knuth, D. E. (1984). *The TEXbook.* Addison-Wesley and the American Mathematical Society.

Lamport, L. (1994). LATEX: *A Document Preparation System.* (2nd edition). Addison-Wesley.

Lewis–Beck M. S. (1993). Applied Regression: An Introduction. In M. S. Lewis–Beck (editor). *Regression Analysis.* International Handbooks of Quantitative Applications in the Social Sciences, Volume 2. Sage Publications.

Lindsey, J. K. (1992). *The Analysis of Stochastic Processes using GLIM.* Springer-Verlag.

Lindsey, J. K. (1993, Reprinted with corrections 1994). *Models for Repeated Measurements.* Oxford University Press.

Lindsey, J. K. (1995). *Introductory Statistics: A Modelling Approach.* Oxford University Press.

Maddala, G. S. (1992). *Introduction to Econometrics.* (2nd edition). MacMillan.

McCullagh, P. and Nelder, J. A. (1989). *Generalized Linear Models.* (2nd edition). Chapman and Hall.

McLean, P. D. and Hakstian, A. R. (1979). Clinical depression: comparative efficacy of outpatient treatments. *Journal of Consulting and Clinical Psychology,* **47**, 818–836.

Menard, S. (1995). *Applied Logistic Regression Analysis.* Quantitative Applications in the Social Sciences, **106**. Sage Publications.

Nelder, J. A. (1997). Don't transform data. *RSS News,* **24**, No. 7, pp5.

Nelder, J. and Wedderburn, R. W. M. (1972). Generalized linear Models. *Journal of the Royal Statistical Society, A,* **135**, 370–384.

Norušis, M. J. (1994). *SPSS® Guide to data analysis.* Prentice Hall.

Ryan, T. P. (1997). *Modern Regression Methods.* John Wiley & Sons.

Scallan, A. (1985). Fitting autoregressive processes in GLIM. *GLIM Newsletter* **6**, 30–37.

Sharma, S. (1996). *Applied Multivariate Techniques.* John Wiley & Sons.

Siegel, S. and Castellan, J. N. (1988). *Nonparametric Statistics for the Social Sciences.* (2nd edition). McGraw-Hill.

SPSS Inc. (1996a). *SPSS Base 7.0 for* Windows™ *User's Guide.* SPSS Inc.

SPSS Inc. (1996b). *SPSS Advanced Statistics 7.0.* SPSS Inc.

SPSS Inc. (1996c). *SPSS Professional Statistics 7.0.* SPSS Inc.

Sternberg, D. E., Ven Kammen, D. P. and Bunney, W. E. (1982). Schizophrenia: Dopamine *b*-hydroxylase activity and treatment response. *Science*, **216**, 1423–1425.

Stevens, J. (1992) *Applied Multivariate Statistics for the Social Sciences.* (2nd edition), Lawrence Erlbaum Associates, Inc.

Swan, A. and Scallan, T. (1995) GLIM Macro: LEV. In *GLIM4 Macro Library Release 4.2.* Scallan, T. and Morgan, G. (editors). Numerical Algorithms Group Ltd.

Tabachnick, B. G. and Fidell, L. S. (1996). *Using Multivariate Statistics.* (3rd edition). Harper Collins.

Whittaker, J. (1990). *Graphical Models in Applied Multivariate Statistics*, John Wiley & Sons.

Wilkinson, G. N. and Rogers, C. E. (1973). Symbolic description of factorial models for analysis of variance. *Applied Statistics*, **22**, 392–399.

Index